Identity and Ritual
in a Japanese Diving Village

Identity and Ritual
in a Japanese Diving Village

The Making and Becoming
of Person and Place

D. P. Martinez

University of Hawai'i Press

HONOLULU

09 08 07 06 05 04   6 5 4 3 2 1

Library of Congress Cataloging-in-Publication Data
Martinez, D. P. (Dolores P.), 1957–
    Identity and ritual in a Japanese diving village : the making and
becoming of person and place / by D. P. Martinez
        p. cm.
    Includes bibliographical references and index.
    ISBN 0–8248–2670–1 (cloth : alk. paper) —
    ISBN 0–8248–2817–8 (pbk. : alk. paper)
    1. Ethnology—Japan—Kuzaki-chō (Toba-shi) 2. Rites and
ceremonies—Japan—Kuzaki-chō (Toba-shi) 3. Japanese—Japan—
Kuzaki-chō (Toba-shi)—Ethnic identity. 4. Fishing villages—Japan—
Kuzaki-chō (Toba-shi) 5. Diving—Japan—Kuzaki-chō (Toba-shi)
6. Kuzaki-chō (Toba-shi, Japan)—Social life and customs. I. Title.

GN635.J2M27 2004
305.8'00952'181—dc22
                                        2003049340

Designed by University of Hawai'i Press Production Staff

Printed by The Maple-Vail Book Manufacturing Group

Contents

Acknowledgments

A book this long in the making owes debts to many people and institutions. It would be wrong to begin this long list of thanks without
acknowledging the greatest debt of all: to the people of Kuzaki who took
me into their midst in 1984 and put up with me during fourteen months of
fieldwork and various return visits afterward. They bore my presence and
queries with endless patience and good humor. On my last visit, all my diving friends and informants, especially, were pleased to see me properly settled with, finally, a family—they never nagged me about the lateness of the
book. Also endlessly supportive while I was in the field were my Tokyo University supervisor, Prof. Itoh Abitoh, and my informal *sensei,* Prof. Kurata
Masakuni, who took me to Kuzaki for the first time in March 1984. My time
in the field was made possible through a Monbusho Research Fellowship as
part of the Oxford-Tokyo Student Exchange Program; the period spent
writing up my dissertation was supported by the Philip Bagby Studentship
at the Institute of Social Anthropology, Oxford. Throughout that time I also
received support from my former partner, Matt Hohenboken.

My supervisors, Dr. James McMullen and Dr. Nick Allen, guided me
through the ups and downs of thesis writing, while my *dōkyūsei,* Dr. Roger
Goodman, has always been able to give good advice and find the humor in
any situation. Prof. Joy Hendry has been both mentor and firm friend
throughout the years. Other such *senpai* include Prof. David Plath, my
external examiner Prof. Arne Kalland, and my coeditor Prof. Jan van Bremen.

After finishing the thesis, many people and events influenced my sub-
sequent rethinking of the material, too numerous to name individually. But
I would be remiss if I did not thank my colleague, Dr. Kit Davis, who, generous with her time and optimism, provided both moral and intellectual
inspiration. Many School of Oriental and African Studies' (SOAS) Ph.D.
and M.A. students throughout the years have both challenged and helped
to redefine my thinking on things Japanese. Without their constant input,

fresh from living in Japan or doing fieldwork, I might have fallen into the trap of thinking I was a great authority on Japan instead of just one of its many explorers. An SOAS conference on Death in Japan, hosted by Dr. John Breen, was crucial at a late stage of writing, when I found myself somewhat blocked. The Faculty of Arts and Humanities Research Committee at SOAS also contributed to the cost of reproducing the photographs for this book, while my friend, Carolyn Clarke, generously gave me permission to reuse the illustrations she so painstakingly prepared for the original thesis. David Frudd gave last-minute technical support, and S. Ballard redrew an old map and scanned illustrations for me.

I also must thank the institutions that made the snatched hours of rewriting possible: Wolfson Day Nursery, whose staff looked after all three of my children in turn, providing them with fun, love, and safety; St. Ebbes School and the European School in Culham for being stimulating places where my children love to be; and Ebbeneezer's After School Club for allowing me an extra two hours in the working day as well as for keeping the children happy. My children—Nick, Martin, and Sofia—have put up fairly well with having parents who are both capable of disappearing upstairs to work, even on weekends; to their great amusement, they also have had to learn to explain just what an anthropologist really is ("No, they don't dig up bones"). My mother-in-law, Susan, has provided extra child care during times when my husband or I have been in the field or away at conferences, gracefully putting up with the obsessive behavior of three anthropologists throughout two generations. Last, but never least, nothing would have been possible without the continued support of my husband David Gellner. For nearly two decades, he has juggled his own writing, sharing of child care, and commuting with providing me advice, proofreading, and intellectual stimulation—all while learning more about Japan than he ever thought he'd need to know.

In a sense, these acknowledgments are also a dedication to everyone who has helped me along the way. But if I had to make a shorter dedication, it would be in memory of my grandmother, Maria Cebrián, and for my mother, Concepción de Benito Cebrián.

CHAPTER 1

On the Anthropologist and Her Subject

In May 1984, during the first few weeks of fieldwork in Kuzaki, I stuck close to the grandmother *(ōbāsan)* of the fishing and diving household that had taken me in. Through her I began my participation in family and community life: I cleaned fishing nets in the morning, helped with the drying of seaweed, went to the fields with her afterward, chatted with her as she prepared meals, sat with her by the television while she repaired nets or supervised the three children of the household, and took her cue about when it was my turn to enter the bath. Along with what at the beginning seemed to me to be impenetrable monologues on Kuzaki history and gossip, she taught me the correct greetings and responses to the family and outsiders. It seemed my Japanese was much too polite and Tokyo-like for a community as close-knit as Kuzaki, where *"ohayo gozaimasu"* (good morning) became the much more breezy and informal *"hayai desune"* (lit., it's early, isn't it?) or even *"hayai ne?"* People of the same generation also referred to each other by a nickname *(aishō),* generally consisting of part of one's first name and the affectionate suffix chan. Thus the grandmother was *bā-chan* to most and Ki-chan (short for Kisa) to the women of her own age.

A short, sturdy woman, *ōbāsan* was baked brown by the sun and—despite her age of seventy-six—was always on the move, always busy. Her hands were rough, cracked, and sometimes clumsy from a lifetime of hard work. Her teeth were brilliantly white and even, as were the teeth of most of the people of her generation; it took me months to understand that they were actually beautifully made, complete dentures. *Ōbāsan* at first seemed eternally cheerful. She was an endlessly patient teacher to the clumsy foreigner who had come to stay in her household, although part of her mode of communication was to shout in the hope that I would understand anything if it was said loudly. She dressed in the conventional trousers *(monpe)* of farming women, over which she wore a blouse and an apron. On ceremonial occasions she wore a kimono, but she only once appeared in a Western-style dress—for a trip to Osaka to visit her grandnieces when their father suddenly died.

After the first few months when fieldwork expanded, I was not always available to help *ōbāsan* with her work. I was watching divers and, in the summer, diving myself; I was spending evenings in Kuzaki inns helping to serve the tourists; or I went out with the men—my only chance to talk to them separately. During the preparations for Kuzaki rituals, I alternated observing what went on in the household with what was being done outside. Thus while I still cleaned nets, I helped less with other tasks. Once, on a busy day when sweet potatoes had to be harvested, I felt I should at least bring in the crop I had helped plant earlier in the year.

It was a gray, cool day and the work was less arduous than I had expected, turning the plants over with a hoe to expose the potatoes underneath and then collecting them in a basket. The field *(hatake)*, like all Kuzaki fields, was a tiny parcel of land tucked away in one of the numerous mountain valleys and was reached by climbing along a series of narrow, winding, intersecting paths that led to other small *hatake*. This field was only large enough to produce vegetables for a family of six, and not all of it had been planted in sweet potatoes. After a few hours of work, as *ōbāsan* and I made our way back for lunch, pushing the wheelbarrow full of tools and potatoes,

Figure 1. Okamoto Kisa harvesting sweet potatoes in 1984 (D. P. Martinez)

we were stopped by two other grandmothers who had been working nearby. This seemingly chance meeting was not the usual cheerful session of making jokes about the foreigner. It appeared that the women had something on their minds to tell me and, being elderly country women, they were direct— there was none of the usual wrapping that foreigners might associate with the Japanese (although the fact that they were probably articulating a concern that was *ōbāsan*'s is an example of another form of indirectness).

"You should not spend so much time in the inns," said one.

"It's not healthy for a young woman to go drinking," lectured another.

"It's good that you are helping *bā-chan* today, that is what you should stick to doing," said the first.

I tried explaining, again, about anthropological fieldwork and what it involved. In reply, I received the surprise of my life. The first grandmother got even more serious with me, and said: "*Wakatta, wakatta* (We know, we know). But if you are really serious about learning what goes on in a household, you should marry one of the young men here, be a *yome-san* (daughter-in-law). *Then* you would know about the *ie* (household) and the village. Instead you are here, away from your husband, at an age when you should be having babies, still a student, doing what?"

It was my first sense that I had crossed a boundary—that in a place where everyone thought they knew what anthropology involved (Kuzaki had had a team of Japanese scholars studying them for ten years in the 1960s), I was causing some anxiety. Previous village studies had involved large teams of scholars, asking everyone questions about diving, household names, fishing techniques, festivals, and so on, and they had stayed for only a few weeks at a time. I was a foreigner, so it was to be expected that language might hold me up, and working alone was certainly an oddity; but as a woman on her own who did not always stay by the grandmother's side, I was causing some worry, or so it seemed to me at the time. Not wanting to cause trouble, I curtailed evenings out with men and stopped going to the inns as often. Other aspects of fieldwork also intervened, as in November village life slowed down and preparations for the New Year and its related ceremonies began.

Yet the statement that I should try being a real *yome-san* struck me as a particularly astute one. I had been incorporated into the household as if I were a new member of it. I had learned the customs of the household and become involved in such a way that I had helped the grandmother with her workload. On the one hand I had not taken on some of the more arduous tasks performed by the actual *yome-san* of the household: getting up first thing in the morning, bathing last, preparing the bath, preparing the rice for the day and making the children's school lunches, cooking, or doing the laundry; but on the other hand I had helped in some tasks that the *yome-san* had refused to do. I realized, when I thought about it, that the women were lamenting a change in the role of daughters-in-law that my presence had helped to magnify: New wives in Kuzaki households often refused to do some of the harder tasks. Net cleaning was one that I was praised for doing, often in the same breath as it was pointed out that so-and-so refused to do it at all. But in contrast to these young brides, I could call upon my research as a way out of the work—and I would eventually leave, so that my help was only a temporary thing, perhaps resented as much as it was appreciated. I realized that I needed to rethink what it was that I was doing.

On Being an Anthropologist

This ambivalence about my presence, about my role, about the value of what I was actually doing not only colored the rest of my fieldwork (upon which I had embarked rather confidently), it has caused me some concern in the years since. It was not a new issue for me: As an undergraduate anthropology major, I had wondered whether as a woman—and in the United States, a member of an ethnic minority—I could even *be* an anthropologist. The realization that anthropology was dominated by white men had, at the end of my third year of college, caused me to change my major—a real shock to friends and family who had heard me saying, since the age of thirteen, that I wanted to be an anthropologist.

This early decision to "study man," as I often joked when challenged as a teenager on this strange choice, did not just come out of what was at the time a common adolescent encounter with Margaret Mead's utopian vision of a sex-filled, happy adolescence in Polynesia. Rather it came out of the sense of recognition that I had when I read her work. "Oh, that," I thought. "I've always done that. It's easy."

By "that," I meant the attempt to understand and interpret—even mediate between—the ways in which other people behaved and interacted. That I had literally always done. I was born in Spain, daughter of a Spaniard mother and an American father. I grew up in an era when people were not hyphenated or transcultural—just products of their nation. Arriving to live in Chicago with three small children, my mother was definitely a foreigner to the way of life she encountered there. More interestingly, it was the mid-seventies before I realized that since my long-dead paternal grandmother was actually a Mescalero Apache, I was a quarter Native American, and my father was half—as we said then—Indian. Not only was I ethnic, I was a real minority.

My embracing of anthropology, however, grew out of a very different sense of being other: This was due to my mother. From a family of political radicals and academics, she clearly found much of American middle-class life alien. Her critical assessments of the American way of life helped form a basis for my seeing the United States as only one possible way of living in the world.[1] Moreover, I was raised to be bilingual (as she had been, with Spanish and French), and I was sent to visit her sister (part of a Spanish expatriate community in Mexico) to keep up reading and writing in Spanish. As the eldest of what became a large family—eight children in all—I seemed to be always explaining, interpreting. And, in the late 1960s and early 1970s, I struggled to reconcile my political beliefs, which found any war barbaric, with my father's service in the U.S. Air Force. Coming across a discipline that seemed designed to understand social and cultural differences was like finally finding the map to help me chart my way through an unknown sea. I was not quite drowning, but I didn't know how to get anywhere any more.

This is a very different description of my discovery of anthropology than, let us say, Lévi-Strauss (1976), who felt it was the only way to combine his range of interests: linguistics, communism, and geography. He presents his embracing of the discipline as an intellectual decision. For me it was an emotional response to being an outsider, which grew into an intellectual position: As a teenager, I chose to continue to be a stranger while at the same time trying to be a hippie, with all the political implications that carried. I was interested in traveling, in other people and other ways of life, and had been lucky enough to have traveled some already and to be literate in my mother tongue as well as in English. What else to be if not an anthropologist—a professional stranger?

After wavering during my undergraduate years, I decided to take a year in Oxford and see if anthropology still attracted me. There I soon encountered others like me: transcultural people who spoke more than one language and who saw no impossibility in the task of understanding others. My experience was not unique, but it was outside of the still dominant discourse of modernity and nationalism: I was supposed to belong somewhere and to only one place. Meeting British students brought up outside the UK, Africans educated in colonial languages (French, English) and later by the Catholic Church, British people whose origins were definitely non-English, did not serve to articulate a dissatisfaction with this model of belonging, but it did allow me to relax. That the founding fathers of anthropology were a Pole (Malinowski) in the UK and a German (Boas) in the United States brought home to me that my decision was not so unusual; other people became anthropologists for reasons similar to mine. So I came back to anthropology.

But I chose to specialize in Japan!

I was drawn to Japan for a variety of reasons, most of them, in hindsight, related to my general antiestablishment attitudes. Anthropology was supposed to be the study of primitive societies, but Japan was not primitive—it was economically booming, modern in the extreme, and seen to be somewhat of a threat to U.S. technology and industry. Nor was it any longer a basically peasant nation-state (the other domain of anthropology) but a democratic society in which literacy was prized and mass culture thrived. It was not a former colony of a Western power (although it had lived with the threat of colonization), and its people bore the reputation of being difficult, if not impossible, to understand—if one could learn the language in the first place! Moreover, my first encounter with Japanese ethnography was through the work of women: Benedict (1947) and Nakane (1970). This attracted me in light of my earlier misgivings: It seemed positive that the famous works on Japan were by women, one of whom was a native.[2] So, loving Japanese film and having been taught that mass culture was an area worthy of study that needed anthropological attention, I decided to learn Japanese and attempt to tackle the anthropology of a modern society.

But as I was at Oxford, where working in such a modern place was seen to be rather wimpish (not as bad as doing a library dissertation, but not far from it), I was steered toward fieldwork in a small, rural community. Looking at the literature on Japan, I found that agricultural communities seemed well covered, but that—oddly enough for an island nation—fishing communities rarely appeared in the ethnographies. Once I had read what was available on fishing communities,[3] it was clear that as a woman I would not really be allowed to go fishing. It was a chance conversation with a friend who had seen pearl divers while on a holiday in Japan that led me to seek more information about diving women (*ama*). Since apparently only one ethnographic book on divers existed in English (Maraini 1962), it struck me that if I was going to be working with women, it might as well be women who were not part of an already large literature on Japanese females. Thus, beginning with the intention of working in a thoroughly modern place, I found myself planning to work on a seemingly exotic and traditional aspect of it. I will return to this issue in the next chapter.

It must be noted, however, that whatever personal and historical moments brought me to Japan in 1984, the fact remains that as a place created and re-created in response to the outside world, Japan exists within a reality of its own. Whatever I brought to it was outweighed by the fact that I was one person living within a society that had its own history, its own accepted view of that past, its own ways of dealing with outsiders, and—even in a place as small as Kuzaki—its own agenda for allowing an anthropologist to stay there. I was at the mercy of large government structures (Monbusho, the Ministry of Education, which gave me leave to study in Japan and a generous grant); a university system (Tokyo University, elite and boasting of its own excellent anthropology department); and the wider world of anthropology (David Plath, a senior American anthropologist, was also studying divers at the same time). And I was reliant on the goodwill of the people with whom I ended up living. I never felt more powerless than when I was in the field. And that, I have decided over the years, is a good thing, even if also frightening.

It has been many years since I submitted my thesis for examination in Oxford and almost twenty years since I left for fieldwork in Japan. In that period, many of the certainties that it seemed my fellow anthropology students had taken for granted—the right to study other peoples, the belief that a person could learn about other societies and theorize about the experience—have been questioned. Yet in my daily life I have continued to teach the subject, albeit framing my lectures on kinship, religion, gender, tourism, or the media with critical and reflexive comments on the state of the discipline. Such comments are not mere lip service to the latest theoretical trends. They grow out of the deep concerns I felt even as I wrote the doctoral thesis.

For example, during the first nine months back from the field, I wondered if I really knew anything about the place in which I had lived and studied for fourteen months of my two years in Japan—whether I had the right to speak as an expert. After all, despite the warm and helpful training I had been given by ōbāsan, it had been made clear that there was a limit to what I could learn. Throughout that time, I veered between writing the same core chapter over and over and asking why my raw field notes were not enough proof that I had done my job as an anthropologist. I resolved my writer's block by going back to the field in 1986 to ask even more questions. The people with whom I had worked thought my return rather amusing. In one way or another, they said, "You have already asked all that; go home and write your thesis." With that blessing, such as it was, I went home and finally sat down to work. The resulting dissertation was typical of the sort of ethnography then on its way out: Full of ethnographic description, it made less of the wider analytical issues than it did of the correct Japanese etymology for the term *"ama"* (diving woman).

Now I find myself looking back on the empirical data in much the same way I did upon my return from the field in 1985. On its own, it does stand as proof that I had done what anthropologists are supposed to do. That is, I had lived, worked, and collected information in a medium-sized village.[4] I had learned the language, followed the rituals, sat for hours talking with people, and I had also lived through the longueurs of illness, boredom, and depression that anthropologists don't like to discuss except with other anthropologists. I had been through the rite of passage that separates ordinary folk—other sorts of scholars, travelers, and tourists—from the anthropologist. I had learned through experience. But the question that haunted me during the writing has bothered me over the years and contributed to the delay in producing this book: Could I do a good job not only of sharing the experience but of giving a clear, honest picture of what life was like for the people of Kuzaki-chō?

This question is not a disingenuous attempt to build up to a postmodernist discourse on the role of the narrator in anthropology, important as that issue may be, but rather frames my attempts at analyzing what I lived through in Japan. For I believe that it is only in trying to unpack the experience that the anthropologist can begin to make clear the complexity of what life in any social reality is like. This is not to say that we are the ultimate authorities on our areas of study, but that by entering the field as strangers who need to be socialized into others' ways, we begin to understand the amazing creativity and diversity that fuels human societies. It is this sense of a shared human ability to form social groupings and to do so in a variety of ways that seems to have disappeared from anthropology. The relativism in which I was educated from the mid-1970s onward celebrated the right of others to be different—but in stressing difference, it allowed for a subtle sort of racism to creep in. If other people in other societies are so different from us—whoever *we* are—then it is not a far step from thinking of them as so alien that they are beyond comprehension. Total deconstruction meant not only seeing society as an arena of negotiable realities, it also led to questioning whether our perceptions of any shared reality were not somehow false. Communication across cultures was made to seem impossible at the same time that global cultures and technologies were being touted as the new terrain of anthropology.

Over the years, I have wrestled with various issues. The question of representing the Japanese who, among other things, have their own anthropologists and their own theories on groups and individuals, and the problem of working within a discourse that seemed to be disappearing below my very feet, are just two of the issues I had. As I've noted, my time has not been spent wandering in a desert but in teaching courses on Japan, on tourism, and on theory in anthropology. In these years I have visited Japan several times; kept in touch through others' work; supervised the dissertations of students who have brought up the very issues that had so worried me in 1986; and I have published articles and edited books on Japan. In short, as a colleague pointed out to me, I was still involved in something that might be called "ethnographic time," and I had not yet come to terms with the fact that I learned more about my subject with every passing year. This concept of ethnographic time has all sorts of implications for understanding a revitalized anthropology, and I want to devote some space here to considering the issue.

Time Machines and Fieldwork

One of the ways in which I had been taught to think about fieldwork was to view it not only as essential to my formation as an anthropologist, but as time *away*. Recent anthropological theory (Fabian 1983; Thomas 1989) has criticized one aspect of this—how the discourse of time in anthropology can lead us to a discussion of others that places them on a continuum that is based on the principle of pre- and post- something or other, and thus always essentially different. Yet it seems to me that this critique has not carried the concept to its logical conclusion. If we can wonder how the doing of anthropology can become a way of writing culture (Clifford and Marcus 1986)— imposing the weight of written texts upon others as well as placing them within a hierarchy of time—we should also think about the way in which we are constituted by these others during our fieldwork. In the end, it is not time away upon which we are embarking, as if climbing aboard Lowenthal's (1985) time machine in order to take part in some sort of ritual suffering only available elsewhere that will turn us into professionals. Fieldwork is part of larger political and economic relationships that should not be viewed as separate from global processes nor as being somehow out of time.

While the transformative aspect of fieldwork has long been implicit, anthropologists have only recently tried to grapple with the issue of where this experience belongs in the larger world. Few anthropologists would argue with the idea that our time in the field can be seen to be both a real and a transformative experience, akin to that of going on a pilgrimage where the merit gained in the journey is not lost upon return.[5] While away we are liminal, taking part in a rite of passage that upon our return will see us slowly reincorporated into our own community (through the act of writing the dissertation), ending with a final ordeal (the viva voce or doctoral examination) of which the successful outcome will be the celebration of our achievement: the conferment of the title, Doctor of Philosophy. And this last part of the rite is generally perceived to be permanently transformative: We are now something other than the students we were. One question concerns *what* we are reincorporated into. Generally, we end up working in the systems of knowledge production, which many anthropologists now label as hegemonic—the Western university system.

I owe the inspiration for some of this formation of the anthropological experience to that grand observer of British anthropologists, Barbara Pym. In her novel, *Less than Angels* (1955), she reflects on the community of London-based Africanists that the narrator, Catherine Oliphant, has come to know through her lover, the anthropologist Tom Mallow. In the search for difference, exoticism, and strangeness, implies the novel, we need look no further than the tribe of anthropologists: They are given to odd behavior understandable only to other anthropologists and tolerated on the grounds that fieldwork, that baptism of fire, is worth the resulting eccentricity. Catherine Oliphant, who as a writer observes not only anthropologists but the city of London around her, is somewhat bemused by their certainty that being in the field is what it is all about—and by their blindness to the fact that the field might well be everywhere. Fieldwork for Catherine involves a state of mind, an interest in human behavior, an attitude; place is less important than an ability to observe, converse, and reflect.

I have often reread this novel in the years since I returned from the field for a variety of reasons. The notion that London was as worthy of anthropological observation as any other place struck me as perceptive of Pym and appealed to me, a foreigner in England. More important was her rather amused examination of the relationships within a group of anthropologists. Her tongue-in-cheek descriptions made bearable the realization that I belonged to this strange tribe. Yet I have also been haunted by her image of field notes as a burden and have long been convinced that writing a novel is the secret ambition of many an anthropologist. Like any writer, we turn lived experience into words on a page; unlike quantitative sociologists, we try and do it mostly in plain language. Unlike travel writers, ambience is not what we are trying to depict—we are after larger human truths. The crux of what we do, however, is in the fact that we have done it somewhere far away, amongst strange people—perhaps even having grand adventures in the process—and we have come back loaded down with proof of our journey. Then the writing up of these notes takes the adventure, flattens it out, and turns it into an intellectual exercise. Perhaps this is necessary lest we be accused of exoticizing others.

But I think the most important lesson to be learned from Pym's novel is that the usual representation of fieldwork as a discrete experience that is over when it is over, and that writing up is a necessary part of our return to the real world, is false. Fieldwork—the embracing of other places and other people—is not a self-contained rite of passage but a process that never ends and can take place anywhere: It *is* a frame of mind. If that was true in the late 1950s when communication was only by letter, parcel, and telegram, it is even more true now, when communications are so much better, air travel is possible almost anywhere in the world, and our informants are just as likely to get on an airplane to come and see us as we are of returning to visit them. Also, that small band of scholars Pym knew has expanded and our students and colleagues keep mining the shaft that we either were the first to explore—or that, as a second or third generation of postwar scholars, we were already reexploring. Ethnographic time, if we think of it as the time spent learning about our subjects, never really ends. Our knowledge is only ever fragmentary, open to criticism and revision, as well as cumulative and interactive. The days of an anthropologist finding one key theme that leads to the complete understanding of a society are over. We must admit that all we do is provide more and more pieces that go into the making of intricate jigsaws. If we travel in time, it is only along the time frame of a young discipline that is ever growing (cf. Cohn 1990), not in a world fragmented by disjunctures of an evolutionary nature.

Thus a return to my field notes after many years is a return with a deeper but not necessarily complete understanding of Japan. I owe this understanding not only to the people of Kuzaki who taught me so much during my time with them but to my fellow scholars who as Japanologists and anthropologists have added to my initial knowledge. Critical as I might occasionally be of others' work, the fact remains that any new work on Japan adds to our understanding of that nation and its people. The book I attempt to write now is very different from the one I would have written a decade ago, although the empirical data upon which it is based remain the same. The book I might wait to write ten years from now would be different as well.

Yet because this book is a product of hindsight as well as fieldwork, it is also a reflection on a variety of issues that have come to the fore in the anthropology of Japan during the 1990s. Not only that, I have chosen to write almost consistently in the past tense. Return visits have shown how things change, even in traditional villages like Kuzaki, and I think it would be wrong to write about 1984 as if it were the present. Still, the overall thrust of the book remains much the same as in my thesis: to understand how a community in the 1980s defined itself both as unique within its region and nation and yet ultimately being as Japanese as anywhere else. More importantly, it is about the making *(tsukuru)* and becoming *(naru)* of place and person. One reason why I do not hold to the idea that single models explain anything about a society is the fact that while I was in the field, people were always telling me what to think and what they thought, but no one ever said exactly the same thing as the next person. Thus, while this book ends by focusing on an analysis based on the concepts of making and becoming, I do not see this as the final word on the subject of understanding Japan. Nor am I introducing a new subject. Making and becoming might well be glossed as structure and agency—familiar subjects in the anthropology of Japan—but I have chosen to use a vocabulary that reflects the way in which the people of Kuzaki talked about their lives, their village, and their rituals. Nor am I the first to use the term "becoming" without reference to wider debates: Hendry's *Becoming Japanese* (1986) examines many of the ways in which a child is "made" by mothers, teachers, group life, and so forth and "becomes" Japanese. The emphasis in her book is on the structures to which this making adheres, an oblique reference perhaps to Bourdieu's "structuring structures which are structured" (1977). I want to balance this meaning of *naru* with the "making" of *tsukuru,* involving the ability of people to act both on themselves and others, creating individuality as opposed to individualism. But it is impossible to make a neat dichotomy between the two terms. Without making, there can be no becoming; without a structure to work within or against, there would be no agency.

The vocabulary of making and becoming reflects not only a certain Japanese attitude but a fact about the researcher. As I have argued, our understanding develops and changes over time as well. For example, I have had to rethink much of my understanding of ritual and religion in writing this book. That is, while much of the symbolism of Japanese religion falls into dichotomies that appear to offer us neat conclusions, I would rather invoke Ricoeur, who in his critique of structuralism noted: "More than one interpretation is justified by the structure of the discourse which permits multiple dimensions of meaning to be realized at the same time" (1968, 94). What Ricoeur argues is that the practice of analyzing words or symbols in opposition to each other ignores the larger structures in which they are embedded. Meaning transcends the single symbol or term; it is the relationships, both diachronic and synchronic, that must be understood.

It is this approach that I have taken in trying to describe and understand both everyday life and religious practice in Kuzaki. While my first attempts fell rather easily into structuralist patterns, I have always been uneasy with the solution offered by this approach. The uneasiness stems from the fact that the practice of religion, like the use of words in sentences, transcends the tidy categories into which we might put implements, figures, offerings, gestures, or actions. Religious practice in Kuzaki always seemed to be about something more than just the worship of the ancestors, deities *(kami),* and the structural principles of the community; it was, as I have come to understand it, also about the making of place and identity and about the way in which a person made the journey through life and death. It is not possible to ignore the fact that, in Kuzaki at least, religious practices not only reaffirmed the importance of the community, they also continued to uphold patriarchal ideals. My first attempts to analyze religion in Kuzaki focused quite strongly on the relationship between male and female as seen through religious practice; I have retained that in this book, but I also try to give a better sense of how polysemous religion in Kuzaki was.

The polysemous aspect of religion in Japan, not just Kuzaki, means that trying to make sense of it all is rather like reading a palimpsest: Some meanings have been written over more than once. Eco (1992) and Ginzburg (1989) both warn of the temptation to make neat Sherlock Holmes–like interpretations, and I have tried to veer away from such analytical tidiness. Religious practices in Kuzaki—and perhaps all of Japan—can be said to be at the core about making and becoming, about an opening out to the manifestations of power and a creation of meaning. It also could be argued that all Japanese rituals mimic the moment of creation when the founder deities stirred up the oceans until land came into being—the beginning of the making and becoming of all things. All rites, then, are a form of mimetic performance; however, the experience and the hoped-for end product are different for different people. Thus, precisely because Japanese rituals are polysemous in meaning, they are also dialogic in their practice (Bahktin 1981; Csordas 1994). Moreover, there exist competing discourses about the interpretation of religious practices.

On an individual level, then, the people of Kuzaki interpreted religious practices in various ways. Some saw them as coercive but necessary; others as important because they believed, whatever that means; others because they hoped for the this-worldly benefits that Reader and Tanabe (1998) discuss; and a few expressed open skepticism. And these categories often overlapped. My introduction to the shrine at Kuzaki involved being taken there on my first day by an innkeeper, who beckoned me in, laughing at my questions about worship. "Here," he said, opening the doors to the inner sanctum, "is where Amaterasu is. Want to see inside?" I hesitated, and he went to pull aside the curtains that veiled whatever the *shintai* (the physical object in which the deity resides) was.[6] As he put his hand on the curtains, he too hesitated: "No, it wouldn't be good." Shutting up the inner shrine, he added, "*Omoshiroi* [meaning both interesting and funny], isn't it?" but he never explained whether it was his pulling back that was interesting or if it was the idea of Amaterasu being inside the shrine that he found funny. It was probably both.

Given the variety of ways in which religion is experienced, then, what does an analysis of ritual practices as being about making and becoming offer us above and beyond such a deconstruction? The concept of making—*tsukuru*—has been written about by Yamaguchi (1991) as an essential part of ritual, performance, and the very thingness of objects.[7] Nor is making opposed to becoming; *naru* can also mean making. In Japanese, becoming is both a natural process and an artificial one. In relation to human beings, becoming is not possible without the effort of making; it is also acknowledged that one is acted on by others—hence the importance of acquiring passive verb forms when learning Japanese. There is no dichotomy. The dead would not become nothing if others did not do the making. A community would have no solidarity if its members did not make an effort. A woman could not become a good diver unless she worked at it. Process, then, always involves effort: The art (in Japan) lies in making such efforts look natural. Rituals such as the ones described in this book "make" at all sorts of levels: in terms of individual need; for the community; in support of patriarchy; to reestablish gender divisions; to mark where the wilderness ends and the social begins, thus making place; and to keep the lines of communication open between humans and the power that is *kami*. Rituals, then, are not just about a one-to-one mode of communication—the channeling of the chaotic into the ordered (cf. Rappaport 1999)—although they might well have that function to some degree. Rather, rituals are about an opening out into the myriad possibilities of human existence. While it could be pragmatically, scientifically argued that rituals change nothing and have no impact on the world, for many practitioners the possibility that they are acting on reality and that something might come of this action is important. As Taussig (1993) put it—albeit speaking of the shaman and his rites—social reality is made through these acts of mimesis.

It should be noted that few are the places in Japan where the fusion of daily life, the community, religious practice, and ritual are as important as they were in Kuzaki in the 1980s. Yet the persistence of ritual in the lives of the vast majority of Japanese requires the student of Japan to rethink some basic assumptions about global processes: the idea that the truth of science will defeat the arcane forces of false religious belief; or that modernity is about secular rationalism in opposition to a premodern irrationality—both bear reexamination (van Bremen 1995). As Evans-Pritchard (1976) argued, witchcraft and oracles make sense if we understand that they explain the Azande experience of reality. The critique is valid that, in trying to explain such a worldview to others, anthropologists reduce experience to a discussion of analytical terms rather than considering the thing itself. It is here that I hope detailed ethnography will save me from such barren reductionism. I have much to say about making and becoming and of how they are not only part of an experience of reality but also essential to its making. My analysis can make sense only in the light of what ritual and daily life were like in Kuzaki. For that reason, the core of this book combines descriptions of the household, fishing, diving, and tourism with the ritual life of the place.

Toward a Conclusion

The above might be taken as a very long explanation, more or less, of my position in the terrain of a postmodern anthropology. I need to add just one or two points. While I will not take Campbell's (1995) line and refuse to use any trendy jargon in this book, I do take seriously Ardorno's (1973) point that jargon is a dangerous and political tool frequently used to justify the wielding of knowledge as power. So I will use some familiar anthropological terms in this book, but in a clear and accessible way. There are, however, three key terms that need defining at the onset: *seken,* role, and identity.

The term *"seken,"* originally Buddhist, means various things: the world, society, life, people, the public. Its usage often implies a person's awareness of others' opinion and can be felt as a very heavy weight. It is "society" in its more Victorian usage: the panoptic eye that evaluates people and judges their actions; it is the "them" of "they say." The term "role" I use in the Maussian sense (Mauss 1985), but it is clearly linked to the concept of *seken:* It is the playing out of a person's status within society, and this implies a multiplicity of roles since people exist in a network of relationships. As an anthropological term, "role" is rarely used these days, although in the study of Japan it is often described as the ideals to which people try to adhere in the making of the self without being clearly defined. I will use the term "identity" to mean the sameness of a group, rather than individual difference. All three terms refer to the very highly organized structuring of Japanese society, which I hope to challenge.

Finally, I should add that the most important outcomes of the debates about anthropology as writing for me have been: (1) to reaffirm the importance of empirical data, but framed by some reflexive comments so that readers can judge and interpret the anthropologist's interpretation for themselves; and (2) to acknowledge the importance of historical context, as well as the national, local, and scholarly contexts that help make sense of the material gathered during fieldwork. This last point, however, must not be taken to an extreme; while an understanding of Kuzaki is all the better for knowing some history, lived experience means that all the dominant discourses fragment on close examination as well. In no case is this truer than when discussing gender, and thus the next chapter is an attempt to bring history, various forms of scholarship, and the anthropology of Japanese women together. Finally, I must note that I will not take a feminist stance (whatever that is), although I acknowledge that postmodernist theory draws on feminist concerns about models that were static, unitary, and rigid. Japan has feminists and feminist theories that its women can choose to adhere to or not. It is not my job as an anthropologist to preach, but to understand. Thus, in this work, I try to analyze how the construction of both male and female roles creates social reality.

When I first tackled these questions, I was still writing within a discourse on Japan that emphasized its homogeneity over its differences. The pendulum has swung the other way now: Japan is being looked at as a place of heterogeneity, and it is perhaps appropriate that I have finally written this book.

CHAPTER 2

Japan and the *Ama*

Where could they be going at this time, in the wrong direction?
Catherine wondered. Was it perhaps significant that two anthropologists, whose business was to study behavior in human societies, should find themselves pushing against the stream? She
hardly knew how to follow up her observation and made no
attempt to do so, only asking herself again where they could
be going. Curiosity has its pains as well as its pleasures, and
the bitterest of its pains must surely be the inability to follow
up everything to its conclusion.
—Barbara Pym, *Less than Angels*

Looking for Divers *(Ama)*

As the conversation opening the last chapter indicates, no anthropologist
arrives in the field totally prepared for what will happen. All anthropologists, however, do some preparation for fieldwork, and I was no exception.
The previous summer (1983), I had received a small traveling scholarship
from the Richard Storry Memorial fund that I used to search for a suitable
fieldwork site. On that trip I had met with Prof. Yoshida Teigo (then at Keio
University) and Prof. Nagashima Nobuhiro (Hitotsubashi University), both
of whom photocopied Japanese material on the locations of remaining diving communities, offered advice, and sent me on my way.

It was my first experience of a hot, humid Japanese summer, and traveling was actually a pleasure as long as I was on air-conditioned trains and
my destination was a seaside town. Yet it was a frustrating trip. Diving communities seemed all to have metamorphosed into large beach resorts, and I
spotted divers in only two places: Shirahama in Chiba Prefecture and the
divers who demonstrated pearl diving at Mikimoto Pearl Island Museum
in Mie Prefecture. I did have luck tracking down some video footage shot
in diving communities by anthropologists (available for viewing at the

National Museum of Ethnography in Osaka). Otherwise, the divers I had spoken to in Shirahama seemed to be more involved in the tourist trade, with diving just a sideline. This actually struck me as interesting: Tourism seemed an underexplored aspect of modern life, and if all divers now worked only for the tourists, this was worth study—or so I decided.

Arriving as a research student at Tokyo University later that year soon changed everything. I was one of a line of female Oxford postgraduates who had come to do the fieldwork for their degrees, and my supervisor, Prof. Itoh Abitoh, obviously felt that I was the most misguided of the recent three. Tourism? Divers? Why didn't I go to Kyūshū and look at the former secret Christians there? His concern was that there was a Japanese literature on divers (a disappearing breed), and that I might be crossing wires with the American anthropologist, Prof. David Plath, who had been working on a diving community in the Shima area for some years. In short, I would just be covering ground already explored by others. I remained adamant. I had been upgraded to doctor of philosophy status on the premise that I was going to study Japanese diving women, and I wasn't sure that I could easily change that. Furthermore, I would sort things out with Prof. Plath (who generously remained unconcerned about me) and read the Japanese literature. Since I wouldn't budge, Prof. Itoh began the process of finding someone who would introduce me to a more appropriate fieldwork site than the too-large Shirahama that I had chosen. Thus, in true Japanese style, through the colleague of a colleague, my supervisor found someone who knew the Mie area and who could introduce me to the village of Kuzaki—a truly traditional diving community. The question was, would Kuzaki want me?

Kuzaki Frozen in a Moment of Time

The contact for Kuzaki was Prof. Kurata Masakuni, an ethnologist who had long studied in the Shima Peninsula area. He was at Tsu University and had arranged for my temporary research assistant Yuko and me to join him on a March 10–11 trip to Kuzaki. This excursion, as I was to learn, actually coincided with a trip Prof. Kurata had already planned to make with a group of his classmates *(dōkyūsei)*.

Our trip began at Tokyo Station, where Yuko and I boarded a bullet train to Nagoya, then changed to a local (Kinetsu) line, getting off at Tsu city (see Figure 2). We spent the night in a small inn, where Prof. Kurata joined us for an excellent seafood meal. Yuko commented that the sushi and fresh sashimi would be typical of what I would eat during fieldwork,

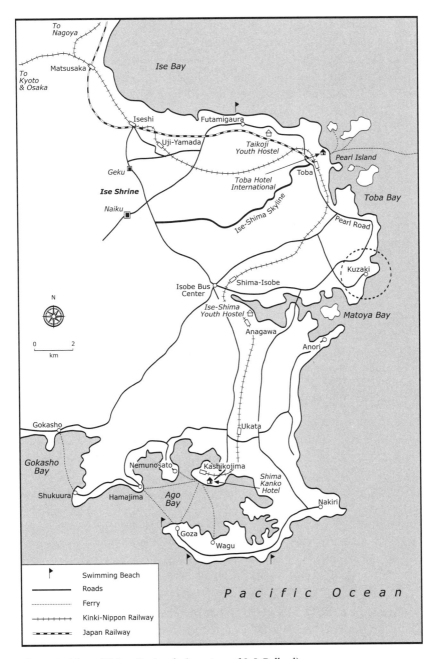

Figure 2. Map of Shima Peninsula (courtesy of S. J. Ballard)

and I would be sleeping on a futon and bathing Japanese style (in which she very carefully instructed me, although I had experienced Japanese baths). Prof. Kurata then spoke to me very seriously about the one-year participant observation that I planned: "Life in an *ama* household will be very severe [*kibeshi*]; besides, not every day will be interesting."

At the time, I was taken aback by his words. Now I often repeat them to my students: Life alone in the field is tough and not every day is one of excitement, despite the fact that ethnographies, with their focus on the events of fieldwork, can make life in the field seem adventurous. When Prof. Kurata told me this, I countered with the query, "Where could I possibly live?" "We'll inquire when we get there," he replied, and he left it until the next day when I got my first taste of traveling in a group of celebrating Japanese.

The journey on the following day was from Tsu City to Toba City, where we stopped off at the local Maritime Museum and I was able to buy several books and journals on the area, on fishing, and on diving. Prof. Kurata showed me the displays of diving equipment and traditional boats with great pride; he had helped collect the data for the exhibits. Then we boarded a van identified by the name Shima no Sato, a Kuzaki inn, and with a group of Kurata's friends (all in their sixties), we were off to Kuzaki. The journey was along the twisting and scenic Pearl Road (a tollway), which I had traveled on a tourist bus the summer before. In contrast to the heat of August, now it was a cold and cloudy March day. The sea I glimpsed as we went around bend after bend was the color of slate and forbidding, while all the vegetation was a shade of gray-green. Those with whom we traveled were unconcerned by this: They were already merry with sake and looking forward to hot baths and a good meal in Kuzaki. Finally, after a rather nerve-wracking twenty-minute drive, we were in the village—a small, narrow place shoved between the mountains and the sea. It seemed cut off by forest and mountain from the rest of Japan. The modern village houses were connected by steep pavement, with little greenery to relieve the concrete. Despite its seeming isolation, we were still officially in Toba City!

This was but a brief glimpse of the village. Immediately we were ensconced in the inn, where the baths and partying began. The group seemed to be united by their experience of Manchuria during the war, but I was more concerned with the fact that the two geisha (see discussion of this term in relation to the *ama* later in this chapter) serving the evening meal, who were kin to the innkeeper, were actually divers. I wanted to ask them about my work, where to live, and so on, but we just watched each other—rather carefully, I thought—after Prof. Kurata announced what I hoped to do. I noted in my personal diary at the time that it seemed that nothing would ever happen.

Wheels were already turning, however. Before leaving the next day (the reunion had been for only the one evening), Prof. Kurata rushed me around to meet the head of the Kuzaki Fishing and Farming Cooperative, who said that one of his executives might have a place in which I could stay. Sure enough, one of his men, Okamoto Takao, said, "We have a spare room," and off we went to visit his house. There, lo and behold, I was greeted by his wife, one of the geisha from the evening before—the woman who had studied me rather speculatively, I had thought. I was shown a room, small but light, with tatami mats and three walls of windows. It looked fine. I was ready to sign a contract, move in the following week—anything. But I was told, "Our grandmother has to decide if she would be able to cope with a stranger in the house." Back to Tokyo we went, where weeks went by before I got a phone call saying I could come. It was April 8 before I finally arrived in Kuzaki, alone.

While I waited, I read about the village and tried to piece together its history. I worked on writing thank-you letters and bought paper, pens, and film for the field. I was settled into a student dormitory and had made friends, so I had acquired a life that I now had to interrupt for the field. I was ready, or so I hoped, but I had already experienced the first lesson I now review for my own students heading out for Japan. It takes at least three or four months to organize the fieldwork part of life. People have to speak to other people, a consensus has to be reached, and the anthropologist has to be incorporated into a household or a place in a way that many a Western society would not be bothered with.

This brings me to the final point I would like to make before disappearing, as it were. While I arrived in Japan open to learning something, the people with whom I worked were also open to finding a place for me. Anthropologists often take this for granted, but this is an important point. I was not the lone stranger, penetrating deep into a place that had not known outsiders before. I was working within a society that had a place for strangers: It treated them with formal hospitality. Yoshida (1983), among others, has written about this mechanism for accepting, incorporating, and sending on their way outside people and objects in Japan. Its premise is that the power held by outsiders is potentially great both for the benefit of the community and for bringing chaos and problems. The way in which this power is channeled into Japan can be metaphorical (the rituals having to do with stranger deities found throughout Japan, which I will discuss later), or practical—witness Tobin's (1992) concept of "re-made in Japan." Ultimately, some strangers are incorporated—daughters-in-law being the most interesting example—through a process that lasts a lifetime (cf. Lebra 1984; Masuda 1975). Since the nineteenth century, foreigners have been placed on this continuum of hospitality and incorporation, and anthropologists, whether Japanese or not, have been slotted into this process as well.

What I am describing is the other side of the coin of Simmel's (1964) classic analysis of the role of the stranger: Outsiders are not created in a vacuum but in an articulated relationship with the other. Thus any visitor to Japan who has stayed longer than a week or two and who has tried to learn the language can speak of shared experiences: the kindness, the encouragement for even the roughest of language skills, the panic in the face of Japanese spoken by someone clearly non-Japanese, the concern over whether we know how to take baths, eat with chopsticks, sleep on the floor, and so forth. This is part of how Japan reacts to outsiders. Longer-staying foreigners also share experiences: the more critical assessment of language skills as they improve, the rejection of the possibility of understanding, the moments of unexpected hostility where once there seemed to be only kindness. (Living in the UK for almost twenty years now, I can say that the rejection of the foreigner who seems to understand all too well is not uniquely Japanese.) All of this is part of the mill through which outsiders are ground when coming to Japan. It would seem that one ethnography of Japan would do for everyone at any given point in time.

Yet individual concerns and historical moments can meet to produce unexpected insights. I arrived with an interest in modernity and was sent to a place that was deemed traditional. The issues of the modern world, of modern Japan, of tourism, and a global fishing industry were important in Kuzaki, small and seemingly cut off as it was. I was someone who had questions about identity and place—and so did the people of Kuzaki, who saw themselves as Japanese despite a history that many outsiders feel marks them as atypical of Japan. In the past, the relationship of villagers as fishermen and women divers to the larger feudal government had raised issues of household organization, inheritance, tax, and, lingering on in the modern era, the relationship between the sexes. The construction of gender identity for the *ama* as understood throughout Japan is interesting; the way in which Kuzaki handled this was also fascinating. Villagers' concerns with the correct role of women also echoed some of my own prefieldwork concerns: Part of my surprise at being asked why I wasn't at home having babies was that I had asked myself that question more than once.

Thus, while I did not explore the issue of consciousness, of the Japanese self, which has come to the fore in recent Japanese studies, I actually found myself straddling issues that pertained to both the older and more modern traditions of Japanese ethnography: How is the identity of a place and its people constructed? In fact, how are identity and social structure seen to be related? What is the relationship between depictions of status, gender relations, and local identity? What are the historical forces that have produced this process? What role do ritual and custom play in this as well? Kuzaki was a fascinating place to encounter these issues, and Japanese diving women were an interesting test case of how to define "Japanese" on the larger, national scale. These are issues that must be considered as larger contexts to my ethnography. What follows is a brief discussion of history, gender, the *ama*, the anthropology of Japan, and some points about maritime anthropology—all of which is meant to frame the ethnography that comes next. In no way is this discussion detailed or complete, but it is extremely relevant.

Japan in the Fast Lane

The Japan I encountered in 1984 was just beginning to enjoy its ride on the cresting wave that eventually washed onto shore in the 1990s recession. After the oil shock of the 1970s, the country was enjoying a growing prosperity and self-confidence that allowed the postwar generation to embrace so-called Japanese values more openly and wholeheartedly than before. The phrase "we Japanese" (*wareware* Nihonjin) seemed to trip off the tongues of people quite naturally, followed by the sort of essentializing phrases that now make anthropologists wince: "We Japanese, unlike foreigners [for which read North Americans], don't like much red meat," or "We Japanese all believe in peace," or "We Japanese communicate silently, through the belly [*haragei*], in a way foreigners can't understand." It was as if a crude form of 1970s' structuralist theory with its emphasis on dichotomies had filtered down into every niche of Japanese life. But I was also lectured on how even the concept of opposing dichotomies could be problematized: "We Japanese do not believe in oppositions like foreigners do. For example, white is not opposed to black for us; it can be opposed to black or red—it depends. It's relational." The main message was: We Japanese are different from you.

This sort of nationalistic mythmaking—its basis the notion that all Japanese everywhere were the same and unlike the peoples of other places —has its roots deep in pre-Meiji (pre-1868) Japanese history (Gluck 1985). United under the Tokugawa shogunate in the seventeenth century, Japan had long been a well-centralized state with a bureaucracy that ruled on everything from the keeping of household records to where feudal lords should live. Religion, travel, taxes, communication with the outside world, the class/caste system—all these were rigidly overseen by a shogunate that ruled for close to 250 years. When forced to open itself to the Western powers, Japan's decision to modernize and turn itself into a nation-state modeled on European and U.S. lines was an event much easier to bring about than it appears to have been for other non-Western states. Building on an already centralized political base, with only occasional resistance, the Japanese state remodeled its education system, its religious ideology, and its form of government. It created a constitution, brought in advisors to design railways, set up universities and factories, and adopted Western sports, clothing, and music. Although allied with the West (fighting alongside the British in the Pacific during the First World War), the Japanese ruling elite always remained aware that their development was in relation to a dominant foreign discourse in which they were the perilous others. Without the benefit of theories on orientalism, they knew that they were at the mercy of the images others had of them. As early as 1881, Japanese statesman Ito Hirobumi wrote during a visit to Europe:

> Since arriving in Europe I have been taking great pains to discern the feelings Europeans have toward us, and I am coming to the conclusion that, from the point of view of both feeling and reason, there is more bad feeling than good toward us. . . . As individuals, when it does not concern their interests, they seem to be kind and cordial, but it goes little beyond that. . . . Should something occur between the Occident and the Orient, all the countries of Europe will consolidate against us in an attempt to override and isolate Japan. The cause lies in differences in race and religion. The morality of Europe is founded on Christianity, and all feel like brothers. They have no intention of sharing their civilization and morality with those of other religions. (Reischauer 1986, 97)

In a series of lectures given by the Oxford historian Anne Waswo, she noted that "if Japan was not a colony in fact, it felt itself to be a colony in spirit." Part of this arose from the fact that all trade treaties with the West were unequal treaties: The Japanese were limited in what they could export to the West, but the West was not limited in what it could export to Japan. Pittau (1967) has nicely documented how the leaders during early Meiji (1868–1889) could have developed in any number of ways, but resistance to foreign pressure on trade and to foreign disapproval of Japan's attempts to expand its territory eventually led to the rise of right-wing forces and the embracing of fascism.

What is of interest for the Japan I was to encounter during the 1980s is the fact that it was during this early era of Japan's nationhood that the study of Japanese folklore—the foundation of Japanese ethnography—was laid. Kawada (1993) has documented the fact that the founding father of Japanese ethnology, Yanagita Kunio, was a keen student of Western anthropology, as well as a nationalist. Fearing the encroachment of Western values and the destructive powers of modernization, Yanagita argued for retaining an agrarian base to Japan's new economy—for loss of this base would be a loss of Japan's "peasant soul." He and his followers did more than anyone else during this era to document the customs and traditions of this vanishing Japan, both preserving what was disappearing as well as lending it an importance others might not have granted the often odd customs of the far reaches of the four islands.[1] Ivy (1995) has written brilliantly on the way in which Yanagita's recording of the *Tales of Tono* seemed to create a cogent subject matter out of odds and ends. In this, she actually admits to echoing the concerns of the Japanese novelist Mishima, that other great Japanese nationalist, who worried about the sort of "soul" Yanagita seemed to have created by this cleaning up of the more gritty and chaotic aspects of rural life.

The gathering of such folkloric data—the validation of disparate customs as somehow national customs—is not a process unique to Japan. Hobsbawm and Ranger (1983) have noted how this is part and parcel of the process of becoming a nation-state; it is, as it were, integral to the creation of Anderson's (1991) imagined community. Yanagita was doing nothing different from what the Brothers Grimm had done for Germany, or what Hollywood—working with less historical depth—was doing for the United States. And by gathering other researchers about him, Yanagita did document much more than would have been possible for a team of foreign researchers. This material exists as an invaluable resource for any study of rural Japan, as well as having formed the basis for Japan's own development of anthropology as a subject. This discipline flourished in the prewar era, with researchers gathering information on Manchuria, Korea, Taiwan, and the Philippines. In the 1930s, Japanese researchers even teamed up with German researchers, a fact not often admitted.

In tracing this trajectory—from studying one's own folklore to looking at one's colonial subjects—Japanese ethnography was following the path trodden by Western anthropology. That the U.S. Occupation (1945–1952) saw a flourishing of foreign team studies of Japan (e.g., Beardsley et al. 1959), as well as of the more traditional individual studies of the country, just added to the sense that anthropology was a valid discipline. In contrast to, say, Nepal, there are large anthropology departments throughout the country, full of students of both Japan and the rest of the world who see themselves as the inheritors both of Yanagita's salvage anthropology and of Western attempts to interpret other societies. The rather paradoxical discourse I heard while at Tokyo University in 1984–1985 was that the lone researcher doing British-style anthropology was *the* way to study others (Latin Americans, Koreans, Chinese, etc.), while team studies of Japan and Okinawa were the way to work at home. Moreover, I heard the beginnings of the discourse on whether Japan needed foreign scholars at all to understand itself: A trained Japanese anthropologist was more than capable of writing on Japan without the orientalist theories of others, thank you very much. Foreigners were, of course, hampered by weak language skills and weak communication skills (as separate from language, perhaps best glossed as the ability to read embodied culture) and thus likely to misunderstand much without hesitating to pontificate on subjects on which the Japanese had already written in some detail. This critical concern with how foreign scholars represent Japan cannot be ignored by anyone writing on the country today.

Moreover, as Aoki (1991) has noted, an interesting silence has surrounded the post-1970s anthropology of Japan. While the early postwar ethnographers—particularly Ronald Dore, Robert Smith, and David Plath —were extremely sensitive to the issues of lives lived in the aftermath of war and defeat, later ethnographers—among them Nakane Chie—have taken this fact as a given and have written about a "new" Japan focusing on the development of the urban middle classes and the changes and continuities within what Yoshino (1992) would term Japan's cultural nationalism. This form of nationalism must be understood as a cautious one. Politicians and other elites of Japan are always aware that an international worry over whether Japan will return to "bad" nationalism colors their place in the global hegemony that is postwar capitalism. For Aoki not to acknowledge this means that anthropologists are not dealing with the real Japan—just with the illusion of a tame and peaceful society.

While I am critical of Aoki simply because I don't know how we can understand Japan if we do not take into account its self-representations along with our own attempts at understanding, I also think he makes an important point. Left unarticulated in the recent work on Japan is the fact that since the Occupation, Japan has been locked within a political and economic relationship with the United States that is also an ideological one. From both sides, this relationship might be summed up as an extreme form of "othering": It is assumed that whatever one is, the other is not. Thus Japan sees itself as opposed to a selfish, individualistic West (for which read the United States), while North American anthropologists (and others) fall back on the group model as the best way to understand Japan. For many anthropologists, their introduction to Japan as a group society is not only Benedict's dated work but Nakane's *Japanese Society*—a rather ironic fact, since Nakane's rhetorical stance in this, comparing Japan to India and caste to class, is a rather interesting attempt to place Japan firmly within capitalist societies while retaining an analysis of the importance of the group for the Japanese. In short, it can be argued that an emphasis on structure has remained important in the anthropology of Japan even while it has become less central in anthropological theory. And interestingly, the study of Japanese women has come to dominate the field, as if this were the only way to understand Japanese individuals and their agency.

If we look at the work on Japan from the late 1980s onward, we can see how the theme of structure and, in some sort of opposition to it, agency, have continued to dominate, but again alluding to the supposedly much freer United States. We get a clear sense of this by examining the reflexive work produced in the 1990s. Kondo (1990), Hamabata (1990), Robertson (1991), and Edwards (1989), to name a few, represent a generation of Japanese Americans or Americans raised in Japan who went to Japan in an era when the larger discourse in the United States was of finding one's roots. In this, they were unlike the earlier generation of scholars who went to study Japan in the aftermath of the Second World War.[2] In terms of the sort of work this new generation of anthropologists has produced, the shift has been from analyses of social structure, its continuities and changes, to what it means to be a person in Japan who must live within the repressive structures of Japaneseness and large-scale patriarchy. Note, however, that one could argue that other anthropologists—European in the main—also have not escaped this largely Durkheimian framework.

It is Kondo's (1990) work that raises various important issues about the anthropological eye/I—about what it means to be a woman who, because she looks Japanese, is subjected to the pressures of conforming to the ideals of being Japanese. Her experience, rather graphically depicted in an encounter with her own momentarily unrecognizable image in a window, is seemingly the basis for her theory of Japanese multiple selves. I have some problems with her theory, simply because Kondo does not tell us enough about the person she thought herself to be in North American terms. The implicit contrast with the United States never deconstructs the ideological assumptions of that society. Moreover, her understanding of the differences between person, role, and individual is quite flawed—something to which I will return in chapter 8.

Yet Kondo's work remains important and stands out for me as the first in which we see the variety of ways in which Japanese—mostly women—deal with life; we are not looking just at a vertical model but at lived reality. Hamabata (1994) is also fascinating here, examining issues that he assumes are not often thought of in relation to Japan, such as the *amour fou*, which can tear an upper-class family apart. His example is important, yet the underlying assumption that outsiders need to know that the Japanese can love, but that for them love must be seen to be in conflict with the core values of society, is rather worrying. The fact is that, as in any society, so much depends on the individual and that person's circumstances: What might cause conflict in one family might not matter much in another. We need an anthropology of Japan that better understands this.

As I have noted, depictions of the conflict between social structure and agency are also to be found in the Japanese literature, and nowhere is this more obvious than in the attempts of historians, artists, folklorists, physiologists, and modern ethnographers to understand the unusual bossy women who are the divers of Japan. The idea of women who do not play by the rules of wider society has fascinated all of these scholars. Thus the *ama* become a particularly interesting example of the collusion between local ideology—in this case, unifying nationalistic representations—and foreign orientalism. All it takes, however, is a bit of careful contextualizing to piece together a different story.

Perceptions of the *Ama*

A year after I had returned from the field, I had the following conversations at a Christmas party:

> *Japanese man:* So what sort of research did you do in Japan?
> *Me:* I worked on the *ama,* the diving women.
> *JM:* Oh, really? They are very different from other Japanese women, aren't they?
> *Me:* No, they are like most Japanese women.
> [Later]
> *Japanese woman:* And what did you do your research on in Japan?
> *Me:* I studied the *ama,* the diving women in Shima Peninsula.
> *JW:* Why? *Ama* are no different than other Japanese women.
> *Me:* No, not really. In some ways they *are* different.

If the anthropology of gender is indeed a separate subdiscipline of its own, then any study of the *ama* would form an illuminating case study. Beyond the Western construction of Japanese women as feminine, sexual, passive, and trapped by a patriarchal society, there is also the occasional reference to the even sexier pearl divers. Within Japan itself, there are also many misconceptions about the *ama* that feed into Western ideas about divers. Their image as strong, tough, and independent women who might be sexually free can be found throughout Japanese popular culture. The process is thus a two-stage one. Where representations of Japanese women could be said to fall into the category of pernicious orientalism, the images of the *ama* go a step further: They may be amazons, but being oriental amazons, they are still rather feminine and sexy. For the Japanese they are also others, and within the cultural imagination, their representation is one in which all Japanese expectations of correct gender behavior and relationships are reversed.

The conversations quoted above are excellent examples of this. Most Japanese react exactly as the person in the first conversation did. In fact, any Japanese who lives near an *ama* community or who has visited one will proceed to explain why the *ama* are so unusual: They are dirty, loud (in speech), free and relaxed in their relations with others, and, most important, the women are often the bosses *(taishō)* of the household—ruling over their husbands—which makes them supposedly unique in Japan. Thus the dominant ideals of both class (in a straightforward Marxist sense) and correct gender relations are seen to be inverted among divers in a way that reveals what the general expectations of women's behavior are (Martinez 1993). Given these attitudes toward the *ama,* it is easy to see why they are considered not quite the people for a foreigner to study: They do not represent the best of what is deemed to be Japanese. I have even been told that I could surely have found a "nicer" community to live in.

The second conversation was extremely unusual for two reasons. It was the first time a Japanese person had ever said to me: "The *ama* are just like other Japanese women," and it was the first time I heard myself saying, "No, they are not." An *ama* is different from a typical middle-class urban housewife in that she works throughout her lifetime, while urban women are said to work only before marriage and, if need be, again later when their children are grown. Paradoxically, *ama* love their work, yet many would like their daughters not to have to dive, preferring that they marry white-collar workers and become middle-class housewives. In this way, *ama* are similar both to Japanese women involved in agricultural labor and to working-class urban women involved in part-time labor. That they are part of a household that functions as the basic unit of production also makes it possible to compare the *ama* to the petite bourgeoisie of Japan—the households that run small family businesses. Thus, my negative reply in the second exchange was based on the problem of defining just which group of Japanese women the *ama* are like. In some ways, the large literature on Japanese women is of little help since it tends to assume commonalties amongst all Japanese women rather than differences. Already mentioned was Kondo, who worked with working-class women. She concludes that the dominant ideal of good mothers and wise wives is so powerful in Japan that the women switched their gender performances depending on the situation, giving rise to her theoretical argument that the Japanese have multiple selves (1990). It would be more correct to argue that in Japan, as in any society, groups of women distinguish amongst themselves by region, by education, by age, by class, by status, and even in terms of the way in which so-called correct gender behavior is constructed—and the ways in which women relate to each other and to men reflect all of these distinctions.

Most of the *ama* I knew, if pushed, would claim themselves to be possessors of all the objects that marked them as middle class and, in their aspirations for their children's education, perhaps even upper middle class. They owned large houses where several generations lived in comfort. They owned plots of land for planting rice and plots of land for growing other produce. They owned cars and scooters, and even nonfishing households owned boats. It was in Kuzaki in 1986 that I first saw a totally modern washing machine, when the rest of Japan still seemed to be using the old watch-every-step-of-the-process machines. People owned huge freezers to store food. Their houses had more than one toilet, with separate baths that in some places were large enough for children to practice swimming. In Weberian terms (1991), they consumed a lifestyle that was middle class, and Clammer (1997) has argued that in postmodern Japan this is enough to constitute a class reality. And yet, other Japanese made a status distinction that often got translated into class terms: Fishing communities have lower status than other communities and, once perhaps, this correlated to poverty and class, but no longer. This problem is one that makes sense only if we consider the issue of status in the Weberian sense, where class and status can be but are not necessarily the same. To make the picture even more complex is the fact that allied with this perception of all fisherfolk as low status in class terms was the more curious representation of the *ama* community as one in which women's ascribed status in relation to men was actually higher than for other Japanese women.

Thus, overriding perceptions of class similarity or difference is the fact that the *ama* are seen to be exotic as well as strangely matriarchal by other Japanese. I use "strangely" here because any Japanese husband with a drink or two in him will tell the listening foreigner that all Japanese men are ruled by their wives. So why are the *ama* as *taishō* seen to be so different? The reasons for this representation of divers are complex and can only be understood through a discussion of the known history of the *ama*, a look at the representation of divers through time, as well as an examination of the position of the modern urban housewife. To paraphrase an idea current in the anthropology of gender, then, the construction of gender relations, as well as the representation of correct gendered behavior, are far too complex to be reduced to that old chestnut of trying to understand why women have secondary status to men. There are historical and political factors to be taken into account as well as variations due to generation, region, and even individuals. The next section attempts to piece together some of these issues in relation to the *ama* and other Japanese women.

The *Ama*, Gender, and Status

Many Japanese would agree with Maraini's definition of the *ama:* They are fisherfolk "who are distinguished from their neighbors by the fact that both men and women are skilled at every kind of fishing and underwater food-gathering" (1962, 17). For several reasons, this is a useful way to describe the *ama*. The fact that they are people skilled at fishing and underwater food gathering is important to note. Many westerners who have heard about *ama* assume that they dive for pearls—that they are pearl divers. This is simply not true, although the *ama* in the Shima area have long been involved in the cultured pearl industry (see chapter 6). Maraini's definition also makes clear that an *ama* can be either a man or a woman; another popular idea about these divers is that only the women dive. Finally, it is important to understand that the term *"ama"* itself can be misleading. Depending on the characters used to write it, the word has various meanings—all describing a person who fishes: fisherman, diving woman, or fisherfolk in general.[3]

There is also some confusion about the etymology of the term. Some writers on the *ama* have used the folk definition of the word: "In the old Japanese language the word originally meant the ocean or the sky. Later the meaning of the word Ama was transferred to the diving fishers" (Nukada 1965, 25). I have heard this folk etymology both on the Chiba Peninsula and in Kuzaki, where this construction of the word added to the way in which village identity was created. Villagers would elaborate this definition somewhat to say that the term *"ama"* originally meant sky or the heavens and is part of the name of the Japanese sun goddess, Amaterasu. Thus, they insist, *ama* was not originally used to describe all sorts of fisherfolk but originated in Kuzaki as a term used to describe their villagers who were part of the sacred guild that serves Amaterasu's shrine in Ise.

Unverifiable as this is, it makes the important point that the term has various meanings not only depending on the way in which it is written but also on the way in which divers and fisherfolk themselves define it. In the Chiba villages that I have visited, *ama* meant only women divers. In Kuzaki, the term could mean divers of either sex or divers and fishermen both; when villagers wanted to talk of fishermen only, they used the term *"ryōshi"* (fish master/teacher).

The use of the term *"ama"* to mean only diving women is often found in the English language literature on divers. I will also adhere to this convention, despite the fact that some men in Kuzaki also dived. According to villagers it is only recently that men have begun to do this; thus it seems appropriate to use the term throughout this book as if it were written with the characters for sea and woman. Yet it is important to keep in mind the various other meanings that the phonetic sounds *ama* can have, for as the anthropologist Kalland has noted, "Any historical study of the *ama* is troubled by the ambiguity of the term itself" (1988, 48n. 1). Records that do not use the Chinese characters for the term could be referring to male divers, female divers, or fishermen. Thus any historical outline of the history of diving in Japan must be cautious about assuming the sex of the diver—or whether the text is referring to a diver at all. In fact, outside of these various usages there also exists the vague division between its use to describe a profession—fishing and diving—and its use to describe the practitioners of that profession as a separate, almost ethnic group.

Many of the sources on the *ama* agree that the tradition is an ancient one in Japan. Physiologist Nukada Minoru states that they have existed for at least two thousand years and points to archaeological findings from the shell mounds of the Neolithic period as proof of this (1965, 27). Kalland also refers to shell mounds in Fukuoka Prefecture, Kyūshū, where there have "been found whalebone tools resembling the iron knives later used to cut the shell loose from rocks" (1988, 30).

Exactly when or where this mode of fishing originated is not really certain, but geographer Birukawa Shōhei notes that "two or three places have been suggested" (1965, 63). While he cites evidence that some Kyūshū divers may have migrated from Korea, he carefully notes that "Ama of Shima in Mie Prefecture and those of Kada, Wakayama Prefecture, both on the Pacific side are presumed to be of different origin"—that is, they are possibly indigenous. The idea that the *ama* of the Pacific coast are indigenous is pursued on the basis of different clothing worn by the women when diving. One must be careful of such analyses, however, since divers traditionally did their work naked; clothing is purely a twentieth-century phenomenon. Also, the relationship of Pacific divers to Ise Shrine might well be part of the reason for arguing that they are not migrants from Korea, as will be discussed.

There do exist records of dive fishing in the central part of Japan from A.D. 220 to 265. The Chinese histories of the Wei dynasty noted: "The people are fond of fishing, regardless of the depth of the water, they dive to capture fish" (translated by Tsunoda 1951, 10). In the Japanese mythical histories, the *Kojiki* and the *Nihongi*, mention of the *ama* is rare and rather vague. Whether fisherman or diver, the fact remains that both groups of people, while central to a construction of a modern Japanese identity ("we are people who eat fish") are also marginal to the dominant history of Japan. As G. B. Sansom noted, "though fishing and hunting were important means of food supply, it seems that the population from an early date was formed into settled agricultural communities," and it was upon these communities that the feudal society was based (1931, 45). Important as well is the fact that the increasingly stratified society of the Tokugawa era placed fishing in that marginal category of *hinnin*—wandering people who, in Buddhist terms, were engaged in polluting work such as hunting, fishing, butchery, or leatherwork. As Ohnuki-Tierney (1987) argues, the history of these people is often to be found recorded in the oddest of places, encoded in symbols and the sorts of relations allowed between those who were pure and those who carried the burden of impurity. Moreover, Ohnuki-Tierney argues that the history of such "special status people" is not really one of symbolic continuity, but one in which the special status accrues different meanings throughout time.

Thus, one place where we find the mention of the *ama* is in the literature and poetry of the inland court during the Heian period (794–1185), where they appear as a metaphor for a life lived away from the constraints of the dominant society. The collection of poems called *Manyōshū* (compiled in the mid-eighth century) has various descriptions of fisherfolk of all sorts and describes the activities of women fishing, diving, and burning salt, an activity associated with the *ama*. The poems found in the *Manyōshū* paint an evocative picture of a simple romantic world. Frequently the diving women of the area are mentioned; there is often a sense of longing in these poems, a nostalgia for the beauty and simplicity of life by the sea.[4]

There seems to have been a very simple but direct opposition in this pre-Tokugawa era between the complicated, intrigue-filled world of the court, as portrayed in *The Tale of the Genji,* and the life of the people on the periphery of Japan—the fisherfolk who were physically as well as metaphorically on the edge of Heian society. The divers in these poems held many associations for the Japanese of the courts: melancholy, solitude, nature, and freedom from the constraints of court society. That divers were more than picturesque—that they were hard-working women—seems to have been perceived only by the very frank Sei Shōnagon, a noblewoman who during her travels in the tenth century saw the divers at work and noted:

> The sea is a frightening thing at the best of times. How much more terrifying it must be for those poor women divers who have to plunge into its depths for their livelihood. One wonders what would happen to them if the cord round their waist were to break. I can imagine men doing this sort of work, but for a woman it must take remarkable courage. After the woman has been lowered into the water, the men sit comfortably in their boats, heartily singing songs as they keep an eye on the mulberry-bark cord that floats on the surface. It is an amazing sight, for they do not show the slightest concern about the risks the woman is taking. When finally she wants to come up, she gives a tug on her cord and the men haul her out of the water with a speed that I can well understand. Soon she is clinging to the side of the boat, her breath coming in painful gasps. The sight is enough to make even an outsider feel the brine dripping. I can hardly imagine this is a job that anyone would covet. (Morris 1967, 247–248)

If we were to add wet suit and face masks, this description could well fit modern divers. The woman below, the man above watching the diver's life cord, the diver surfacing, clinging to the side of the boat, and gasping for breath—all this remains the same.

Later, in the fourteenth and fifteenth centuries, there were Noh plays in which a change of themes can be discerned. The divers are no longer romantic figures seen at a distance who evoke feelings of longing and nostalgia; rather, they themselves have become the objects of romance. Thus, Seami's *Ama* and Kan'ami's *Matsukaze* both portray the *ama* as forlorn women, abandoned by their lovers to die and who return as ghosts. *Matsukaze* is based on *Ama* and, like the "Exile at Suma" chapter in *The Tale of Genji,* is inspired by the "exile of Ariwara no Yukihara (818–891), a famous poet, courtier, and scholar" (Keene 1970, 18). It is here that there appears to occur a conflation of several concepts central to Japanese culture—concepts that eventually came together to form the image of the *ama* as sexy and erotic women, an image that continues to exist despite the addition to it of the Tokugawa and modern images of divers as women whose household life is decidedly different from that of mainstream Japan.

One strand of the representation of divers as erotic comes from the simple fact that there has long existed a strong association between water, origins, and the female sex in Japan: The sea is female, as is the sea god; so are boats. Blacker (1975, 79) follows Hori and other folklorists in positing that the Japanese originally worshipped deities who came from the sea; then, with the unification of Japan under the emperors, this worship eventually shifted inland, both geographically and metaphorically, to the worship of mountains. The introduction of Buddhism might well have been part of this process; it is very likely that the Buddhism brought overland from China had a place for mountain worship in it as well. We might see this shift from sea to mountains as a symbolic echo of the shift from a female-centered society to a male-dominated one, as some feminists who write on Japan have done (Paulson 1976). Whatever such a shift might imply, the fact remains that, as Dalby has noted, "women, water and sexual emotions are concepts that have tended to cluster throughout Japanese history" (1983, 27). The world of the geisha is part of the "floating world" or the "water trade" *(mizu shōbai),* and she cites various sex and water-related terms used by the geisha.

There is an interesting opposition that existed between the geisha and *ama* during the Tokugawa era, mediated by (in structuralist terms) or created in relation to (in Japanese terms) the sea.[5] It is an opposition that makes sense. The multi-kimonoed geisha with their masks of makeup and their various skills in the world of art and culture were considered the embodiment of all that was most feminine in Japanese culture. *Ama,* in contrast, worked almost naked in the sea, which coarsened their skins, and they were famed for their rough and easy manners—obviously female, but not feminine. Geisha were part of a symbolically watery world, a world controlled by the patronage of men; while the *ama* were completely immersed in the real stuff and were said to be controlled by no one—least of all their husbands. One way in which this difference was also perceived was that the *ama* were seen as being sexually free, while the geisha were sexually attractive and, literally, expensive. In the most simplistic way, the differences can be summed up as shown in Table 1.

Listing these oppositions simplifies a complex reality. This is made clear by looking at the eighteenth-century prints that Utamaro made of diving women: What we actually see is a conflation of symbols. The divers in these prints often stand in the elegant poses of the sort that were used to portray geisha, but they are half-clothed, resting after dives, or flirting with small boys. By the twentieth century, the geisha had become a smaller group, too expensive for all but the richest of Japanese. Further, any opposition between the two groups collapsed in that any kimonoed server at a dinner party called herself geisha—and this included *ama* working in seaside inns (as I encountered in my very first visit to Kuzaki).

Yet it was also in the twentieth century that an older theme related to divers reemerged and was reworked to identify divers not only with the rural landscape but also with the values lost by a westernized Japan. This is best epitomized in Mishima's novel, *The Sound of Waves* (1957), which was based on his experiences on Kamishima, an island not far from Kuzaki. This is a romance in which the men fish on large boats and the sturdy, honest women dive for seafood. These women are contrasted with the city-educated daughter of the island lighthouse keeper. This young girl is selfish in contrast to the divers' selflessness, fat compared with their healthy sturdiness, and tainted by Western ways rather than being pure Japanese—an important tension in all of Mishima's works.

Some of these themes recur in the already-mentioned work of Fosco Maraini. His book on the divers of Hekura Island plays up the erotic element of naked divers (in contrast to Mishima, who sees only a healthy sexuality). For Maraini, the *ama* are healthy, bronzed sea nymphs, and the book contains dozens of photographs to ensure that the reader does not miss the point. Not intended as a sociological study, the book is meant to be a descriptive account of a summer spent with these people, who "live a life distinct from that of the ordinary Japanese, by whom they are considered rather as gipsies with us" (Maraini 1962, 72). He portrays the *ama* as the remnants of something truly Japanese, untouched by the influence of imported culture throughout the centuries, but he offers no proof of this

Table 1. Structural oppositions relating to the image of the *ama*

ocean	land
female	male
nature	culture
countryside	court
sexual freedom	sexual constraint
ama	geisha

aside from their vocabulary, which "includes numerous words which are peculiar to them" and the fact that "women seem to occupy a much more important position in the community and the family than is usual in Japan" (18).

The fact that Japanese researchers themselves are uncertain of the origins of divers—Korea or Japan—is not part of the picture Maraini paints. The question of whether there ever was an ancient Japanese matriarchy that is still alive among divers must also be asked, and it will be considered later. Yet Maraini's work had a profound influence on the touristic image of the divers outside Japan. Ian Fleming used large chunks from *Hekura Island* when he wrote *You Only Live Twice* (1964), in which he created the improbable *ama* Kissy Suzuki. Americans found the image of the sexy diver irresistible (there was also a film based on this Bond novel), and there was a time when one could find *ama* diving demonstrations in Florida and California. These blond, blue-eyed divers were billed as "Japanese *Ama*, or Pearl-Divers."

Alongside the symbolic role divers have played in Japanese history, there is another history waiting to be researched. The main catch of divers has always been abalone *(awabi)*, a shellfish much valued among the ruling class. The sale and presentation to feudal lords of abalone during the Tokugawa era, as well as the exportation of the shellfish to China, mean that economic records of the *ama* in relation to trade do exist. Some preliminary work on this has been published by Arne Kalland (1988), whose research centered on the history of diving in Kanezaki in Fukuoka Prefecture, Kyūshū, the village which some hold to be the origin of all diving in Japan. It is from this article that we get a picture of the *ama* as highly mobile, with entire families traveling on boats to different feudal domains in order to dive. Warfare seems to have caused the *ama* to migrate permanently or to obtain fishing rights in distant waters. The seventeenth-century diary of English Captain John Saris offers a glimpse of the *ama* during this time. He writes of "women divers, that lived with their household and family upon the water, as in Holland they do the like." He added that as a result of regularly diving "eight fathom deep . . . their eyes . . . do grow as red as blood" (Tames 1981, 56).

Kalland also documents the way in which he believes that the rigidity of Tokugawa organization helped to destroy the *ama* way of life in Kanezaki. The tension between the different marriage and inheritance strategies followed by diving communities and the dominant ideals of Tokugawa patriarchy created a rift between the life of *ama* wandering and the land-based ideology of this period. Other sorts of problems could arise between feudal lord and divers, as will be seen in the history of Kuzaki itself. But it was the marginality of divers that seems to have fueled the interest of post-Meiji folklorists and ethnographers. In this way divers became part, as I have noted, of the salvage anthropology done by Yanagita Kunio and his followers. The interest of Japanese folklorists fits into the nationalist project of recording all the true customs of a vanishing Japan, while also delineating the way in which these communities were different from rural and urban Japanese.

Modern Studies on the *Ama*

This construction of *ama* identity, allied with the symbolic representations of divers, underpins the work of the ethnographers and physiologists who have collected so much data on modern divers. The endurance of these once-naked divers to low water temperatures sparked a great deal of research on their ability: Was this an evolutionary adaptation? Was it a racial characteristic? Why didn't the men dive? Throughout the 1950s, the *ama* provided the main test subjects for experiments on how the body coped with cold water, pressure in deep waters, the building up of large amounts of carbon dioxide in the body, and other areas essential to the development of subaqua diving. This interest was prefigured by Teruoka's work in the 1930s when he provided a detailed description of diving methods and equipment, which he wrote with a German colleague. It appears that Teruoka's work on the *ama* inspired some of the more grotesque and horrifying of the Nazi experiments on hypothermia and hypoxia. These tests also formed the basis for later American and British research on the human body's endurance while in water (Keatinge 1969), ensuring interest in the *ama* up to the 1970s.

Alongside studies by the U.S. Office of Naval Research (1965), various articles have also been published in the *Journal of Applied Physiology*, frequently written by the same small group of researchers that included Japanese, Americans, and Koreans. Among the major issues were whether women in general were better suited to diving in cold water than men and why; and—even more important—whether *ama* physical traits such as broader backs, greater lung capacity, and lower shiver factor were results of changes in the gene pool, whether they related to a particular group of people only, or whether all human beings were capable of such an adaptation. In support of the notion that the *ama* were not like other Japanese, physiologists used the data of ethnographers and, I believe, relied on popular conceptions to assert that the *ama* held higher status and had stronger positions in their households than did women in other rural communities. All of this interest faded when the introduction of wet suits returned the *ama*'s cold water tolerance to the same level as other people's.

One legacy of all this research is that when I asked Kuzaki *ama* why it was that women do all the diving, especially in the cold weather season, the response was one that came straight from the physiologists who had studied them: "Because we have fat [unlike men]" *(abura ga oru kara)*. So convinced were they of the correctness of this learned interpretation that it was the only explanation that they offered. Any other explanation of the factors—and there must have been several—that led to the particular division of labor where men fished and women dived did not seem to exist (remember that the Chinese noted that all Japanese dived). Both David Plath and I observed that in seasons when fishing was poor, men would take over diving. This seems to imply that diving, lucrative as it can be, is even lower-status work than fishing. The equation, then, between those lowest in status doing the least-valued and most dangerous work seems an obvious one. Yet the myth that the women in diving households had higher status and more authority over their men than other Japanese women persists, and physiologists reconfirmed it with their "scientific" research.

The source for this misconception appears to be a misreading of the work done by folklorists. Initially the work done on fishing villages did not distinguish between ordinary fisherfolk and divers but centered on the ritual life of maritime villages. This was an area that had always fascinated the great Yanagita Kunio, and he noted in the introduction to his *Kaisan seikatsu no kenkyū* (Research on the customs of coastal villages, reprinted 1981) that folklore studies had concentrated on mountain villages, ignoring how they were different from maritime villages and not taking into consideration the way in which coastal and small island villages were similar to each other. Many Japanese ethnologists have continued the work begun by Yanagita on maritime communities,[6] but the most important of his followers for *ama* studies was ethnologist Segawa Kiyoko, who gathered vast amounts of material in the 1930s and 1940s and whose work is referred to by all students of *ama* communities.

Segawa's work always centered on women, especially women from the maritime communities. Her huge work on women peddlers, *Han onna, josei to shōgyō* (Female peddlers, women and trade, reprinted 1971), includes a great deal of material on women from these coastal villages and even notes that until the 1920s, some women divers still did migrant labor, traveling on boats to areas where abalone was plentiful. Her great contribution to the study of women divers, however, came in the form of the seminal work

Ama (1956). A large part of this book covers the history and customs of the Wajima / Hekura Island *ama* who so fascinated Maraini, but it also includes sections on the women divers of Shima Peninsula. During her visit to Kuzaki in Shima, Segawa notes that she met a lone, unhappy Korean diver (19). Her interview with this woman is typical of Segawa's approach: Her work is always full of quoted conversations with the women she met and interviewed.

It is from Segawa's work that the notion of the *ama* as strong, individualistic women seems to have been built up. Her interviews with Hekura Island divers on the subject of marriage include the following loosely translated comment: "A woman's talent can differ from a factor of 1 to 10: a very talented daughter-in-law will bring much money to a household but, as for men, their talent is all the same, only their faces are different" (1956, 65). Peppered with comments of this sort, it is no surprise that the book presents the *ama* as earthy women—a decided contrast to urban middle-class women. Yet Segawa herself notes in the book's introduction that the high value accorded to a diver's work did *not* imply female dominance in the family or in the community.

Still, the idea of divers as members of communities in which the strict patrilineal ideal of household inheritance did not hold can be found in Segawa's section on marriage. Her discussion of how parents tried to hold onto a daughter who was a good diver, thus putting off marriage and often encouraging short-term matrilocal marriages seems to have struck a chord among other scholars. Could the *ama* be the remnants of the original Japanese who were said by the Chinese to have been characterized by the high status of women?

This theme of matrilocality and the status of women in the *ama* household is only partially dealt with by modern researchers. For example, Iwata Junichi, who writes extensively on the divers of Shima, notes that he was frequently told, "In that village women are the bosses, in this village men are the bosses" (Iwata 1931, 81; 1961, 1). Iwata believed that women held the power in *ama* communities and that men said such things only as a way of dismissing that power. One problem with this reading of the statement is that the use of the demonstrative adjective "that" (*ano*) is vague. "*Ano*" is used to refer to a place that is partially and normatively removed; in this case, it might best be translated as "some other place where such things occur." Just where were these villages in which women were the bosses? Iwata's belief that these statements were meant to dismiss the real situation of women's high status is not enough; if the men sat around in boats, waiting for the women to do all the hard work, can we really say that this is a sign of women's power?

That there was short-term matrilocality in *ama* communities is verified by the work of Segawa (1956). Kalland (1988, 47–48) also attributes the decline of diving to many factors as noted above, but he includes the tension between matrilocality and the virilocal ideal as one central factor. Divers may have even lived virilocally and sent money, for years after marrying, to their parents; yet as an argument for *ama* as women who held higher status within the household, this is also flawed. One of the problems with this view is simply that until the change of marriage laws during the Meiji Restoration, marriage and inheritance patterns throughout Japan were varied and by no means always patrilineal (Bachnik 1983; Befu 1963, 1,329; Hendry 1981, 16). This did not, however, ensure a higher status for women in agricultural or merchant households.

What I learned from interviews with Kuzaki grandmothers (sixty to seventy years of age in 1984–1985) is that even in prewar Japan, married *ama* spent many years doing migrant labor *(degaseki)* away from their villages. While they worked, their husbands either did some husband service for the wife's household (e.g., working for the household) or were occupied in migrant labor of their own (in fact, many of the Kuzaki grandfathers had been in the navy). Other divers traveled with their husbands and children while working and thus were free from the constraints of being a daughter-in-law. It is this freedom from the mother-in-law that might well have contributed to the development of strong personalities in divers. Living away from the household also gave the young women a chance to become close to their husbands, leading to the development of an affectionate and good working partnership. Kuzaki was the first place in Japan where I ever heard men openly say affectionate things about their wives. That the huge earning power of a diver as compared to that of her husband led to a woman's higher status, as Linhart posits (1988), seems dubious to me. As I have argued elsewhere (Martinez 1988), all money earned by anyone in a household went into the coffers of the household as a whole and did not affect the Confucian patrilineal ideals on which the household was modeled. This, of course, leads us to ask: What were the ideal relationships between men and women, as well as between older and younger women? To whom or to what exactly were the *ama* constantly being compared?

Women and Status in Japan

Many of the women anthropologists who have written about Japanese women[7] have worked on the assumption that a male bias in the ethnography of village and urban Japan needed to be corrected.[8] In this they mirrored the work of feminist anthropologists elsewhere. It is not that women do not figure in these ethnographies—they do—nor even that they are all written by men, but that they present the male view of Japanese society with little input from women. There has been a vast change in the recent studies on Japan,[9] but it should be noted that Japanese feminists (cf. Ueno 1987 and Iwao 1993) have criticized the Western bias in these studies of Japanese women. As with the person who warned me against using Western dichotomies in Japan, these two Japanese feminists are concerned more with equivalencies—valuing women's separate and different roles in life—rather than equality with men.

What has resulted is that the analysis of Japanese masculinity has fallen somewhat by the wayside. Smith noted this as early as 1988 in an overview of the "new wave" of gendered studies in Japan:

> It is indeed the case that the focus on "women's roles" in Japan has led to an emphasis on the domestic and the familial, on exceptional female-dominated domains such as those of the geisha and bar hostess and on the few women who compete successfully in male-dominated domains. While I would never dismiss that literature as unimportant, I agree that it is time to move on to broader areas of investigation. . . . To describe the situation only of one sex is to imply something about the other and therein lies a problem, for the implication may be wide of the mark. (1988, 1)

I refer to this because it seems to point to one of the central problems with the discussions of status in *ama* communities. To tell us that *ama* have high status without telling us more about what men do (except that they are lazy and sit in boats) is to imply something that may indeed be wide of the mark. What we do not learn about the *ama* from historical or fictive accounts is: Who held the political power in *ama* villages? Whose name went on the household register as household head, the man's or the woman's? Who dealt with and made contracts with the feudal overlords beyond the villages? Last but not least, who took the most important roles in village festivals and rituals? The answer to all these questions, I suspect, is the men.

If the external system of village and state political power gave men higher status than women, can it be said that within the household it was possible for the women to have higher status than the men? In order for this to be possible, it would have to be assumed that *ama* did not comply with the traditional Confucian precepts about the role of the family in Japanese society that governed status relations in other classes—the hierarchical structure of the group in which women were instructed to obey first their father, then their husband, and finally their sons. That a woman could be valued as a hard worker within this system is not the same as according her higher status than the men in the household.

There is, of course, another side to this: the supposed history of the destruction of the matriarchal system that once ruled Japan. Paulson argues that Buddhism and Confucianism "abolished the matriarchal system inherent in Japan's clan organization. They established a patriarchal system" (1978, 4–5). If the *ama* could truly be seen as the bearers of these older Japanese traditions, then what more proof would be needed that such a system did once exist?

There are various problems with this approach, the first being that a true matriarchal system has never been described by an ethnographer and that anthropologists now refer only to matrilineal or matrifocal societies. As Paula Webster tells us, matriarchy is a vision: "The only *vision* we have of a society in which women have power, or at least one in which men do not" (1975, 145). Matriarchy was probably an important and necessary vision for the Japanese feminists of the 1920s and 1930s who adopted Hiratsuka Haroko's motto: "In the beginning, there was sun, and it was woman" (*genshi, josei wa taiyo de atta*) (Miyamoto 1975, 192). This refers, of course, to the sun goddess Amaterasu, and it would be truly fitting if it could be proven that the women who claim to be named for her really were the descendants of an ancient matriarchy. Yet if we look at the historical sources for this matriarchy, we find very little.

There is some evidence that women held political office in ancient Japan (Sansom 1931, 29, 33), but it would appear that this was based on their magical and religious power and did not correlate to the secular position of other women in the wider society.[10] It is true that the first recorded Japanese ruler was Empress Pimiko, who ruled in conjunction with her brother/ lover/uncle (different sources do not agree on his relation to her), but her rule appears to have encompassed only a small area of Japan—not even all of the main island. As for women who were not shamans or rulers, the Chinese chronicles tell us that "when men break a law, their wives and children are confiscated; when the offense is serious the offender's family is extirpated" (Tsunoda 1951, 2). Women were treated little better than property; they were considered polluting and dangerous (Sansom 1931, 51; Segawa 1963), and they were often associated with ghosts, underwater deities, and evil spirits (Blacker 1975; Hori 1968). While such power could be construed in such a way as to make the bearer of it valued or special, this appears to have happened only rarely; in general, the attributes of pollution and the like are typical of what Rosaldo and Lamphere (1975, 67) call the "secondary status of women."

Historical fragments, unfortunately, do not inform us about the relationship between different classes of women. What was dangerous in some women might have been politically necessary for others, such as the occasional empress in this early part of Japanese history. We just don't know.

If we look at the status of women during the feudal period of Japan, we are presented with the fact, again, that the historians of the Japanese prewar era "neglected the role of the masses" in their work (Takeuchi 1982, 273), and the few women we glimpse in these histories are all from the upper classes. We know, for example, that during the Heian period women of the feudal court produced some of the greatest literature to be found in Japanese: *The Tale of Genji, The Pillow Book of Sei Shōnagon,* and the diary entitled *Sarashina Nikki.* All three of these works give us hints of the life of court women: their physical isolation, which was punctuated by clandestine romances; the care with which clothes were chosen or poems written; and the long pilgrimages the noblewomen took. There is no hint of resentment at this mode of circumscribed life, as Sei Shōnagon noted: "When I make myself imagine what it is like to be one of those women who live at home, faithfully serving their husbands—women who have not a single exciting prospect in life yet who believe they are perfectly happy—I am filled with scorn" (Morris 1967, 39). In this extremely hierarchical society, these women may have been subordinate to men, yet they felt themselves of higher status than the women of the lower classes, with greater freedom to enjoy the pleasures of life—to travel, to write, to take lovers. But this does not include the right to consider themselves equal or superior to men.

Noblewomen seem to have lost some power with the rise of the warrior clans during the Kamakura period (1185–1333), but there were still the occasional political figures such as Masa-ko, better known as the Ama Shōgun or Nun General (Sansom 1952, 304). It was during this period that patterns of inheritance were changed for the samurai class, and "accordingly there grew up the privilege of masculinity and the custom of primogeniture, and it is from this period that begins the subordination of women" (365). But as Reischauer notes: "Among the peasantry women always retained their importance as co-workers with men in the fields and consequently retained a more earthy independence as individuals" (1977, 205).

This split between samurai and peasant classes became wider during the Tokugawa period, when the laws of inheritance were much more widely followed by the aristocrats than the peasants. If in the past the rights and status of women had varied, now only the peasants appeared to allow flexibility in this area, while the samurai strove to adhere to the new codes and the merchants tried to emulate them. If we group divers together with peasant women, their independence is not so much a marker of higher status as a sign of their value in a poor working household, where all good workers were valued despite their subordination to the men and older women. In this, *ama* differ only in the potential to be free of a life of servitude to their mothers-in-law. A brief look at other lower-class women gives us some idea of how true this might be.

Isabella Bird, the intrepid English traveler, is a good source for comments on Japanese women of the nineteenth century. From her we get glimpses of widows who "keep *yadoyas* (inns) and shops and cultivate farms as truly as men"; of alcoholic women who "when their husbands give them money to pay bills at the end of the month, . . . often spend it on *sake*"; and of sturdy women working in the paddy fields alongside their husbands (1880, 173, 248). Miss Bird also noted that: "According to our notions, the Japanese wife is happier in the poorer than the richer classes. She works hard, but it is rather as a partner than the drudge of her husband. Nor, in the same class, are the unmarried girls secluded, but within certain limits, they possess complete freedom" (295).

We get a similar picture of rural women engaged in agriculture from the work of the first foreign ethnographers of Japan, John Embree and his wife Ella Wiswell, who did fieldwork in the village of Suye in the 1930s. Unlike in the upper classes, widow remarriage existed and often the widow was seen as a sexually free agent. Wiswell tells us: "To an extent not suggested by the literature on Japanese rural society, the women of Suye displayed a remarkable and quite unexpected degree of independence in the matter of marriage and divorce. Many of them had been married more than once, and what is astonishing is that it was not at all uncommon for the woman herself to terminate the marriage, whether it had been formalized or was a common-law one" (Wiswell and Smith 1978, 149).

Although the divorce laws had been changed after the Meiji Restoration, these women appeared to follow a much more traditional pattern of just abandoning their husbands, running away with lovers, or returning to their parents' home. Both Embrees, as well, express surprise at the sexual license in Suye and describe premarital and extramarital affairs, frequent quarrels between spouses, and the bawdiness of older women—all of which presents a different picture of the Japanese woman from the submissive, gentle female of Western romances. Oddly enough, the divers I spoke to of this generation had much less tumultuous lives (or so they made it sound). A life lived on a boat with husband and children made such adventurous sexual freedom more difficult. Often I was told—pointedly perhaps—that a diver needed to have complete trust in her spouse since her life lay, literally, in his hands. Affairs were obviously not going on.

In farming villages, too, a similar picture of strong women holds, despite differences perceived to exist between the two. The differences relate to the degree of freedom. Norbeck (1954) gives us a brief description of women in fishing rather than diving villages of the 1950s and notes that the fishermen themselves felt that "fishermen's wives ordinarily have more freedom than wives of farmers for the reason that they must run the households and make decisions on at least small matters much of the time while the men are at sea" (49).[11]

What, then, about urban housewives? How were they different from the *ama?* Marriage, divorce, and education laws for women had changed with the new constitutions of the Meiji and postwar governments, and this would seem to imply that women of all classes had more freedom in the twentieth century. Yet the consequences of industrialization and the breaking down of class barriers that resulted in what Befu (1971, 32) calls the "samuraization" of the lower classes affected the status of middle-class women far more than did the government's legal stance. These values included arranged marriages, which had not been traditional for all classes and restricted women's choice in this sphere (Blood 1967). That this samurai practice was not rejected by women but rather had become part of modern Japanese life along with calligraphy, the tea ceremony, and flower arranging classes (all samurai arts) indicates the greater importance of social status versus personal independence.

The growing middle class that adopted these values was created from the peasant and merchant classes who moved to urban centers and became the cheap labor of Japanese industry. As historian Hane Mikiso points out, during the interwar period women in particular became the cheap and often abused laborers of the Japanese industrial revolution (1982, 172–225). In the recession after the war, women were forced to leave their jobs to men, and they took up the role of "good wife, wise mother" that Kamishima Jirō (1977) believes was imported from the West. Imported or not, this emphasis on the important role of the housewife accords with feminist theories that claim that the subordinate woman reproduces her class for the greater good of capitalism. You cannot have an independent, freely divorced, and frequently remarried woman doing this, for her autonomy contravenes what the capitalist workforce is meant to embody. This was a large shift for the older peasant and merchant classes whose women were often partners in the economic unit, which was the household.

This is perhaps one of the great differences between the *ama* and the middle-class women I knew in the 1980s: The latter's standing in the household was based on their ability to be good wives and mothers who helped their male children get into the best universities and hence the best jobs, while the former exerted their effect on household standing within the community by the income earned through their diving. While middle-class women take their status from their husband's job, divers take it from their household's relative standing in the community.

The picture that emerges is that of urban middle-class women who— despite the equal rights clause in the postwar constitution and despite the 1986 Equal Opportunities Law and later amendments—are circumscribed by middle-class ideals of feminine behavior derived from highly ideological notions of the importance of the mother and wife in terms of class reproduction. That all Japanese women might not be happy with this role has been pointed out by many writers on Japan (Koyama 1961; Davis 1980; Lock 1980; Ueno 1987), but what is interesting is that the value most women place on proper feminine behavior colors their view of the *ama*. The *ama* might not have high class status, but they are freer in their behavior and in their language than urban women. The money a diver makes from her work does not give her power over the men of the household, but it does contribute to her feeling of self-worth. A good diver is also valued by her mother-in-law and husband and is thus almost always better treated than the typical daughter-in-law of the urban middle class. Yet to outsiders she seems a rough, tough, almost vulgar figure and, by implication, if free in her manner, then most probably free in her sexual behavior.

All of this supports Norr's assertion that the generalization frequently found in maritime anthropology—maritime women are more independent than other women—does not take into account other factors such as wider social class (Norr and Norr 1974, 249). Many of the classic studies on fishing fail to place their subjects in the context of the wider society and make the women found in these communities seem very unusual. Yet a close look at the larger social context would, as the Korean anthropologist Cho Hae-joang notes on the subject of Korean divers, show "that neither do women develop a matriarchy nor are men the housekeepers" (1979, 1). As Cho shows, female autonomy, solidarity in the diving huts, and authority within the household do not undermine patrilineality or virilocality. "Strong" fishermen's wives or "independent" diving women are a matter of relative perception. Such perceptions reflect different modes of appropriate behavior, not necessarily different levels of power or status.

While such issues of status and household roles occupy the literature on divers, the divers themselves were aware of others' perceptions of their low-class status and, in Kuzaki at least, worked hard to adhere to the middle-class model of a good wife and wise mother. Diving had become part-time, as will be discussed in chapter 5, so that there was time to devote to children's schoolwork, the Parent-Teacher's Association, and to classes in singing, dancing, and kimono wearing. More importantly, divers worked hard to provide all their children with a good education, but especially so that their daughters might not have to be divers when they married. The image others held of them was rejected with statements such as "we are just like other Japanese," at the same time that their concerns about their children's future showed that they were aware they did not fit dominant class models. Furthermore, the touristic image of sexy divers was both laughed at and at the same time manipulated in order to earn income, precisely so that their daughters would not have to be *ama*.

Yet the sense of pride in their work, the skill of being a good diver, and the warmth of relationships with other divers and with husbands were striking throughout my fieldwork. There were good things about living in Kuzaki, about diving, fishing, and farming—so I was often told. Economies could expand and decrease, but as long as you knew how to plant a field, irrigate a rice paddy, and dive into the ocean, you would never go hungry. This, villagers felt, marked the difference between them and urban Japanese—they were independent of the vagaries of the capitalist economy, a rather prescient feeling on their part, it now seems. But fisherfolk the world over are like that: They never trust in luck, wealth, or what tomorrow will bring. What is important is the weather, the sea, and a person's own knowledge and skill. This applied to men and women equally, and it marked what to me seemed the real difference between *ama* and other Japanese. In Kuzaki the marking of time, the observance of ritual, and the adherence to notions of purity and pollution formed a coherent whole necessary to the maintenance of the daily life of work and to social interaction for all members of the community. In this sense, then, it was a traditional community, but we must take this representation on board with caution. Fishermen and divers alike spoke readily of traveling the length and breadth of Japan as well as in the world outside; they were not an isolated community caught in some time warp, but one in which the modern world had made many inroads, as I shall describe in the next chapter.

CHAPTER 3

Kuzaki

Making Place and Identity

In contrast to the associations with the term *"ama,"* being identified as someone from Kuzaki was straightforwardly a matter of pride. Not everyone in the community had been born in Kuzaki—in 1984–1985 there were many women who had married into the village, and not a small number of men who had done the same—yet the idea that life could be better anywhere else was only ever put forth by some of the unmarried young men and women. Most older and married villagers agreed that Kuzaki was a nice solution to the problems of life in modern Japan: You could work in the city, Toba, which was not too bad—not as inhospitable and impersonal a place as, say, Tokyo—and continue to live securely in a small, traditional community. Even disgruntled young men who worried about meeting girls had to admit that it was possible to have some sort of social life, without parents overseeing every aspect of it, by simply getting into a car or on a motorbike and going to Toba. "No one ever goes hungry in a place like this," I was told more than once. "In the city if you lose your job, that's it—you could be on the streets, family and all. Here, there is always family to help and work to do, even if it is only farming and fishing."

Thus it could be said that community solidarity remained strong. There was little population loss due to urban migration: Kuzaki was politically part of a city. Young people did move away, of course—there had always been migration into and out of the village. But the possibility of inheriting a large house and owning some land was better for those who stayed behind, so young people who could find jobs in Toba usually stayed and commuted. The school system was integrated so that primary school was in Kuzaki, middle school was in the *chō* next door, Ōsatsu, and secondary school was in Toba. Most young villagers had friends scattered in various places, and the buses to Toba on weekends were often full of teenagers traveling to meet schoolmates for shopping or just general hanging out. There might well be a wider world out there; school trips and honeymoons were arranged to see more of Japan or more of the Pacific, but ultimately there was no place like home.

In a way, then, Kuzaki could be seen to be like the ideal hometown (*furusato*) that has come to have such an important place in the imagination of the modern Japanese. It would seem to be the real embodiment of what others have argued is an imaginary, nostalgic construction (Ivy 1995). Yet, as Ardener noted in his comments on remote areas (1987), the reality of daily life was as mundane in Kuzaki as anywhere else. In my time there, incidents of violence seem to have been rare—a few drunken arguments that almost became fights, and some mention of domestic violence. Women's gossip circled around the unfaithfulness of husbands; there was a certain stoicism about it, as well as a lot of ribald humor. It was clear that people depended very much on the friends of their childhood or of their own generation (if they had married into the village) as one way of coping with the stresses of living in a small place. The closeness could seem claustrophobic to a Western outsider, but it had a warmth and supportiveness to it that could give strength to the mother of a four-year-old who was dying of cancer and make it possible for disabled men and women, widows, and even divorcees to have a life. "We are all related in the end," many people told me. "If you go back far enough, we are all family." Certainly the mode of address—the nicknames I mentioned in chapter 1 and the far from polite language used in everyday life—made the atmosphere extremely relaxed, as if, indeed, everyone was family.

The other side of the coin is obvious. Old quarrels between households would sometimes be mentioned, and competition between households in terms of land size, houses, children's education, money earned, fish caught, and the like could be fierce. Entering such a world was obviously not going to be easy. There was no way I could have rented a house and lived on my own, as I had once dared to hope. I had to be adopted by a household and given a role. My general title was "elder sister" *(one-chan),* although some people later called me Lola-chan. For despite the fact that fishing villages are famed for their independent characters, and Kuzaki certainly had its share of those, a lone stranger on her own was too dangerous. Who knew what I might be up to? Even the reassurance that I was married was not enough; I was there on my own and thus doubly suspect as a sexually mature woman who might want to have some of what she was missing (or so people kept telling me—fisherfolk are not above detailed discussions of others' sex lives). I needed the safety net of a household and the village needed the safety valve of having me overseen by a household. The Okamotos bravely took on this task and, after them, the younger Seiko family adopted me as well. To both these families I am eternally grateful, and I could well begin a discussion of life in Kuzaki by outlining the important role households like theirs played in the community. But before I realized how important it was that I had been taken in by a household, I learned how important being a resident of Kuzaki was to its people. These next two chapters, then, parallel my discovery of place, household, and community groups.

Kuzaki: Historical Background

Kuzaki, as already noted, was once a village and is now a ward of Toba City in Mie Ken (Prefecture). The city and prefecture are both part of the Shima Peninsula, an area recognizable as the setting for many of the prints of the artist Utamaro Kitagawa (1753–1806). Large sections of Mie are now included in a national park and protected from industrialization, so the scenery is still strikingly like that depicted in the old prints: a few wind-blown pines on the rocky cliffs that overlook the sea.[1] Off the coast are piles of rock that natives call islands *(shima)*, although they are rarely more than 5–10 feet wide. It is stark, sparse, and beautiful scenery. Seen from the observation area halfway along the tollway, Pearl Road, this mountainous terrain is revealed to be dotted with narrow terraces in which small vegetable fields and rice paddies stand out like neat cultivated jewels. The climate is subtropical: extremely hot in the summer, with cool winters and a typhoon season that runs from late July through September and occasionally into October.

Kuzaki is not visible from Pearl Road, crammed as it is between the Pacific and the sacred mountain Sengen, squeezed between the mountain and the sea. In the past, grandmothers especially liked to recall, since walking out of Kuzaki to anywhere else took days, all travel was by family boat on which everyone took turns rowing the single huge oar. Back and forth, back and forth, the grandmothers would mime the movement for me. Total flatland area was very small. The village households were built close together with doors and windows overlooking one another, and no one in the village was far from either of the two harbors where the households docked their powerboats. Kuzaki had always been a half-farming, half-fishing village; the people survived by diving, fishing, and by working the rice paddies and small fields tucked away in the hidden terraces.

The village histories claim that Kuzaki is two thousand years old and has always existed as it does now—a small community physically cut off from nearby villages by the mountains. In fact, the characters that make up the village's name are *kuni* and *saki,* which the older villagers used to mean "land's end." This is an archaic (about eighth-century) use of the word *kuni,* which can also mean "country" and suggests how isolated the village once felt itself to be. The villagers spoke, when needed, standard Japanese (learned in school) and the broader village dialect, *Kuzaki ben,* which was both more relaxed in levels of politeness and typical of Kansai Japanese (spoken in southwestern Japan), where the verb "to be" does not distinguish between the animate *(iru)* and inanimate *(aru),* but is the same for both *(oru).* Added to this are village terms relating to fishing and diving that are not the same as those found even in nearby diving villages.

The claim to being two thousand years old is interesting. Many villages in Japan have recorded histories going back centuries, but only the large urban centers can claim a thousand years or more of continuous history. Most regions in Japan do have museums with exhibits on the archaeological findings indicating that there were settled inhabitants in that area from the very dawn of Japanese prehistory. Kuzaki's claim to have existed as a distinct place since prehistory goes one step further: It implies a continuity that links villagers to the very land itself.

Modern Japanese history concedes that the four islands' original inhabitants were the Ainu, and that other people migrated there through (never *from*) the Korean Peninsula. Kuzaki's claim to have always been there reaffirms its links with Ise Shrine and Amaterasu, the deity who rules the heavens and, through her son, is ancestress to all the Japanese; this places Kuzaki at the very center of Japaneseness.[2] There is also the claim that Ise Shrine is two thousand years old, with a temple architecture that supposedly predates all Chinese and other foreign influences. Kuzaki's village deity is Amaterasu herself (not unique in Japan), and in the past, the village's strongest connection to the outside world was its annual tribute of *noshi awabi*[3] to the sacred shrines at Ise, a tribute it still made in the 1980s. Thus the village was still called a sacred guild *(kambe)* that served the deities at Ise.

One village legend has it that this relationship with Ise began in 5 B.C., when Princess Yamato made a tour of Ise Shrine's domain and found herself in Kuzaki. The local history, *Kuzaki Kambeshi,* places the time in the twenty-sixth year of the reign of Emperor Suinin (or about 3 B.C.). These legends are recorded by both Kurata (1974) and Iwata (1961) in various versions, and I heard one variation of it on the very day after I arrived in the village, when I was taken especially to hear Okuda Mohei (then eighty-three years old) tell me the story. As a foreigner with poor Japanese, I was given the brief version that I was to hear from many other people during my stay in Kuzaki: "One thousand years ago [*sic*], Princess Yamato came to Kuzaki and saw the women diving for *awabi*. She asked a diver to let her taste the *awabi* and, upon eating it, found it the most delicious she had ever had. So she commanded that the village send *awabi* three times a year to Ise Shrine."

Kurata's and Iwata's versions were told to them by Ota Hitoshi, who died before my time in Kuzaki, and they were more elaborate:

> Departing from the place in which our ancestress Amaterasu-ō-mi-kami is enshrined, the Princess Yamato wandered here and there until she came to Kuzaki in Shima.
>
> On that day there was such good weather that it was possible to see to the bottom of the sea. Exactly at the tip of Yoroizaki there was an *ama* called Oben diving in the sea. Out of great curiosity, Princess Yamato asked the diver, "What sort of thing is it that you are bringing up?" "It is *awabi* to make into *noshi* [*awabi*] (dried *awabi*)," she [Oben] said. Then she said, "If you were to try and eat it, you would find that it is a delicious food. Won't you eat one?" Princess Yamato replied, "Well then, thank you very much."
>
> The Princess was incredibly delighted: "This is the most delicious thing I have ever eaten! I would like to have this *awabi* made into *noshi* and to present it to the place where our ancestress is enshrined." When the Princess returned home, she told the people of her home about these things. Thereupon, as soon as she told them of her visit to Kuzaki, the Princess' party went again to Kuzaki village. The villagers gave a great reception (for the princess) at the village's entrance. The returning Princess Yamato said, "Please supply us at Izuzukawa, the place where our ancestress is enshrined, with this *noshi awabi*."
>
> All the villagers promised, "That is a very little thing." So it is that from that time until now, in April, August, and November,[4] three times [a year], Ise Shrine is supplied with *noshi awabi*. (My translation from Kurata 1974)

This version of the story holds various clues to Kuzaki's view of its connection to the wider Japan. Amaterasu is identified as "our ancestress," although it is not clear whether this is meant to include all Japanese or is a specific reference to Kuzaki's own enshrinement of Amaterasu in the village. Older villagers, however, were clear that "*ama*," as far as they were concerned, was their title because they were descendants of Amaterasu, thus implying that they, privileged over others, really were descended from Amaterasu as all true Japanese are meant to be. So, the Princess of Yamato (the old name for Japan) meets the divers, who in some way were also her kin (both descended from Amaterasu), and she asks them to supply the *noshi awabi* not as tribute but as a small thing to give to them in the place where Amaterasu is enshrined.

The second version of the story was one I never heard in the village, although both Iwata (1961) and Kurata (1974) recorded versions of it. The informant, a woman named Hashimoto Tora, claimed that she was a descendent of the diver Oben, a woman of the Tsuji line, a household that only ever allowed men to marry in rather than women out. This is interesting, since it is clear from her surname that Tora had married out, and no Tsuji ever made this claim of matrifocal marriage to me. Hers is a later version of the tale, set not in prehistory but in feudal Japan:

It is a thing of long ago.

On that day, grandfather Haku-Hatsu came to Yoroizaki in Kuzaki village, leaning on his cane. Exactly at that time, an *ama* called Oben was in her home by Yoriozaki making *awabi* into *noshi* [*awabi*]. When the grandfather saw this, he asked, "That is a very skillfully done thing, what is this thing called?"

Oben said, "It is an *awabi* and it is food. It can be eaten raw or cooked." Then grandfather Haku-Hatsu said, "It is the first time I have ever seen this beautiful, this finely made thing. I want to take some of this Kuzaki *noshi awabi* to the place where it is said that there is a festival for our ancestress Amaterasu-ō-mi-kami." Then the diver Oben said and promised: "During my lifetime I will give [*noshi awabi*]."

Grandfather Haku-Hatsu established forty small shrines in this area and brought ancestors and eighty small shrines to the land of Ise. Because of that, Kuzaki village had shrines to the Moon, the Wind, a shrine to Haku-Hatsu, an Izawa shrine, etc. There were forty shrines. Truly, every house also had about two shrines and performed rites for the deities.

The *ama* Oben made the promised *noshi awabi* and gave it to Ise. For that reason at the small shrine of Amagozen there is a festival.[5] There are found the divers' deity and the fishermen's deity. Oben's household continues to this very day in Kuzaki, Tsuji we call ourselves. In this household, for generations, the daughters have taken husbands (i.e., married uxorilocally). (My translation from Kurata 1974)[6]

This version is newer than the other because Haku-Hatsu is identified in other sources with a feudal lord. In this story he is not called lord, but only grandfather, as if he were just a wandering elderly man who in exchange for being introduced to *awabi* seems to bring religion to the area in the form of shrines and ancestors. In both versions, the wanderers must be from inland, since they do not know what an *awabi* is, but in the latter version it is encountered only in its already dried and cut form, while Princess Yamato is offered the fresh and probably still living form to eat. It would be possible to launch into a variety of interpretations here based on the shape of abalone. In other contexts, I was constantly being told it was just like a woman's vulva (see Figure 3), and locals stressed its powerful ability to make ill people well and impotent men vigorous, but no one ever made such jokes in reference to these stories.[7]

The differences between these two origin tales are interesting. In one, a woman discovers the wonderfulness of *awabi* and demands it in Ise. This could be historically correct, since imperial princesses have served as the chief priestesses at Ise on and off throughout recorded history. The shrines and connection to the native Shinto religion are taken for granted. In contrast, the feudal era is represented by a man who brings shrines and ancestors to the land. Again, this appears to echo actual historical events, since it was the centralizing feudal governments that administered Buddhism especially as the religion of all Japan—and Buddhism is, for most people, the

Figure 3. Fresh *awabi* (D. P. Martinez)

religion of ancestor worship as well as an imported religion. The role of Oben is also interesting. In the first version, she is spokesperson for the whole village; in the second she speaks only for her household, and they preserve this heritage by bringing men into the community by marriage (in implied contrast to the other village households). The tension here would seem to be between the community as a whole agreeing to pay tribute to their ancestress and one person making the bargain with the feudal lord. This is a rather more difficult point to follow, but since historical records on Kuzaki do note that they were well known for resenting their dual allegiance—to Ise on the one hand as a sacred guild and to the feudal lord who controlled the price of *awabi* on the other—it could be said that the two stories are symbolic narratives about the two ways in which Kuzaki was tied to the wider area.

The researchers from Aichi University, who spent ten years working on Kuzaki, cast polite doubt on the older version of the legend that places the princess' wandering in prehistoric times, but are able to cite documentation on Ise Shrine–Kuzaki relations that date back to the sixth and seventh centuries c.e. (Aichi Daigaku 1966, 16–17), which is when the Japanese first began recording their own history. The relationship is better documented, however, for the Ise Naikū (interior) Shrine from 1111 c.e. *(Ten'ei ninen).* As in the stories, this recorded tribute consisted of a thrice-yearly offering; but the records include fresh abalone for the Ise priests, dried sea snail *(sazaya),* and *noshi awabi* to be given to the deities. Interesting to note is that another nearby village called Ōtsu also paid this tribute to Ise, but since Ōtsu became part of Kuzaki in 1499 *(Meiō shichinen),* the villagers are correct when they say that Kuzaki is the only village in Japan to make the deities' food (but not necessarily the only source for *noshi awabi* for other uses).

According to the Aichi report (1966, 16), Kuzaki was placed under the domain of the Toba Han during the Tokugawa era. This resulted in a great deal of economic hardship because Kuzaki remained part of the Ise domain with the Ise priestesses—known as Yamato hime-san—responsible for overseeing the village's tribute. In fact, Kuzaki was one of several *kambe;* other villages grew the rice for offerings and/or priests' food, and these villages appear to have been tied together by a series of rituals and worship at shrines that Kuzaki dwellers would travel to attend. This practice of taking part in other *kambe*'s rites no longer exists, although I was taken to see one such festival at an inland village so that I would know what they "used to do in the past."

The twofold rule of Ise and feudal lord was the cause of unrest on the part of the villagers, who resented both the fixed price Ise paid them for their abalone and the feudal lord's control of abalone prices. As we shall see in later chapters, modern villagers do not recall these relationships as having been oppressive but instead celebrate their ancient connection with Ise and the feudal system. Given the highly rigid structure of social organization during the Tokugawa era especially, this is a triumph of nostalgic mythologizing over grim historical reality.

The dual allegiance came to an end, politically, with the Meiji Restoration when the giving of tribute to Ise was briefly stopped (*Kuzaki Kambeshi* 1936, 66). It was sometime during 1878–1890 that the gift of *noshi awabi* was resumed and it was then, according to some of the oldest women in Kuzaki, that a major shift occurred. The women had made the *noshi awabi* for Ise (as in the stories); with the resumption of the gift under State Shinto, the women had to teach the men to do this, and the men have done the work ever since. When asked why this occurred, one woman laughed and said, "Because the grandfathers had nothing better to do." It may well be that the raising of status of Shinto practices (which had been subsumed within a Buddhist framework for centuries) meant that it was considered more appropriate for men to do the work. This change appears to predate the arrival of any Shinto priest in the village (as separate from the Buddhist priest), but since I found no evidence of this beyond what women told me, I can only speculate here.

The village that had been part of the Toba domain also became part of the new Toba Prefecture at this time. In 1877, Toba-ken became Toba-shi (city) and was incorporated into the larger Mie Prefecture. Kuzaki was joined with its northern neighbor, Ijika, to be administered as one village. In 1890, again for administrative purposes, the village became part of a *mura* made up of five neighboring villages and called Nagaoka (*Kuzaki Kambeshi* 1939, 67). At the head of this administrative unit was Kuzaki's southern neighbor, Ōsatsu, a relationship that Kuzaki resented. Ōsatsu was larger and had always been "that bad place to the south,"—not worthy to be placed above Kuzaki, with its unique connection to Ise. It was a welcome solution when all five villages were incorporated into Toba City proper and were made wards of the city in 1955–1956.

The 1950s and 1960s saw a crisis in most of the Shima Peninsula fishing communities. Industrial pollution along the Pacific coast and generations of overfishing created what are continuing problems in the diving and fishing villages: dwindling catches, the killing off of the ocean flora and fauna, and changes in the ocean floor. The 1963 opening of Pearl Road (Pēru Rōdo), which runs along the coast from Toba City to Kashikojima, brought many changes. Not only does it connect formerly isolated villages, it has brought an important economic change: the growth of the domestic tourist industry.

Until the opening of the road, many villages in Shima had turned to pearl and nori (laver, a type of seaweed) cultivation as added sources of income. Both these types of cultivation are possible only in areas where there are protected bays, and the villages along the more open coast could not take up these industries. In the 1980s, tourism as a household's main source of income was rapidly replacing diving and fishing in many places. Kuzaki was no exception to this, as is discussed in chapter 6.

Although it is not technically correct to refer to Kuzaki as a village, as previously noted, it still felt like one. It maintained its own traditions and a sense of distance from Toba. The trip into the city—for those who did not drive or who did not want to use the toll road—took an hour by bus and public roads. Most older villagers disliked this trip and saw themselves as essentially remote from the city, despite using it as a place to shop or visit the doctor. The fact that they were administered from Toba and via Ōsatsu was rarely referred to. Nevertheless, this was the case, and it was therefore difficult for me to collect household information because I was constantly being told it was all in Toba. After several futile attempts to look at records in Toba, I was finally referred to the Ōsatsu ward head, who kindly allowed me to have copies of the household records for Kuzaki.

Political and Geographical Organization

Politically, Kuzaki was organized as if it were an autonomous unit. The main form of local government was the Fishing and Farming Cooperative (Gyogyō Kyōdō Kumi-ai), which was established in 1903. This Cooperative (Kumi-ai) oversaw all aspects of village economic life: deciding when to fish, when to dive, when to take in any harvest, negotiating sales of produce and catch for the households, acting as a bank, organizing local festivals, and overseeing the increasing tourism in the area. Most importantly, it maintained Kuzaki's ancient connection with Ise Shrine. Political life outside the village was also part of the Kumi-ai's function and had been since the office of ward head and Cooperative *chō* were merged in 1955. It was easy for villagers to ignore the relations with Toba, but some *chō* found the burden of representing Kuzaki to outsiders an onerous one. The sense that Kuzaki really remained its own place meant that having to deal with outsiders who did not have the best interests of the place at heart felt like one battle after another.

The internal organization of Kuzaki as a community that works together is discussed in chapter 4. It is appropriate to note here, however, that village subdivisions were established and used by the Kumi-ai to organize village labor; they were also important on ritual occasions. Like many traditional villages in Japan, Kuzaki was divided into two large sections that were further subdivided into two, making a total of four subdivisions in the village. These divisions were Kaikan-tani (ocean valley), which was subdivided into Kainaka (between oceans) and Ōtsu (big harbor);[8] and Sato-tani (village valley), which was subdivided into Sato-naka (between villages) and Hozune (treasure). The two large divisions were used to facilitate the organization of events. For example, when divers had to bring in their catch at the end of the day, the Kumi-ai would ask the women of Sato-tani to come first at 3 P.M. This meant that only fifty or so women would appear at that time. Then at 3:30, Kaikan-tani divers would be asked to come to have their catches weighed. The docking of fishing boats at the main harbor, as well as the side of the harbor on which a family chose to sit and clean their nets, was determined by this Kaikan-tani and Sato-tani division. During school sports events, the parents might be asked to team up according to these divisions. Members of one section of the village would claim that they did not know the household members of other sections very well or at all. There was also a bit of competitive feeling between these geographical divisions: Fishing and diving catches were compared not only between individuals and households but overall between village sections. In village rituals, the two large divisions determined on which side the men would sit in the shrine or temple,[9] and the organization of large village feasts would be done by the four subdivisions, so that men whose households were based in Hozune, for example, would all eat in a household in the Hozune area.

The original village record of households was divided up according to the four smaller sections, and any calculation of household religious needs (for example, which grandmothers go where to pray; see chapter 7) was done by the old divisions. Occasionally, households with the same surname but located in different village sections would claim that "we might have once been related to such and such a household, but not now." This may indicate that in the past, moving to another section of the village was a way of splitting a household. In fact, in a modern fashion, some households were split, grandparents living in the older house or a newly built one, while a younger couple who desired some privacy would occupy the newly built house or the leftover old home. Larger houses and young couples wanting to set up their own homes meant that new houses had sprung up at the very boundaries of the village. Many villagers would describe such locations to me as "lonely," but this also indicated a concern with the spreading out of the community, which for some people had little to do with solidarity and much to do with the dangers of being on the margins.

One way to understand this sense of place is to look at the village in terms of its boundaries. It was not only cut off by the mountain and the sea but marked its borders very clearly. On the south side of the village, at the beginning of the road to Ōsatsu, was the village graveyard, and the boundary between Kuzaki proper and the graveyard was marked by the figures of six *rokuji* or bodhisattva. The southeastern bay—the main harbor for the village—had Kaminoshima, a small island with a Shinto shrine on it, as its boundary marker. The northeastern bay—the sacred area of Yoroizaki where Princess Yamato stopped to watch Oben dive—had the Buddhist temple on one headland and an old Shinto shrine on the other. The road up to Pearl Road, which joined the northern and western sections of the village and was known as the Ijika Road since it led to that village, had a figure of Jizō-sama (see chapter 5) and the new (1926) village Shinto shrine marking that village boundary. This was also the way up to Mt. Sengen, where various small shrines—Shinto, Buddhist, and even Confucian—were located. In 1984 I learned that for older villagers and for children as well, these markers were important. Beyond these boundaries, all sorts of bogey creatures might well be found (so the children told me), and the grandparents confirmed that it was dangerous for me to go wandering outside the village boundaries on my own (I had started jogging in the evenings up the western road).

"Why is it dangerous?" I asked. "You never know what terrible things might be there; at the very least there are monkeys and wild boar," was one grandmother's reply. When I tried the more modern middle generation, I got a laugh at the mention of terrible things, but I also got a warning: "There *are* still wild boar. No one has seen a monkey in a long time, but the other day a boar startled Me-chan who was alone in a field, and in her panic to get away, she slipped and fell, hurting her head." I stuck to the road, but even on my trips to the *hatake* with the household's grandmother, I never glimpsed a boar, let alone a monkey.

It was only after fieldwork that I came to realize that this concern with village boundaries—in terms of the physical markers, the geographical distance, and of the more spiritual domain (as the sacred markers along roads and harbors would indicate)—defined the village in another way, which accorded with a large literature on Japanese folk religion. The world outside settled areas is a dangerous one: You bury your dead there and they might well linger as ghosts and werefoxes. There are witches and goblins, as well as other mythical creatures—of which monkeys are a very interesting manifestation (see Ohnuki-Tierney 1989). In Kuzaki, with its orientation toward life on the sea, the feeling that the woods around the village could be dangerous was felt even by the young people who did not believe in ghosts and goblins but were willing to express their worries in the form of a fear of wild animals. The sea, on the other hand, was also a dangerous place, but appeared to be somehow tame. All the bays and beaches were named, and the waters off the village shores were known intimately. Divers knew the ocean floor, and fishermen lay claim to secret knowledge of areas where the catches of certain fish were always good. This knowledge was passed along within families.

This conception of the village—not just as a historical and political entity, but as a place physically opposed to the more dangerous world of spirits and as a civilized and sacred domain that was opposed to the more secular and wild world outside—was one that took me a long time to understand. It is, perhaps, a vision of Kuzaki that was dying out, but I encountered it again and again without realizing at the time what it was that I was being told. If the marking of village boundaries was a concrete manifestation of an abstract concept—the division between inside and outside *(uchi* and *soto)*, which created a sense of place—there were other ways in which abstract concepts such as Kuzaki's historical continuity, its relation to Ise Shrine, and the correct relationship between various groups of villagers were made visible generally during ritual events *(matsuri)*. The ritual in which all of these themes became obvious was the celebration of Ise-Kuzaki relations called Hi-nichi (lit., Sun Day).

Hi-nichi: The Big Festival

As with all village *matsuri,* the Hi-nichi had multiple meanings. Not only was it part of the way in which village history and its connection to Amaterasu and Ise were celebrated, but it was also a festival that marked the mid-season of women's diving. It was a festival, as I was first told, meant to thank the villagers for their work as a *kambe* of Ise. In a more traditional sense, it was a festival that recreated the village, or as Bernier (1975) has termed it, recreated the cosmic circle or sense of *uchi* (insideness) that united all the villagers. Symbolically, as a festival in which outsiders—in this case, representatives of Ise—come to the village, like the dead during Obon or the deity of war, Hachiman, in January, it was also a ritual celebration of the need for interaction with the *soto* (outside). This last leads me to argue that even the more recent relativistic models of *uchi* and *soto* relations (Nakane 1970;

Hendry 1995; Bachnik 1994) are too simplistic. If we go back to the work of Yamaguchi (1990), Hori (1968), and Yoshida (1983) on the stranger deity, it becomes clear that the *uchi/soto* dichotomy is not just strongly situational (Quinn and Bachnik 1994), there is also sometimes a conceptualization of the *uchi/soto* relation as a clear opposition that depends on the interpenetration of one by the other in order for the social to exist. Thus, on the one hand it is possible to construct a sense of belonging or *uchi* that is contextual—that is, dependent on place, time, and opposition to that which is outside *(soto):* the family versus village, the village versus the city, the city versus the next prefecture, and so on. On the other hand, however, in rituals such as the Hi-nichi, these abstract principles must be seen as absolutely separate in order that the one can enter and imbue the other with power or *kami.*

"*Kami*" is a term sometimes difficult to grasp from a Judeo-Christian point of view. It is an honorific term for sacred spirits, and all beings have such spirits. Herbert claims that to understand the term we need to include cognate words that relate to the idea of master: the Ainu word for "he who (or that which) overcovers or overshadows"; the words meaning to brew, ferment; to grow and germinate; a fungus; a mirror; all-seeing; as well as subsidiary meanings such as the top of the head, hair, the headwaters of a river, and paper (1967, 24–25). Ultimately, the list of things that are sacred and therefore *kami* includes "qualities of growth, fertility, and production; natural phenomena, such as wind and thunder; natural objects such as the sun, mountains, rivers, trees and rocks; some animals; and ancestral spirits" (Ono 1962, 6).

Kami is an idea of the sacred and the potential for life, as well as power manifested, and in the end it can be embodied in anything from stones and mirrors to the flesh of living beings.[10] While necessary for all that is important and good in life, *kami* can also be dangerous and must be controlled. This is one way to understand the elaborate rituals surrounding *kami,* even in modern Japan. In most *matsuri,* the *kami* is carried around the village, neighborhood, or area in a closed, portable shrine that sways—not because of its inebriated bearers, but because the power of the *kami* is so great that it causes the men who carry it to stagger and weave. So great is a *kami* that whatever its manifested form (jewel, mirror, or stone) within the permanent Shinto shrine, it must rarely be revealed. To this end, shrines are always "wrapped," as Hendry (1993) has termed it.

The Amakajikime Shrine in Kuzaki (see Figure 4) was no exception. Physically it was separated from the road by a row of sacred trees, and wor-

The priest then handed the *sakaki* back to each representative, who laid them on a single altar. As each branch was presented, different members of the village bowed their heads and clapped their hands in prayer in unison with their representative. When all the *sakaki* had been presented, the Ise priest went to the small altar, knelt, and lifted it up, down, and to the sides as more music was played. The gifts, touched by the *kami,* now were returned to the worshippers. Then the village priest, starting on the left, bowed, stood, and closed the *honden* doors. Once more the music played was eerie, the musicians adding groans to their playing. The key to the door was returned to the Ise priest, both priests bowed in the center of the shrine, the village priest made a speech of thanks, and the drum beat once more to mark the end of the ceremony.

Outside the shrine all the villagers got a drink of sake, which was served in rough clay saucers that they all got to keep. Protective amulets were also handed out at this point to all present. The Ise priests and grandfathers stayed at the shrine to share a meal, while the women of the village gathered in the Cooperative hall to celebrate the "great day." The younger women had been preparing food for this since the previous day, while the older women had also prepared food for the four feasts each village section held. These smaller banquets were attended by all the village men and, in the absence of the village women, some of the sections had collected money to hire Toba geisha to serve the food and entertain them. In the women's celebration, the entertainment consisted of a speech by an invited dignitary (in 1984, this was the Toba Aquarium head) and the women's own singing.

This outline of the ritual and the day's celebrations suffices to highlight many of the major themes involved in all village ceremony. Purification— and thus some sort of resultant benefit—is symbolized both by the *sakaki* and the gifts the worshippers receive after the ceremony. The solidarity of the village is clear, as each section of the village is represented during the ceremony. The careful ordering of the village organizations and representatives symbolizes the importance of hierarchical and gendered divisions in Kuzaki. I will discuss these divisions in more detail in chapter 4 and relate them to another ritual—that of the Two Boats Festival (Nifune matsuri). What needs to be explored here is Hi-nichi's importance as a rite that celebrates the village as a place with deep historical roots and connections to the outside world.

Important to note is that this is the only village rite that called on outsiders for its performance.[13] It takes no deep analysis to understand the presence of Ise priests in the village for this ritual that involves the chief *kami* of all Japan—the goddess Amaterasu, who is worshipped in Ise as well as Kuzaki. The shrine might be in Kuzaki, but Ise hands over the key that opens the door to the *kami*'s inner shrine; it is the priests who bring the dancers for the goddess' entertainment (although village grandmothers claimed that in the past, young, unmarried village girls would act the part of the *miko*); and Ise who sent the carpenters who rebuilt the shrine torii the month before the ceremony. It could be said that much as Kuzaki saw itself as physically isolated, it was joined to Ise, and—through Amaterasu and Ise—to all of Japan. Through the rite that recalls the first shamanic dance, a historical continuity is alluded to as well. Thus, although the shrine was called Amakajikime (the Fishermen's and Diving Women's Shrine), with all that might imply in terms of the *ama*'s debated origins, it was the place where a primordial Japanese event was enacted. While other Japanese and experts might argue over the origins of the *ama* or whether they should or should not be studied as representatives of modern Japan, the people of Kuzaki assert through this ritual that they *are* Japanese. In fact, they lay claim to being more Japanese than anyone else—save, perhaps, the imperial family itself. Yet as with so many groups that lay claim to pure Japaneseness (aristocrats, or *yakuza*, for example), the *ama* are also marginal, existing on the edges of that supposedly homogeneous middle class that now sees itself as representative of the modern nation-state.

The ceremony is also important for another way in which it reveals a tension at the heart of what is taken to be central to an understanding of Japanese culture and society: the dichotomy between *uchi* and *soto*. As already mentioned, this dichotomy has long been analyzed as a relational or situational one, shifting as the self must in her relationship to society. Bachnik (1994) argues that we might see the self—the I—as the zero point in this indexical ordering of Japanese society. She hints at but veers away from considering moments in which this relationship is necessarily symbolized as being completely polar. That this opposition is temporary and ends in what I would call the interpenetration of the one by the other would appear to be a concrete enactment of what is often symbolized by the conventional depiction of yin and yang.

Yin and yang must not be considered as separate, for without each other they would not exist and together they form a necessary whole; nor must they be thought of as absolute in their opposition, since each contains aspects of the other. Structuralist analysis would see these oppositions as complementary, but they are more than that: They are creative forces that need the other to exist. Thus we might depict all the contradictions at the heart of the Hi-nichi ceremony as impossibilities that are necessary: Amaterasu is found wrapped inside the very heart of the shrine—which, however, stands on a village boundary. Like all *kami,* she is both there and not there, for she also dwells in Ise and other shrines in Japan. Her power is both creative—as sun goddess, the world, let alone Japan, would not exist without her—but also destructive, and she must be summoned or coaxed out only on carefully ritualized occasions.

Kuzaki itself might well be seen as contradictory in its existence: Fiercely proud of being a self-sufficient village, it formed and still forms part of a larger whole tied to the support of Ise Shrine. Historically, like all Japanese villages, it was ruled by a feudal lord whom it supported through taxes and by performing the duty of guarding the coast; now it is tied to the civic through the ward system of Toba City. Through marriage ties, it continues to be linked to other villages in the area. Through the practice of migrant labor, its young men and women wandered up and down the Japanese coasts, traveling to Korea sometimes; and despite the end of such migrant work for women, since the 1950s Kuzaki fishermen have been sailors in Japan's global fishing fleet. Most importantly for the villagers, it is tied through their ancestress, Amaterasu, to the imperial family—tendentious though this claim might be.

As traditional villages are meant to do, Kuzaki guarded its boundaries; yet these were ever permeable, constantly being breached by people, events, *kami,* and even the dead. Every ritual I witnessed during fieldwork might be seen as an attempt to shore up these boundaries, to remake them—but paradoxically, the shoring up involved the inviting in of the very forces that might destroy it (cf. Bernier 1975): Amaterasu, young *kami,* Hachiman, the dead, as well as other guests such as officials from the local government. The inviting in, the ceremonies full of offerings, also possibly served to reanimate these various powers. It was not just the village that benefited but also the *kami* who were worshipped—the fulfillment of a contract that empowered both sides. It might be argued that this symbolic enactment of the village's empowerment is a form of resistance to a fact both historical and modern: Kuzaki exists and existed enmeshed in a series of political relationships that often have made its residents feel powerless. Obliged to make offerings of good food to Ise; owing loyalty to the feudal lord; geographically redefined by changing governments; at the mercy of business interests that would bring more tourist development to the coast; competing with neighboring villages for a voice on the city council (Ōsatsu, it was always claimed, got the best of them); the object of domestic tourism in which they were seen as exotic others—Kuzaki was anything but the self-sufficient, independent place villagers always liked to assert it was. Hi-nichi, however, reaffirmed a feeling of specialness and superiority for the villagers. In the

1980s it was not a festival open to outsiders, and the NHK crew was not allowed to film the event for its documentary.

Thus Hi-nichi celebrates a historical or geographic continuity that might be viewed as a natural process—a becoming—to do with the realities of life and the passing of time. At the same time, it is a continuity that depends on human agency, as represented by the various sectors of village society. As a ceremonial and religious event, however, it raises questions about the role of religion not just in the village but in Japan as well. Were the people of Kuzaki more religious than other Japanese because they were a *kambe?* What does it mean, anyway, to be religious in Japan? These are questions that need to be answered in some part, since rituals in Kuzaki were very much part of everyday life.

Religious Japanese?

There are two questions to be addressed here. First of all, what is the nature of religion in Japan? Secondly, what role does the performance of ritual play in the lives of the Japanese? These two questions echo larger questions that have caused great debate in anthropology: How to define religion, and why does religion continue to play such an important role in human societies? That is, given the idea that our modern or even postmodern societies accept many of the premises of science, why do religious ideas, beliefs, and practices continue to exist and develop in human society? The example of Japan is one that begs discussion of all these issues.

We also need to ask why religion is often discussed as a separate part of life in modern Japan. This seems a false dichotomy given the statistics quoted by Reader (1990) to the effect that while most Japanese say they are not religious, if you ask them what they do in terms of rituals, the number of adherents to Buddhist sects, new religions, and Shinto practices is higher than the entire population of Japan. Anthropologists and religious studies specialists of Japan argue that the reason for this has to do with an understanding of religion as being about belief: The Japanese feel no need to *believe* (as they see Christianity and new religious movements demanding)—they just *do*.[14] Thus Shinto is the "way of the *kami*," while Buddhism is the "teachings of Buddha" (Bukkyo). Religious behavior in Japan, argue Reader and Tanabe (1998), is so embedded in daily life that it is part of the fabric of that life—it is about being *practically* religious. This is an important issue to understand about religion in general, not just about Japan: The doing of religion in many societies is distinct from the issue of belief so

All Kuzaki population records were kept by household surname, of which there were only twenty-nine in the village. Some 105 households shared eighteen surnames: Seiko (17), Okamoto (11), Matsui (9), Ota (9), Hashimoto (7), Sakaguchi (6), Okuda (6), Tsuji (6), Kusuki (5), Yamaguchi (5), Oguchi (4), Sakai (4), Tsumagari (4), Murayama (4), Kukuchi (2), Yamamoto (2), Norita (2), and Nakayama (2). Eleven households had individual surnames: Hatai, Kawamura, Makino, Nakasato, Obata, Ohata, Okayama, Ono, Sakata, Suidani, and Yagura. In order to preserve some anonymity for the people in Kuzaki, I will refer to people by their surnames only. In the cases discussed in chapter 8, I use pseudonyms and have combined various people into two case studies to further protect anonymity.

All birth, death, and marriage dates were recorded under the name of the household head. The head *(shujin)* was generally the oldest male in the household who had inherited both the house and associated property. There are exceptions to this rule, throughout Japan and especially in Kuzaki. A man who has reached his sixties or seventies frequently allows his middle-aged son to take over the responsibilities of the *ie*. This need not always be the eldest son. Kuzaki long had the custom that any son able to find employment outside the village would leave for jobs in Osaka or Nagoya. Often it was a middle or youngest son who stayed behind to fish or run the family inn, and it was this son who inherited the *ie*.[3] In some cases, the widowed mother of the *ie* was listed as *shujin;* occasionally the only man in the household was the adopted son-in-law, and the mother-in-law would be reluctant to relinquish control to him. There were even some young widowed women who held the position of *shujin*.

The main *(honke)* and stem *(bunke)* household organizational unit known as *dōzoku* found in many parts of Japan was not common in Kuzaki. Occasionally, people referred to another household as their *honke,* but this was only at times such as when funerals or large Obon celebrations were being planned and help from all one's kin was needed. As one man told me, the *dōzoku* system depended on landownership, so that the households could be organized around the labor of irrigation, planting, and harvesting rice paddies and fields. The basic premise of the system is that the head family is richer than the others, who fulfill their stem family obligations by offering labor to the main household. As this Kuzaki informant noted: "Fishermen are too poor to have such relationships; one year you have a good season, another a very poor one. You can't fulfill the obligations of *honke* and *bunke* when you might be too poor to fulfill your duties."[4] The people of Kuzaki used a much more general term for their kin—"*shinseki*" (actually, *shinrui,* meaning relatives)—and existed in a very wide and loose network of patrilateral kin relations. Matrilineal kin were considered important only while a woman was alive. That is, a woman would remember her kin and count them among the household *shinseki*. At her death, however, that matrilineal connection would be forgotten. Daughters-in-law still spent the first month after a baby's birth at their parents' house, and villagers used the term *"mago-bāsan"* (grandchild's grandmother) for a child's matrilineal grandmother.

As the basic unit of village organization, the household had one vote it could cast during the village Kumi-ai elections, and it was responsible for ensuring that one representative from the household was present during the elections. This person could be the wife, daughter, son, or household head. In modern Japan, this decidedly republican practice was rather archaic. For local and national elections, all eligible adult members of the household were encouraged to cast their vote.

Village tasks were also allotted by household. If the Kumi-ai decided that it needed the harbor cleaned, it would request one or two members from each *ie* to come to the harbor and work. When, in August, the seaweed *arame* was gathered and sold, all the money went to the Kumi-ai and all the labor for this was voluntary, with different members of the household coming out to work as their schedule allowed. Households who sent no one to work were fined; each village *ie* had to be represented, and it could be anyone. During my fieldwork, when the members of the Okamoto household felt too busy to take part in such work, I was an acceptable substitute —although it meant bearing the brunt of various jokes about being a second wife. Important festivals also fell into this category, although as many members of the *ie* as possible would try to attend major ceremonies; smaller ones often saw only grandparents—and during my stay, the anthropologist—in attendance.

These practices of participation and representation of the *ie* in village life and organization go back to Tokugawa Japan, when the village priest would keep track of household records *(koseki)* as well as of household participation. One way in which this continuity was still made tangible in Kuzaki was during the *nembutsu* (sutra reciting) the grandfathers performed on Buddha's birthday (April 6th). As they and the village Buddhist priest recited the sutras, they opened and closed the villagers' *koseki*. This sutra chanting is termed *"tendoku"* (skipping) by some and "chasing the *mushi* out" by others; here *"mushi"* can mean, literally, bugs such as moths, but also evil influences (cf. Stefánsson 1993). Many areas in Japan had or have similar ceremonies in which evil spirits are sent out of the village. The performance of this rite by the grandfathers points to another way in which the social and ritual life of the village had long been organized—that is, through horizontally organized groups that have been described as "age-grades" (Norbeck 1953). Perhaps it is no surprise that in a place not organized along *dōzoku* principles, age-grades should dominate.

Age-Grades

Age-grade organization can be seen as a level of organization above that of the household. Ueno (1987) argues that the existence of these horizontal groupings constitutes an important exception to Nakane's vertical society theory, giving us a picture of a much more egalitarian Japan. In Kuzaki, the various village organizations were called by a specific name that was often followed by the term *"kai"* (group).[5] These organizations were based on the principle of *dōkyūsei*, or "same-age classmate."[6] As Bestor has noted, "relationships among classmates may last a lifetime, cutting across occupational and status lines attained in adult life" (1985, 128). This relationship was especially close-knit in Kuzaki among the men and women who had not left the village; a *dōkyūsei* friend was a friend for life, and duties as well as responsibilities are inherent in this relationship.

Yet despite its horizontal nature, age-grade organization parallels the hierarchical organization of the *ie*. The various groups within the village could be seen as forming one large household, with men in their fifties as the head (the officers of the Kumi-ai); younger men waiting to inherit the political mantle; women as housewives, mothers, and daughters; and the retired men and women being responsible for various aspects of village ritual life, just as household grandparents were often the most responsible for the *ie* ancestors and *kami*.[7]

It is doubtful whether this traditional type of village organization—or even the cohabiting, multigenerational *ie*—was to be found in such a complete form in prewar Kuzaki. Given that young married couples and their children lived on boats and performed migrant labor outside the village for large parts of the year, and given that even after the war, married men often worked on large fishing vessels, the household and age-grades must have relied mostly on the presence of older men and women in the past. It is a rather postmodernist irony that just at the time when the *ie* and age-grades were believed to have disappeared from Japan, Kuzaki had enough of a locally based population to support households of up to four generations whose members also were integrated into a wider village organization. Thus the seemingly quite traditional aspect of life in Kuzaki that I am about to describe was, I suspect, a very modern development.

The *Dōkyūsei*

The basis of the modern age-grade groupings is the school-age group. All children born between March of one year and February of the following are grouped together as classmates. School begins for most children at the age of five, and their classmates for that first year of primary school *(shōgakkō)* will continue to be classmates throughout middle school *(chūgaku)* and secondary school *(kōtōgakkō)*. In Kuzaki, the first six years of schooling took place in the village, and one's classmates were one's constant playmates both inside and outside of school. Children might play with older or younger friends, but the school reinforced the principles of hierarchy based on age or *senpai* (one's senior). During school events, distinctions between the grades were carefully observed, the first-year students always coming at the end of the queue or being the first to perform during the school open house, while the older children were given more time and more elaborate speeches to do during special school events. Young schoolchildren would often introduce their friends by saying, "He/she is my *dōkyūsei*," so that an adult would know that they were about the same age and to be treated as equals.

By middle school, the Kuzaki children went to Ōsatsu Chūgaku, and the group expanded to fit in Ōsatsu children. Other divisions occurred here; the groups were crosscut by school clubs such as volleyball or baseball. Yet within these clubs, age hierarchy was always maintained. Graduation to secondary school meant attending classes in Toba City or, if the student was very bright, at the more prestigious Ise City Kōtōgakkō. Again the group expanded to include children from other places in these cities, but these connections might well turn out to be tenuous. The farther away from the village, the less likely were the *dōkyūsei* relations to be continued once school had ended, unless people coincided in the workplace or some other organization. This was frequent in the 1980s with men who found themselves working in construction or belonging to the regional innkeepers group with old classmates.

After graduation from secondary school, the young men who remained in the village became members of the Seinendan—the young men's group. Most members continued in the Seinendan until the age of twenty-five or marriage. Young girls had no equivalent group, although in the 1980s a few had joined the unisex Toba City Seinendan.

Kuzaki Seinendan members had a special club kimono—a distinctive abstract blue pattern on a white background—that they wore on ceremonial occasions. These occasions included four important village events. The most important festival from the young men's point of view was Obon, the Buddhist festival of the dead, which took place during August. The Seinendan was responsible for organizing the three nights of dancing during Obon. To do this, they would raise money by weeding and spraying along the roads of the village. The Kumi-ai paid for this, and individual households also made donations if the Seinendan cleaned an area directly outside their home. The money earned in this way was used to buy prizes for the best dancers and costumes worn during Obon; the members of the club acted as judges during the dancing. Seinendan members also taught children the traditional village dance, often carrying the smallest children as they danced. They also arranged for modern rock music to be played after midnight during Obon and taught the current dances to others.

Next, on September 15—Old Folks' Day—the Seinendan helped the Wives' Club with the entertainment and food preparation for the grandparents who attended a luncheon feast in the village hall. In the past, it was said, the young men did all the work for this, including the raising of money for the food, but in 1984 the Kumi-ai distributed Toba City funds for this and the more efficient Wives' Club did the cooking.

On November 18, ten young men from the Seinendan (the ten oldest) were selected to row the old boats used in the Nifune festival. This complicated ritual required that one of the two boats row out to an island called Kaminoshima (god's island) and replace the ritual objects at the god's small shrine. This ritual will be described in more detail at the end of this chapter.

On January 5, the Seinendan also participated in another important festival involving Hachiman-san, the god of war (see chapter 7). Three of these occasions that so involve the young men (Obon, Nifune, and Hachiman-san festivals) can also be seen as occasions when village boundaries were restructured and community solidarity was reaffirmed. Thus any young man who remained in Kuzaki, working, hoping to marry and inherit the household, was from very early on involved in the symbolic maintenance of the village. Finally, on an occasional basis, the Seinendan organized bowling and a yearly holiday taken by the club members.

After the age of twenty-five or marriage, a young man joined the volunteer firemen (Shōbōdan). These volunteers were on call during the typhoon season, drilled once a month, and were responsible for the maintenance of the fire equipment, which was stored throughout the village. The monthly drills ended in dinner and drinking in the village restaurant and were seen as a social event. In this way, the Shōbōdan also served as a way for the young men who worked outside the village to keep up with their friends. Men continued in the firemen's group until the age of thirty-five or so, when it was time for them to begin considering their role in the political realm.

There was no special group for the men between the ages of thirty-five and fifty, but this was the time when men who had some free time—generally fishermen and inn owners—began to take part in village political life. This could include taking one of the minor offices in the Kumi-ai such as beach officer or some role in the PTA. In fact, only men held offices in the PTA, and its head was always chosen from among the fathers who had children in the sixth and final year of primary school. Being PTA head was seen as an important step toward any other role in Kuzaki political life.

Men over sixty—the grandfathers *(ojii-san)*—took part in three separate groups. There was the elders' club (Rōjin-kai),[8] the Buddhist Nembutsu kai (sutra-reciting group), which met three times a year, and the Shinto group that made the *noshi awabi* and participated in special Shinto festivals. The last group included only men who had not had a recent death (in the previous year) in their household and therefore varied in its membership. Hierarchy was maintained in all three groups, with the Rōjin-kai being the most flexible; only the most active grandfathers in the age range of seventy would serve as head and secretary for this club, which met to hear lectures on topics such as "A healthy old age" or to clean up the temple and shrine sacred areas. For the Buddhist and Shinto groups, the eldest sat at the front and taught younger men the prayers and practices pertaining to each occasion.

Although women did not have organizations equivalent to the men's Seinendan or Shōbōdan, they too talked of "my *dōkyūsei*" and began active participation in age-grade activities after their marriage. The assumption was that unmarried women in the village would probably marry out and that there was no need to involve these young women, early on, in village organization. Once married, not only did women automatically belong to the wives' club (Fujin-kai), but through this group they were also linked to the divers' group, which was subsumed within the wives' club. That is, a woman took part in all the social events of the wives' club until the age of forty-one, when officially she could no longer be a member. Yet since the club also served the divers, older women would attend meetings and some of the special festivals until their fifties. But they no longer took part in arranging dances for the School Sports Day and were no longer responsible for the club's organization.

Women of forty-one to fifty-nine years of age were referred to as *chūbāsan*. They were practicing to become part of the Buddhist sutra (Nembutsu-bāsan) group. The group was not very active, although grandmothers spoke of a time when they met regularly and had good times.

Grandmothers aged sixty to seventy-one who had not had a recent death in the family belonged to the Nembutsu-bāsan group. It was an important part of village religious life, marked by an initiation for the sixty-year old women on February 15 each year. The head of the group was the oldest woman present. The Nembutsu-bāsan prayed for the souls of household and village dead. All grandmothers over sixty belonged to the Rōjin-kai, as did the men.

Other Groups

There were three groups in the village that did not fall into the age-grade type of organization: the families of the war dead group; the young village intellectuals who formed the Kambe-kai[9] and printed a village newsletter; and the Ryokan Kumi-ai, the Inn Cooperative, which worked to bring tourism to the village.

In 1984–1986, the last two groups were marginal, but in the years between 1986 and 1991 they became more important. By 1987 an innkeeper had become head of the Kuzaki Fishing and Farming Cooperative for the first time, clearly marking the end of fishing as the dominant economic form in village life. As we shall see in chapter 6, fishing had long been in decline in Kuzaki, but fishermen had continued to dominate the offices of the Cooperative. Shifting to electing an innkeeper symbolically conceded the point that tourism had become more important as a source of income villagewide, while innkeepers who did not commute out of the village to work and owned their own businesses neatly filled the role of men who could devote two years of their life to running the Cooperative. In 1991 the leader of the Kambe-kai was selected to be Hachiman for the festival described in chapter 7, signaling this socialist rebel's incorporation into more mainstream village life.

The Kumi-ai

All these organizations and activities were overseen by the village Cooperative: the household, the clubs, and even the village divisions described in the previous chapter. The Kuzaki Gyogyō Kyōdō Kumi-ai was part of the larger regional and national fishing cooperatives that were important in setting national guidelines for fishing and diving. These larger organizations monitored current literature on pollution levels, overfishing, and the cultivation of scarce ocean resources and made this information available to the smaller cooperatives throughout Japan; they were also the headquarters for the Fishermen's Rescue Fund and other financial aid organizations. As independent as the Kuzaki Kumi-ai tried to be from city and national politics, it was closely allied with the national Fishing Cooperative Organization. Like most Japanese fishing cooperatives, the Kuzaki Kumi-ai also provided a variety of services for the villagers: It gave loans to members; transported, processed, and sold fish, shellfish, and seaweed catches; trained fishermen in new types of fishing and conservation techniques; maintained quays and anchorages; provided insurance and banking facilities for the whole village; and stocked spares and supplies for boats.

The Kumi-ai in Kuzaki had six paid officers and three full-time secretaries. The officers were all men and included the head *(chō),* who was also head of Kuzaki as a city ward; the second in charge *(semmu-san);*[11] and four officers called the *riji.* There was a seventh officer, the beach officer *(hama-riji),* who was unpaid. Elections for the Cooperative were held every other year. Kumi-ai finances were provided by taking a percentage of all profits made by divers and fishermen in the village; it also did its own fishing for profit in November (lobster) and August (the seaweed called *arame).* The Kumi-ai also arranged and charged fees for any groups who might come to Kuzaki to film documentaries or to photograph divers. The money was then used either to promote more tourism to the village or—in the case of the funds earned through several documentaries I witnessed during fieldwork —to repair and rebuild areas associated with Kuzaki's sacred role as the producer of *noshi awabi.*

Twice a year, in November and February, the officers of the Cooperative prepared a report on all the finances of the village and held a meeting to which a representative from each household came. This report included money earned in the year by all fishermen and divers, the percentage the Kumi-ai had taken in the sale of the catches, and an accounting of all money spent. The Cooperative oversaw not only the fishing in the village but was also involved in making and enforcing village regulations. Its position as ward office for Kuzaki meant that it served as the vital connection to Toba City administration and bureaucracy. It was also involved in all community religious life, administered the funds for public works such as road widening, undertook public relations for the village to encourage tourism, took in taxes, acted as a savings bank for households, and generally organized village life. In fact, "being a member of the village is very much like being a member of an organization like a school or a factory. One is organized. The social contract contains quite a lot of fine print" (Dore 1978, 211). A description of the responsibilities of some of the Kumi-ai officers gives a clear idea of just how organized this can all seem.

The *chō* was the man who made the introductory speeches at all social events, from PTA meetings to wives' club meetings; he oversaw all the daily weighing of fish and *awabi;* acted as salesman during the auctioning of the catches; met with the heads of all Kuzaki groups; administered money to these groups; prepared the biannual financial report; went to Toba City meetings to represent the village; and had innumerable other tasks. The *chō* was expected to make the first announcements over the village loudspeaker every day at 5:45 A.M. and to be available at the Cooperative until 7 or 8 P.M. It was a lot of hard work for very little money. For example, the head in 1986, Okamoto-san, was paid 180,000 yen per month, which was about U.S. $1,160 a month or $13,920 a year (this was more or less the same amount I received as a Monbusho research student).

According to Kumi-ai records in 1985, the average income per annum of a full-time fisherman (which the *chō* always had been) was 200 *man yen* or U.S. $12,500. The *chō* would appear to be getting the better of the deal, but the people of Kuzaki did not see it that way. It was not just the income from fishing that was lost but all the extras that came with independent fishing: the fish that was brought home to eat; the days when there was a huge catch, increasing the average take; the free time spent on growing vegetables in the fields or planting rice paddies; the time spent repairing equipment; and, most importantly, the part-time jobs that all fishermen had to earn extra income—helping in an inn or taking tourists fishing or scuba diving.

Thus, being *chō* was seen as a great deal of work for little financial gain. The man who was elected had to be able to cope with all the work, had to be able to afford a break in his fishing, and needed to know how to make good speeches and look serious on special occasions—but it also helped if he was a nice guy who knew how to relax, drink, and dance with the best of them. These qualities were not decided on at the moment when such a man was chosen; it became clear to me during my fieldwork that likely men were spotted as early as their mid-thirties, when they were offered key ceremonial roles and minor political offices that appeared to mark their progress through life as worthy men. Fifty was seen as the right age to ask a man who was both responsible and nice to take on the job: He was not too old, his children were grown, he was financially secure, and most men would have shown their true colors by then.

It is not surprising, however, that most men were not interested in the job, and the major part of the Kumi-ai election was convincing the right man that he wanted to do it. The next step was finding a vice president—*semmu-san*—who had the same qualities as the head, with the added skill of being a good accountant *and* being able to get along with the *chō*. This man was paid only $10,900 a year for all his work, but he was allowed a little more free time in which to fish and attend to his own work. It was considered essential that he be younger than the *chō*.

The other four officers, the *riji,* were men in their mid-forties who might eventually be selected to be head; serving a term as a minor officer in the Kumi-ai was another way of determining if a man was capable of handling responsibility. The youngest officer, the beach officer, was in charge of beach safety during diving. He often was in his thirties and a man who was trying to be accepted in village life.

It is important to understand that being a Kumi-ai officer was not considered a way to gain power in village life. It was, as Dore has noted (1978, 206), a way to attain status, but it was also seen as a nuisance, and most Kuzaki villagers pointed out that the position of Co-op officer was not really a political one—or at least not one that they understood as political. As an informant explained: "The two-year term is not long enough for a man to begin to know the job well or even to make the sort of connections a good political leader needs to make. It takes a full year to learn the job properly, and just as they are becoming very good at it, it's time for the next elections." In many ways, it was an ingenious system that kept any single man from building up a personal power base. This was well understood by the villagers themselves, who pointed out how their city representative, who had held the post for seventeen years or so, had become so powerful that it verged on the corrupt. Also, it would appear that the Cooperative alternated between efficient years when the *chō* knew what he was doing and those when he didn't. The three female secretaries who remained in their jobs from year to year and oversaw the running of the place were the basis of the effective functioning of the Kumi-ai. If anyone had real power in their hands, it was this small group of generally friendly and unassuming women who worked in a not very well paid office job because it kept them close to home and their children. This is an extremely important point to understand about village organization: The men are at the forefront of everything, but it is the women who do most of the work. This is the core of much if not all of village life, and the two examples below will, I hope, make this very clear.

Village Elections in 1985

In 1985, the process of electing new officers began on Sunday, February 17. For divers and fishermen, February was a slow month. The whole village was quiet after the festivities of the New Year, which took up most of January; the sea remained too rough and cold for any diving; and there was little fishing. On the other hand, inns were very busy at this time of year; domestic tourism in the form of office trips and weekend visits seemed at a winter peak.

In keeping with the tempo of February, the 1985 elections were due to begin at 8 A.M., and I dutifully rolled up at the village hall at that time only to be met by a lone villager, Hashimoto-san, who laughed at me for not yet knowing that 8 A.M. really meant 9 A.M. Kuzaki time! Sure enough, by 9, the hall had filled with one representative from each household in Kuzaki. There was a large proportion of women because so many village men worked regular jobs outside of Kuzaki and could not be there to represent their households. In fact, the identity of the voter at the elections appeared to somewhat flexible: Men and women both, as the days proceeded, came and went to do chores, and someone else would come to take their place—a grandparent, the husband home from work, or a wife after collecting the children from school.

The first task of February 17 was to collect the packet for each household that the Co-op officers had spent days preparing. Inside the packet were the fiscal year's form for tax returns, health insurance forms, copies of receipts for any money paid directly to the Cooperative, and a record of all sales by the Co-op of seaweed, shellfish, fish, and so on. As people filtered in, two interesting things seemed to occur naturally: No one sat in the front rows facing the stage where the officers were seated; and the right-hand side of the hall (facing the stage) filled up with men, while the left-hand side—very much at the back—filled up with women in huddled groups.

The meeting began with an open vote to select the meeting's chairman and secretary. In 1985, the men selected to this post were a former Kumi-ai *chō*, Seiko-san, and the head of the Seinendan, Takahashi-san. The meeting was then formally opened with a short speech by the older Seiko-san and proceeded to what seemed like a grilling session, as different members of the audience asked questions about the year's financial report. At each question, we'd be asked to turn to such-and-such a page, which would then be read aloud by either the *chō* or the *semmu-san*. This was actually a very aggressive session, and at one point the original financial records were passed around so that anyone who had any questions could check the original documents themselves. After this, everyone began to relax a bit. One of the village men known as a bit of a joker, Matsui-san, caused an uproar when examining the PTA records (he was head at the time) by shouting out: "Look! Every night a bill from Maru-no-ichi [a village pub]!" Finally, this part of the elections ended with a look at two separate handouts: one a breakdown of general village expenses and the other of money made from fishing. At 10:50 there was a twenty-five minute break, and at 11:15 or so we reconvened to ask questions on how the money earned from local taxes had been spent. This session was punctuated by one young man who kept questioning the percentage that had been taken by the Co-op from what was then the village's only large-scale fishing boat *(Oshiki)*.

Yet there was an air of nitpicking done out of duty. People asked their questions, but the background noise was the murmur of gossip. It was then that a friend told me these elections would take at least another four days. At noon there was a vote taken as to whether everyone was satisfied and would agree to accept the financial report as it stood; the "yeas" had it, and we broke for lunch.

The early afternoon of the first day was devoted to how city money had been spent that year, the widening of two roads being the most prominent. When the *chō* and the *semmu-san* had finished with this report, they bowed to general applause, closed their books, and left; all Cooperative business was in suspension until the elections were over. The head and his second were officially stepping down, although the other officers remained onstage. A general meeting began at this point, and votes were taken on several small matters: whether the large-scale fishing boat would be allowed to continue to operate; whether the expectations of large earnings from *arame* gathering were too great and needed to be reconsidered; and how the areas for net casting should be changed.

The last matter dominated the latter half of the afternoon. Various fishermen came to explain why the areas should be changed, taking into account the weather, changes in the ocean floor, and the problems of overfishing. The decision on this measure was taken by secret ballot, with the result being seventy-nine households for the change and eighteen against. As a result of this, it was also decided that the projected earnings for the coming year should be adjusted by 10 *man yen*, as fishing should be more profitable. The young leader of the Kambe-kai gave a speech asking the new Cooperative to pay more attention to agricultural matters, and the village eccentric gave what seemed to me a lampoon speech that set everyone to laughing.

The issue of whether the ban on the use of more than one wet suit per diving household was raised, and the discussion of this—by the women—was interrupted by a question on whether the Cooperative should get a freezer in which to store fishing catches. Eventually the refrigerator question was shelved because ice had so far served the village well, and no one knew what the large freezer would cost; and the women spoke up again about the wet suits. The interruption had been, not surprisingly, a male one, and when the issue was reopened, it was almost immediately put to a vote by Takahashi-san, who explained that the rule kept the non-wet-suited people from being tempted to stay on diving for longer and longer periods and thus prevented overfishing. A quick vote was taken in which the male hands outnumbered the female, and while several women tried to make themselves heard at this point—repeating that the rule made no sense because no one was allowed to dive for longer than an hour at a time anyway—the matter was declared closed.

Finally, after another break for tea, someone asked whether the Co-op head and the vice president should get raises. By 5 P.M. this remained unresolved, and the discussion turned to whether the meeting should continue or start again the next day. The men who commuted to jobs Monday through Friday tried to keep the discussion going, but they were outvoted by the fishermen/innkeepers contingent. So the meeting dragged on with a disjointed discussion of parking spaces in the village, coupled with a return to the freezer question (how much would the electricity cost), before breaking up at 6:30.

On the second day of elections, Monday, the 8 A.M. meeting again started at 9, after a general cleanup of the hall by the women. The minutes from the day before were read and interruptions from people who had missed the Sunday meeting were heard as well as questions from people who had carefully read the financial report overnight. In my corner, the discussion was whether or not such questions should be accepted, as that part of the meeting had been officially closed the day before. I found that this sort of discussion was common throughout the elections—people grouping and regrouping to ask each other whether they should bring up X or Y. If a group decided it would be good to raise the issue, then one person would get up to speak while the others offered support. Rather than rehashing finances, it was decided that we move on to the elections; a break was called so people could begin to discuss candidates.

At this point, debate became intense among the men, while the bored young women began to organize the making of tea as they told me that Fujin-kai elections were not only more organized but much quicker. "We decide in five minutes," one woman reassured me. In the meantime, nominations appeared to be made in person to Seiko-san, who was still chairing the meeting; individual men went up to give him names of likely candidates. The meeting splintered into very fluid discussion groups, people came and went, a group might merge with its neighbor, but there were some broad divisions: one large group of almost all the fishermen; the older women in their own group (eating as they chatted); and several smaller groups composed of neighbors, kin, or headed by a *dōkyūsei* head such as the *chō* of the volunteer firemen or the Rōjin-kai. At one point a woman, Okamoto-san, was called out of her group, consulted by a small group of men, and sent back to the women! The end result of these discussions was that the officers for the Cooperative and the beach officer would be nominated before taking a decision on who should be considered for the top two positions. The names of candidates were quickly decided and discussions became gossip sessions. The meeting was finally readjourned at 11 A.M., the minutes reread, the proposal for a lunch break entertained, and we broke up until 12:40.

The afternoon discussion was to consider the candidates in some detail. The five men whose names were being considered for the officers' posts were asked to leave (five men and only five positions to fill), and again there were small groups formed. There was an unscheduled break when a car failed to brake and ran into a beached boat; all the men went out to haul the car back in the pouring rain. While the issue of the five officers seemed mostly settled, the question of the *semmu-san* for this election seemed to be presenting problems. To pass the time, or so it seemed, the unsettled issue of salaries was brought up; in fact, it became clear that this was actually an important question, since the willingness of a man to be *semmu-san* depended on the salary he would receive.

Outside, I noted, the nominees for the other offices were having an intense discussion of their own; inside the hall, some people were so bored that they took to checking my notes—trying hard to read my bad handwriting and English. At 4 P.M. the women in the hall were asked to prepare the evening meal, which we finally were served at 7. At 7:30, the question of whether or not we should break was tabled when someone asked if we really needed to discuss and vote on *that,* and everyone laughed. But it was 8 P.M. before a vote was taken as to whether the five nominees were acceptable. At this point, the first roll call of all village households was taken, and eighty-seven *ie* were represented; then all names were called again. When it was asked if everyone had been called, a joker called out that my name had been missed.

For a third time, the names of all the households were called to check who was present. It was then 9 P.M., the checking of household names was still continuing, and it was decided to reconvene the next day.

Tuesday, the third day, began with cleaning again, another roll call to see who was present, and finally ballot boxes were brought out. Each household was again called, votes were placed in the boxes—one for the *chō* and one for the *semmu-san*—and at 9:58 volunteers were counting the ballots. It was not long before the new head was named: Okamoto-san, who garnered sixty-seven votes. The new *semmu-san* was Ohata-san. Elections for the *riji* were then called and quickly decided, since there was really no contest for these positions. At 10:30 all the elected officials went home to consult with their families and give thanks at the household altars.

Yet this was not the end of events. The young women were once more asked to make lunch, while the older women who remained sat back to compare notes on the year's diving, taking turns declaring themselves the best diver in the village. One young grandmother, a woman in her fifties, had brought in a bottle of *chū-hi* (a mixture of rice vodka and tonic water), and several women began to sneak drinks. The discussion turned to others' drinking habits and how to pretend you were sober when drunk. After lunch people gave up even the pretence of seriousness; some left, others lay down in the hall for naps, and small chitchat occurred. At 5 P.M. we went home for dinner; at 6 we were back waiting in the hall. I had brought along a deck of cards to play solitaire and found myself being asked to read fortunes instead. My knowledge of terms related to disaster or good fortune and any knowledge I had of village affairs were stretched to their limits at this point.

From fortune-telling, we moved onto comparative anthropology. I was asked if it was true that American women could refuse to have sex with their husbands if they had a headache, as they had seen in U.S. films and television programs. I asked what Japanese wives did and was told that you could not say no to your husband—but also that there was the problem of the woman wanting to make love and the husband being too drunk to proceed. "Still," I was asked once more, "could American women say no?" In theory, they could, I replied. "Ahhh!" was the group comment.

It seemed, I eventually learned, despite the small role women appeared to play in the elections and their inability to refuse their husbands' sexual demands, that the final moment of the elections—officially accepting the job—was being held up by discussions at home for both the *chō* and *semmu-*

san with their wives. In both cases, the women were unconvinced that the household would be able to survive the cut in income that holding these offices would entail. Without their wives' consent, it appeared, the men could not accept the offices they had been offered. At 8:30, these issues still being unresolved, we all voted to go home until the next day.

By the next morning the rumor was that the whole issue was so complex that it might well be a ten-day matter—ten days of waiting for the negotiations at home to conclude before the elections were finalized! So, four days into elections, people began to dissipate. I did some errands in Toba, an insurance salesman was brought in to talk to the few people still sitting in the village hall, and the real action was taking place with visits to the households of the would-be *chō* and *semmu-san*. Women actually took the lead in these visits, taking turns to have long chats with the wives of Okamoto-san and Ohata-san. Finally it was explained to me that the *semmu-san*–elect had only a two-generation household—his wife and sickly daughter—and they were worried about how their rice paddies would get planted if he took the office. When I asked why Ohata-san had allowed others to nominate him, I was told that it was "an honor and a duty," and he could not have really refused.

The day dragged to an end for me with a discussion of why the term *"mame"* (bean) was a slang term for penis. "I don't know," I said. "Because Japanese men all have small and wrinkly penises like a bean," said one of the men. When I said that I really had no point of comparison, a grandmother said she knew that Western men were huge compared to Japanese because she had seen Western penises in a soft-core video (obviously a pirated edition, since the legal versions in those days had little clouds floating over the male and female genitalia). I wrote in my field notes: "What a blow for symbolic anthropology. Penises are not like *mame* because they sprout, germinate, grow and reproduce as much as they are like beans because they're small and covered with a wrinkled skin. Lévi-Strauss would cry."

In the end, the ten-day affair took only five. On the fifth day it was agreed that Ohata-san would alternate his office with another officer who was close to him in age, and thus he would have one year of being *semmu-san* and another of only part-time work as a *riji*. The village women, it seemed, had also offered to help the Ohata household during rice-planting season, as well as offering Okamoto-san help in finding a daughter-in-law for his household (his wife, not to be outdone by the Ohata wife, had declared that with no daughter-in-law, how could she do all the work needed for the two years her husband was *chō?*). Finally, at 11:28 P.M. on Thursday, February 21, the new Kumi-ai officers were formally introduced to the village. The women went home at this point, while the men stayed behind to celebrate the completed elections.

Before analyzing the events of the election in detail, I would like to describe the Nifune festival that takes place in November. Although very different events, there exist similarities and parallels between the election and the festival that need to be considered before contrasting the ways in which village organization actually worked with a model of how it was supposed to work.

The Nifune Festival

"*Nifune*" literally means "two boats," and the ceremony did involve two different sets of boats. The deity honored during Nifune was known throughout the village as the Wakai kamisama (the young deity) because, as one grandfather told me, the original sanctuary *(honden)* for the deity was on an island farther out than today's Kaminoshima (literally, "god's island"). A typhoon in 1935 destroyed the *honden* and—he implied—the deity, so a new one was brought from Ise and installed on a small island just off the southern shore of Kuzaki. Although this *kami* was apparently nameless, there were several attributes that the villagers ascribed to it: The *kami* was male; he was a sea deity; he protected the village and fishermen's boats, especially during the lucrative winter lobster trapping season; and he appeared to have some relationship with war.[12] According to Sakai (n.d., 15), the original deity was named Haku-hatsu-daimyō and would seem to be the enshrined feudal lord who, in some versions of the *noshi awabi* legend, was responsible for the tribute of *awabi* to Ise.[13]

The festival itself was made up of a series of events beginning on November 15, when the Kumi-ai's *semmu-san* made a trip to Ise Shrine. Special prayers and offerings were made in front of the second gate to the sacred shrines.[14] Then in a small shrine, the Ise priests performed a short ceremony "just for the people of Kuzaki." The object was to bless the special Ise sake that would be offered two days later to the Shinto deity on Kaminoshima. That same evening, after the officer's return to Kuzaki, he was required to attend the dinner held by the Fujin-kai for all the women divers in the village. This was an evening of eating, drinking, singing, and dancing that was proceeded by the women's visit to the beach across from Kaminoshima. There they lit floating candles and set them off in the direction of the island where the deity's shrine was located. This was in thanks for the protection the deity had given divers during the diving season.

This ritual was performed with little ceremony. In 1984 it was raining so hard that only a few of the women rushed out to light the candles, which promptly sank. No one took this as a bad omen. Laughing it off, the women settled down to the important part of the evening: evaluating the karaoke performances of all the members of the Fujin-kai. Between eating and singing, everyone switched tables and stopped to chat and laugh with friends and relatives. In the all-female atmosphere, the jokes got rowdy, occasional snippets of gossip were malicious, and everyone broke their rule of "mothers shouldn't drink," mixing beer and sake. For the women of the village, this was the most important part of the five-day festival; the rest of the ceremonies required their labor, but this was the bit that acknowledged them. As with the women's party on Hi-nichi, it would be easy to see this banquet as the main event since it involved the divers, yet Nifune was another example of how village ritual life was about everyone in the end.

At dawn the next day, November 16, the grandfathers were purified in the Shinto shrine. They arrived early for this and wore the *hakama* and kimono, which indicated that they were laymen performing a ritual function. After the Shinto priest purified them, the men rested in the priest's house and drank some sweet sake *(amazake),* which the wives' club had prepared the day before. This was partially fermented sake, still resembling a mash, and was served warm. After this breakfast, the men split up into three groups: Two men went to work in the workshop of a grandfather, Seiko-san, who lived across from the shrine; another two worked outside the shrine, making small wooden boats; and the other five worked inside the shrine itself. These were the same men who made the *noshi awabi* for Ise Shrine, save that no man older than seventy-nine could take part in this work, while the oldest grandfather who made *noshi awabi* was close to ninety years of age. The number of grandfathers also varied from year to year, since any man whose family member had died in the last year was too polluted to take part in this work.

The grandfathers in the shrine spent the day making what they called *shige,* which looked like very small (four- or five-inch-long) arrows without tips.[15] The *shige* were made, as I was told, from any useless wood. These were given to all the families in the village that had not had a death in that year and were objects that were to be given as offerings at the household Shinto shrine; some *shige* were also left in public places such as the doors to the huts that housed the fire brigade's pumps. The 1984 list from which the grandfathers worked had twenty-seven eligible households in Kainaka, eighteen in Ōtsu, twenty-three in Sato-naka, and twenty-two in Hozume. Extra *shige* were made for the two different ceremonies that formed the main part of the *matsuri:* Thirteen were made for what the grandfathers call the *daikke* (large) ritual on the morning of November 18 and the *shōgge* (small) ritual performed on November 19. The grandfathers also made larger arrows that they fitted with shavings to represent feathers. There were two sets of these types of arrows, one set 8 inches in length and another set 6 inches in length.

Outside the shrine, wood was whittled into the shape of forty-eight small boats representing the number of active fishing boats left in Kuzaki.[16] The two grandfathers in the workshop made two far more elaborate boats called *senkokufune* (literally, "one thousand stone boat")—an old form of a cargo ship. The villagers insisted, however, that it was a war boat used in the past. All the work was done cheerfully with a great deal of gossiping (daughters-in-law and potential granddaughters-in-law were important topics) and joking. Yet the grandfathers did tire easily, especially as the weather was cold and they were working without heating of any sort, so there were several breaks in the day during which food was served. These meals were all prepared by the wives of the Kumi-ai *chō* and the *semmu-san.* The 10 A.M. break included a traditional meal of four pieces of dried octopus *(tako),* pickled horseradish (daikon), and a paste of soybean *(daizu),* which was eaten with crudely shaped bamboo chopsticks. I tried asking whether the food had any significance and was told: "In the past, food was not very plentiful at this time of year, and this meal represents what was the typical autumnal fare—especially the *tako,* which could survive all the days of the ritual without refrigeration." As in the dawn ceremony, *amazake* was drunk at this meal.

After the morning break, the men in the shrine moved on to tying the *shige* into bundles of five using rice straw rope *(wara nawa),* and a sprig of sacred *sakaki* was added to the center of these bundles. The 6-inch arrows were also tied into bundles of five, but the rope around these bundles was wrapped counterclockwise, the opposite direction in which the *shige* were wrapped. The 8-inch arrows were tied onto a longer, thicker stick to form a sort of crown. In alternate years *(toshi),* there were twelve sets of these tied with five arrows each; in the other years *(uradoshi),* there were thirteen sets. These were to be given away in what one grandfather said was *kubaru* (the giving of goods to the poor). Outside the shrine, one of the two grandfathers began to whittle wood into the shape of a sword *(katana),* while the other continued making the small boats.

The Shinto priest arrived after a simple lunch of regular food and began to fold white paper that would hang from a thick rope of rice straw used in Shinto rituals *(shimenawa)* that a grandfather had made by twisting various strands of the straw together. The paper was folded to resemble two fish tied together (symbolizing fertility and good fortune), and the priest also made a purification wand *(gohei)* from paper. Another grandfather tied rice straw rope into a shape called *kakonoyuna,* and this was to be hung with two fresh sea bream on the following day. The symbolism of the sea bream is most frequently used in wedding ceremonies and, for once, this piece of information about symbolism was offered by a grandfather.

By the end of the day there were 113 bunches of *shige,* an extra 23 bundles having been made to give to the *kami* as well as for placing in sacred public places. The end of the day's labor coincided with the end of school, and suddenly the grandfathers were surrounded by children who wanted to see the sword making. The grandfather who did this work had made two beautiful wooden *katana* for the deity—one long and one short sword as the samurai always carried. For the children, who begged repeatedly, he made rougher versions of these swords, and the afternoon ended with the children fencing and begging *amazake* from the grandfathers' tea, which was another meal that included octopus, pickles, and bean paste.

A final division of *shige* was made: Five trays were filled, four according to the village's geographical divisions and one with the extra twenty-three *shige.* Finally, the day ended with another ceremonial meal of *kenchin* salad, persimmons, oranges, octopus, and sake.

On November 18, the ceremony began on Yoroizaki Beach. Early in the morning, the Cooperative brought out two canoe-shaped boats that the young men of the village had to row. One would go to Kaminoshima with the implements for the deity (the *gohei, shimenawa, katana,* and Ise sake in a container called *sunodaru*); the other would start out at the same time but take a different direction to fool any demons. These objects had to be purified in a Shinto ceremony in the shrine. This purification *(harau)* ceremony was so special that I was asked not to be present, but I was allowed to note the offerings laid out before Amaterasu's *honden.* These offerings were grouped into five sets containing respectively three, three, two, four, and one items as follows: (1) rice cakes, uncooked rice, and sake; (2) *wakame,* fish, and one of the big boats; (3) all the small boats on a tray and the tray of *shige;* (4) cabbage, a lobster crowned with paper, fruit, and salt; (5) a tray of *sakaki.* A grandfather told me that although the catch of the season should always be offered to the *kami,* lobster (with a season of November to April) was offered only twice in the ritual year—once in Nifune and again during the Hachiman festival. This link between the two festivals will be discussed later, but it should be noted that one way of understanding

Nifune is to see it as a festival that marks the end of the diving year for women and the beginning of men's more intensive fishing.

During the morning the grandmothers were out in full force, leaving offerings of dried fish, rice, and adzuki beans at various sacred points in the village: unusual rocks, the family boat, in front of small shrines, and so forth. At 1 P.M. the wives' club held a banquet in the town hall for the ten young men who were to row the two boats. The men had to be members of the Seinendan—that is, under twenty-five years of age and not married. The two boat crews represented the two main village geographical divisions: Sato-naka and Kainaka. During the banquet, these men sat facing each other as if in challenge, with the Sato-naka men on the left and the Kainaka men on the right.

Slowly, full of the sake they had drunk for courage, the men headed for Yoroizaki Beach. Waiting there were their grandmothers and a few young married men who had rowed in recent years. These people helped dress the rowers for their work. First the men stripped down to white *tabi* and purified themselves in the already wintry sea by jumping into it (this is again paralleled in the Hachiman ceremony). When they came running out, their grandmothers helped them put on a loincloth and a white kimono. Younger boys were hanging about learning how to tie a loincloth, and the married men offered advice on how best to put on the sacred garb. The first and second rowers of the Sato-naka crew dressed first and, carrying their oars over their shoulders, went to the shrine to collect the offerings. At this point, one of the grandmothers told me that it was good luck for an unmarried man to row on Nifune: It meant he would find a wife within the year. One young man kept repeating this to his grandmother: "Surely after this year, I will have a wife." Another man told me that this was a rare instance in Kuzaki of a boat in which women could not ride.

Once the rowers returned with the deity's offerings, the Sato-naka boat started out for Kaminoshima. With a slight delay, the decoy Kainaka boat followed, rowing to Ōtsu Harbor. This sounds simpler than it was, for the boats were narrow, with hard wooden seats that were covered only with rice straw—and they leaked. Also, the young men worked on brute strength rather than skill, since they had little if any practice at rowing. By the time the Sato-naka boat reached Kaminoshima, the sea was full of fishermen's boats following the men to the island. In 1984, one of these carried a news camera crew to record the event. The first rower leapt from the boat to the island, removed the previous year's offerings, and replaced them with the new offerings. The old things were taken ashore when the men rowed to

Kaminoshima Beach; there they started a fire and burned the old sacred objects. Some of the older men waiting on the beach gave the rowers more sake to drink. Meanwhile, the Kainaka boat at Ōtsu lit their own warming fire and shared sake with returning fishermen. While all of this was occurring, the grandfathers were distributing *shige* throughout the village, and the nonfishing village men in their forties and fifties gathered in their smaller village divisions for an afternoon and evening of eating and drinking.

When the Sato-naka crew felt energetic enough to row again (before dark), the rowers got back into the boat and began the return journey to Yoroizaki Beach. At the sight of the other boat approaching Ōtsu, the waiting Kainaka crew climbed back into their boat and rowed out to meet it. The two boats had to return at the same time. On Yoroizaki Beach, the grandmothers were cleaning up and building a fire. All the married village men and the children, women, and young girls began to gather on the beach, bringing old rice straw (saved from the summer rice harvest) and dumping it onto the bonfire until it grew large enough to be seen by the boat crews who were now rowing in twilight. The mothers of the rowers brought large buckets full of hot water and barrels of *amazake* for everyone to drink.

Trying to land at the same time took the boats several tries. Each attempt to land that would have one boat landing before the other meant that they had to row back out, then the Sato-naka boat circled to the left and the Kainaka boat to the right before attempting to land once more. One

Figure 5. The Nifune decoy crew waiting for the first boat to return (D. P. Martinez)

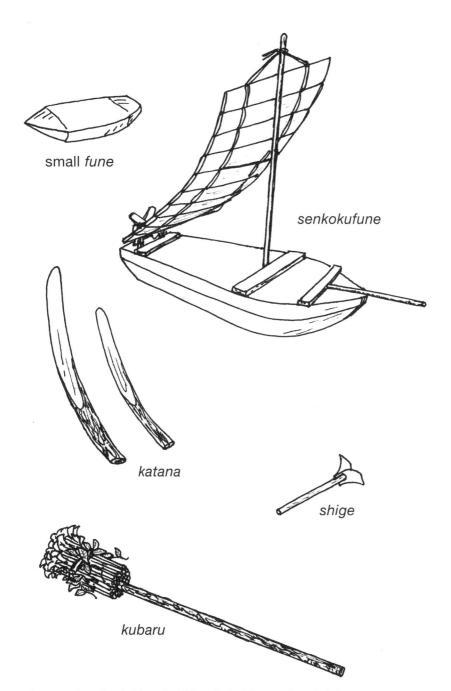

small *fune*

senkokufune

katana

shige

kubaru

Figure 6. Completed objects for Nifune festival (by Carolyn Clarke)

grandmother told me that in the past, the men would have spent days practicing for this and, by the day of the festival, the boats would be able to land together on the first try. "Nowadays," she added, "they all have jobs outside the village and can't practice, so they have to keep trying. It is bad luck for one side of the village if its boat lands after the other. For both Sato-naka and Kainaka to have good luck and a prosperous year, the boats must land together." [17] In 1984, it took six attempts before the boats landed. Once on shore, the young men washed, dressed, drank, and eventually went off to a celebration held by the Seinendan. The older men returned to their drinking and the women and children went home.

November 19

At 8 A.M. on November 19, the grandfathers once again met with the priest at the village shrine. The *honden* was clear of offerings save for a few *shige* and one of the two large boats. Inside the *haiden,* the following offerings were arranged to the left: the small boats and *shige;* the second of the two large boats; uncooked rice and *sakaki.* The drum used during the New Year was also out, next to the alms box, and was struck to announce the start of the ceremony. It was the basic Shinto ritual of purification and offerings; on this occasion, the final prayer thanked the deity for the successful completion of the Nifune festival. Bowing three times to the grandfathers, the priest ended the ceremony with the words, "Everyone, it has ended."

A final meal for the grandfathers was served by the wives of the Cooperative executives inside the shrine itself. Again there was a tray shared between two men, the food (octopus, bean paste, and pickles) was eaten with bamboo chopsticks, and there was sake and *amazake* to drink. At the end of the meal, the grandfathers rolled up the tatami in the shrine and opened a hearth that was set into the floor. They made a charcoal fire and sat near it, chatting.

In 1984 this became the second occasion during which village men spoke to me about the Second World War. The experiences they described were those of feeling confused, perhaps a contrast to what the samurai of old—who Nifune appeared to honor—felt in battle. The navy ships the men had served on were crowded and dirty, and planes always came from out of nowhere to attack. One grandfather said he still dreamed of the sound of droning American fighters; another refused to watch war films on television, as it was too upsetting. Another man recalled the horror of being wounded and sent to an understaffed, under-equipped hospital where there was no food, no water, and the excrement was never cleared away because of staff shortages. The hospital, they all agreed, was almost worse than any battle. In the end, they all reassured me, war was horrible.

Any attempt on my part to turn the conversation to the meaning of Nifune was met with clear if functionalist answers: The small boats represented the old fishing boats; the two large boats were the war boats on which Kuzaki men had served coast guard duty for their feudal lord in the Edo period. To possess one of the these boats brought good luck to a household, and for that reason the Co-op always had bidders for the auction in which the remaining boat was sold (the money earned at this auction helped pay for the festival expenses). Finally, my questions were met with the reply, "It is just something that we do—we don't know the meaning of it."

Clearly, Nifune could be described as a ritual that parallels and opposes Hi-nichi. In the former, Kuzaki goes to Ise and the villagers row out to the deity; in the latter, Ise comes to Kuzaki, as does Amaterasu. Hi-nichi is meant to be the divers' festival, Nifune the fishermen's, although both festivals involve the whole village. The July festival celebrates the village's links to Japan's prehistory, while the November ceremony celebrates the village's links to the feudal era. Both festivals are about reaffirming connections and reestablishing boundaries.

On both occasions, women—old and young—are in the background, while the men appear as the central actors. Yet an essential aspect of the rituals, the feasts in which all participate, relies on the labor of women. This is obviously also what happened during the elections in the village: All discussion and all the decisions appeared to be the men's, but the women in the background provided the food that oiled the wheels of sociality, and sometimes they acted as the brakes that put a stop, or at least a pause, to the actions of the men. The women's voices served as punctuation to the lives of men—remembering smaller deities while men worshipped the main gods; reiterating gossip; saying no to an addition of household duties; giving advice and support. Thus, life in Kuzaki was experienced as an interweaving of gender, age, and status—a never-ending negotiation with one's family, neighbors, and deities. Interlinked at almost every step of the way were the civic and the religious domains: The age-grades had set roles in both areas, and each individual was expected to take part at one time or another. In this, the social person becomes the site of a series of duties and responsibilities to the state (through the village), the deities, and—as we shall see later—their families, as well as the dead. The next two chapters describe how both duty and responsibility are situated within the *ie,* made manifest through the work of diving and fishing, and how they are central to rituals.

CHAPTER 5

Keeping the *Ie* Afloat
Part 1. Diving and Women's Rituals

When introducing themselves, almost everyone in Kuzaki added which *ie* they belonged to, referring to the household by its shop name. The use of these shop names indicates how strongly the *ie* was still perceived to be an economic as well as a kin unit. Almost every village household still retained the shop names that they used before the Cooperative took over the marketing of the *ie*'s produce. Under these names—generally composed of a favorite Chinese character around which the names of most of the men in the family were constructed and the word *"ya"* (shop) added— a household would do business. Many households also had a sign *(shirushi)* associated with it, and all their equipment was marked with the *ie* sign. Villagers claimed that the *shirushi* were a leftover from an era when fisherfolk did not know how to read but had to mark all their nets, diving equipment, and other tools. Moreover, in contrast to urban middle-class families, the *ie* in Kuzaki still depended on the labor of nearly all its members to survive.

As well as using the household name when introducing oneself, speakers might clarify things, if they were young, by indicating whether they were an elder son or oldest daughter within the household. Perhaps they were the *yome*, and they might let me know this by telling me how long they had been married. For the villagers who did not come to know me well, these principles applied: Rather than calling me Lola, they would refer to me as an *one-chan* (eldest daughter) from Genroku-ya, the household in which I was living. When I spent a second period of fieldwork with another household, I was identified as being part of Tamago-ya. Young children often called me *oba-san* or auntie. The point is that not only were people seen to be members of a particular household and so identified, but they were seen to fill particular roles within the household and, as with the organization of the village, they were meant to have certain duties and responsibilities that went along with that role. A large part of these responsibilities involved the labor that kept the *ie* economically viable. I will outline the general features of each generation and then go on to describe relationships between these household members.

Children and Young Adults

While in the past the labor of even young children was necessary for fishing and diving, with teenagers contributing wages if they worked, modern compulsory education meant that the children of Kuzaki no longer contributed wages but were still expected to contribute labor. Young boys might go out fishing with their parents on the weekends or during school holidays; girls would help in the inns doing maid service. Children did not help with housework since the school insisted that they be free to do their studying in the evenings. Mothers and grandmothers did most household chores.

This modern emphasis on studying also changed attitudes toward a child's future. Most parents hoped that their children would continue their schooling and go on to some form of higher education, thus perhaps becoming or marrying white-collar workers rather than divers or fishermen. One fisherman told me that any idiot could buy a boat and nets and take to fishing; Kuzaki men had higher hopes for their sons. Women as well would comment on each other's children, saying: "So-and-so is bright and will go far; but such-and-such is not so bright and will have to be a fisherman." The idea that daughters should go on to higher education was often expressed.[1]

By 1984–1986 there existed a generation of young adults between eighteen and thirty years of age who did not want to work as divers or fishermen. In this generation were several young wives who only did *ryokan* (inn) work or who had jobs in Toba City, as well as several young men who did construction work or work for the city government. As previously mentioned, these young people did not see a need to leave Kuzaki but were often happy to commute. In keeping with the idea that the *ie* is a lineal rather than an extended family, however, it was only one child—generally male—who stayed in the village. Other sons and daughters married out or sought work in the large urban areas. Frequently it appeared to be the second or third son who stayed behind to work in the area and, eventually, inherit the household. Despite the theoretical importance of primogeniture in Kuzaki, the village seems always to have lost its elder sons to the larger cities.

Women

It should be kept in mind that until the early 1960s, the diving woman of Kuzaki provided the main source of income for her household, mostly through diving for abalone. This pattern involved work away from home *(dekasegi)* for a young diver before and even after marriage (sixteen to forty years of age), followed by a life of diving in the village (often until sixty-five years of age). Although the sea had been overfished and abalone was scarce, it remained one of the more expensive shellfish in Japan. This meant that in the 1980s a diver did not gather as much abalone as in the past, and since she was no longer the main contributor to the household's income, several part-time jobs were added to a diver's regular schedule. For example, a Kuzaki woman would work in a nearby inn or help run a shop or pub as well as dive; if not the major contributor to the household income, she remained an important contributor.

In the past, older women would tell me, a diver in the village could rely on her in-laws for child care while she spent the day in the sea. A woman was also responsible for work in the fields and rice paddies as well as for the sale of her catches. Without the period of migrant diving outside the village and no longer spending a large part of the day diving, the modern *yome-san* might work part-time, and she was still responsible for helping her mother-in-law in the fields and paddies.

Men

In the past, a married man would either do migrant work with his wife or on his own in order to earn enough money to purchase his own boat.[2] Generally, a man would be engaged in full-time fishing in the village by the time he reached his forties. As a grandfather past the age of being active in village politics, a man might work in the fields, have a full ritual calendar, and quite frequently be responsible for a large portion of the baby minding. In the 1980s I still saw little old men with babies in push chairs or on their backs meeting up on the quay of Ōtsu Harbor, where, rocking gently to and fro, they would discuss the weather and fishing conditions and comment on the current village gossip for hours on end.

In the 1980s there were ninety-two households in Kuzaki that did not practice full-time fishing, and in 70.6 percent of these households the man had become the major wage earner through outside labor. Yet because in the past a number of men had always worked outside the village, this new pattern of commuting daily to Toba or Ise to work was not seen as making much of a difference to the structure of the household. As already noted, upon retirement a man could still become involved in village life, performing ritual work, doing some subsistence fishing, or helping with labor in some other way.

What is essential to note is that the backbone of the *ie* remained the husband and wife working together. They were seen as a team—the basic economic unit upon which the household was founded. That this partnership was essential to the villagers' concept of the structure of labor was clearly evidenced by the fact that Kuzaki was one of the few villages in which women also worked on fishing boats as their husbands' partners. As already mentioned, there were no taboos in Kuzaki about women bringing bad luck to a fishing boat.

Relationships between Household Members

So far I have outlined a traditional pattern of labor for the old diving and fishing households, which remained pretty much the same for the modern Kuzaki *ie*. My fieldwork, however, focused on the few remaining full-time fishing and diving *ie* in Kuzaki, so my observations about the family stem from the long hours I spent with these particular members of the village.

Yet whether it was a fishing household or not, there remained a basic assumption about the interdependence of the various members of the *ie* for aid in diving, agricultural labor, fishing, and, increasingly, as economic partners. That is, it was still expected that all adult members of the *ie* contributed in one way or another to the household economy. I met no full-time housewives during my Kuzaki fieldwork; all women did something besides looking after the house and children. This assumption resulted in relationships that might well be termed partnerships. All decisions—about crops, times to plant, times to fish, what to put the nets out for, or what the household earnings were to be spent on—were made by the entire household, often with women having the last word. In fact, some women were considered more knowledgeable than their husbands about the weather or which fish might be running, and a husband would rely on her expertise. If neither partner was sure about conditions, grandfathers were always consulted for the final word on whether to fish or not. In the households that ran inns, the woman often did all the reservations and bookkeeping for the business. In households where men worked outside the village, women actually made more of the day-to-day decisions on their own. Thus it could be said that the men within the *ie* respected the women of the household for their opinions and valued them for their labor.

This picture of a working partnership contradicts the ideal of the Confucian precept that a woman must follow: to obey first her father, then her husband, and finally her son. But despite a partnership in external labor and internal decision making, a woman's work *within* the *ie* still held to the patriarchal pattern of most if not all of Japan. A woman would be the first up and the last to bed each day. She would do the cooking, the cleaning and laundry, attend to the household gods and ancestors, be sure to serve her husband first, and bathe last; she also supplied most of the help for the children with their schoolwork. Of course, a grandmother would help her *yome-san* with this work. Yet even in this traditional pattern of household labor, the men were flexible. Men did all the sashimi preparation and had taken up the preparation of most meat dishes as well. Although they claimed, rather proudly, that they never did any cleaning, minor tidying up was within the male realm, and it was not unusual to see the men doing the shopping for the household in Toba City. Some fluidity within household chores was possible.

The most important aspect of this partnership was the building up of what seemed to me to be truly affectionate marriages. I was not privy to everyone's private lives, but when comparing the litany of complaints I heard from urban married women and the stories Kuzaki women told, I felt that many men and women here were content with their marriage partners. Kuzaki remains the only place in Japan where I heard men openly praise their wives: "Isn't she marvelous?" I might be asked. Young couples, married and with children, might still go out to dinner together or with friends, and I would sometimes glimpse an earnest husband helping a wife fold clean laundry as they discussed their day. Or someone would reveal that theirs had been a love match, not an arranged marriage. Jokes about sex and drinking sometimes masked bad marriages, but many times I would find a couple laughing together about their work or lives in a way that indicated their understanding of each other. "He/she is not really so bad" was another openly affectionate claim a husband or wife might make. Men were closer to their children than their middle-class counterparts, and evenings were often family affairs: watching television as each member went off for a bath (although children might bathe with their father or with each other); drying wet hair with a hair dryer that was passed around; cleaning out ears; asking for neck rubs; or checking, last minute, that homework was done. The stereotypic Japan where children slaved at schoolwork while overanxious mothers acted as servants and fathers spent only two hours a week awake and chatting with their family seemed far, far away.

The basic partnership—the married couple, the core of all this—was important at all levels of household labor and was most apparent when looking at the way in which diving and fishing were organized. I have already set the scene by outlining the role of the Cooperative in both enterprises, but I will return to some of those points here and in the next chapter in order to build up an understanding of how gender was constructed.

Diving

The first spring diving session of 1984 was my introduction to the sight of some of the older women diving. As I sat waiting for the divers to return to shore, a little grandmother in her seventies appeared from the sea. She was dressed in layers and layers of white cotton sea wear *(amagi)* and shivering from the cold. After she built up the fire, she put the few abalone she had brought up and three sweet potatoes onto it and insisted on feeding me. As I ate, she changed back into her work clothes and I saw that she had a huge scar that marked where her left breast had been removed. Why had she gone diving if she was old, ill, and felt the cold so terribly?

I asked her this question in my still fumbling Japanese and got the answer that I was to hear in various ways over and over throughout my fieldwork: "I love it."

When the weather grew warmer, there were more and more groups of grandmothers who came to dive just for the pleasure of being in the sea once more and for the fun of the hours by the fire after diving, full of food and gossip. Whenever I interviewed the grandmothers of Kuzaki, the conversation would quickly turn to their youth and the fun they recalled working *dekasegi,* the songs they had sung, and the number of kilos of *awabi* they had brought up as young divers. Even the young divers in Kuzaki seemed to feel this same pleasure in diving: They too lingered after dives for long chats and short naps. Sometimes I would find the women still in a diving hut two or three hours after the work was over, slowly tidying up, cleaning, and gossiping.

As I was to learn when I began diving myself, however, there were levels of skill and knowledge that had to be mastered before being able to dive successfully. As one woman put it when a television crew tried to get her to lend me her wet suit: "I can't, really I can't. Diving is my business, my work —if my wet suit were damaged, it would be bad for my work." She didn't trust me as a diver, and this included knowing how to correctly put on a wet suit.

Diving might have been a pastime for the older women of the village— a rather nostalgic pastime—but for the younger women it was also hard work. They enjoyed the work and the leisure after diving, but first and foremost, it was how they earned a part of their living. To understand diving in Kuzaki it is important to remember that it was a mode of production essential to the economy of the *ie,* and it was embedded within household relationships as well. It was also a dangerous job. The ways diving was arranged —the tools and gear that were used, where one dived, how one dived, and the rituals performed for the safety of divers—were necessary details that had to be mastered before a woman could relax and enjoy diving purely for its own sake. Moreover, it must be added that skill at diving, as well as at other forms of labor, was a crucial way in which a woman was evaluated as a person.

In Kuzaki there had always been two types of divers: *kachido* and *funado.*[3] *Kachido* (walking people) were the shore divers—that is, they generally waded into the sea from a beach and went no farther than 500 or 1,000 meters offshore. Sometimes if a diving area was inaccessible from a beach, *kachido* went out in small boats in groups of six to eight, leaving the anchored boat to swim and dive in the immediate area. Sometimes a *kachido* would swim so far off that she would find another closer boat to take her back to the harbor. Most *kachido* were between the ages of thirty and forty, while in the hot summer, some of the women in their sixties and seventies also dived as *kachido.* A *kachido* would dive to 5 or 6 meters in depth and

Figure 7. *Kachido* taking a break during summer diving (D. P. Martinez)

stay underwater for twenty to thirty seconds with rests of about twenty seconds between dives. In 1984–1986 in Kuzaki there were about eighty *kachido,* twenty of whom were men.[4] These men were often from households that practiced full-time fishing and whose wives were also diving as *kachido.*

Funado (boat people) were the older, more experienced, highly skilled divers between the ages of forty and sixty who always dived from boats during the abalone season. In 1984–1986 there were only twenty *funado* in Kuzaki; nineteen were husband-wife teams and one was a woman who dived with her son—an unmarried man of thirty-five—as boatman. These women dived in areas that were more than a kilometer offshore and dived to depths of 10 to 15 meters, holding their breath for an average of one minute. Many could go for as long as three minutes underwater, but they paced themselves with shorter dives and rests of twenty or thirty seconds between dives. Many *funado* claimed that the *kachido* of Kuzaki would never advance to their stage, since the latter included many women who had only seriously taken to diving after marriage and the birth of their children. These women would never amass the knowledge or develop the skill of a *funado,* who usually came from a generation of women who had been diving professionally from the age of sixteen.

Normally, a *funado* did not dive in a group but alone, with just her husband in the boat. She wore a rope around her waist to serve as a safety line and held a large counterweight that was tied to a line to aid her in making a fast descent. Once on the seafloor, she let go of the weight, which her husband then pulled back up alongside the boat. The rope around her waist was for use in an emergency—that is, if an unconscious or hurt woman had to be pulled up. A man would be very familiar with his wife's diving pattern and could judge accurately if she was in trouble. Most husbands also gave added help during the diver's ascent by pulling the rope in when they noticed that she had begun her return to the surface. Thus the diver wasted neither breath nor energy in swimming up or down from the seafloor; all her energy was expended at the bottom, looking for abalone.

Japanese ethnographers have always stressed the need for understanding and harmony between *funado* couples, for a woman's life literally depended on her husband's competence. Early during fieldwork, I timed both *kachido* and *funado* divers and found that whenever I did *funado* times I could check my figures against the mental count of the boatman, who always knew the number of dives and the length of time a diver spent underwater as accurately as I did with my notes and stopwatch. A common joke in Kuzaki was that no *funado* could afford to quarrel with her husband, for he literally held her life in his hands; conversely, especially in the past, no husband could afford to quarrel with the woman who earned so much money through her diving.

This *funado/kachido* division was important only during the abalone diving season. During the rest of the year, when diving for seaweed, only women would dive and all would dive from boats in small groups of five or six. Generally, these groups were made up of a woman's kin: mother, sisters, and cousins on the maternal side. If a diver had married into the village, it was her mother-in-law's group that she would join. During these sorts of diving sessions, there would be two men in the boat who would keep track of the divers and also empty the full barrels *(iso-oke)* into which the diver loaded the seaweed. These men did not need to be kin; rather they often were a pair of husbands who were free for the day. If women were diving for shellfish, they grouped according to the major geographical village divisions and waded in from the shore.

All twenty men who dived in the village during the summers of 1984–1986 claimed to have always dived. Even some of the grandfathers maintained that they dived in their youth. All village children did play at diving in the summer, so it does seem plausible that all men in Kuzaki had always learned to dive, even if most stopped as they grew older. The men who dived claimed that with the introduction of the wet suit they could

Figure 8. A *funado* leaping into the sea (D. P. Martinez)

stand the cold water as well as the women, so they could dive for longer periods of time.

As divers, of course, the men were classed as *kachido* and, with the exception of *hijiki* (a seaweed) gathering, dived only for abalone. A man could never progress to the *funado* category. When I asked the villagers if this would be possible, I was told "no" because no woman was strong enough to pull a man back into the boat. Actually, with the use of mechanized pulleys it might have been possible for a woman to do this, but the villagers found this suggestion very funny. Still, the idea of working with one's wife as a team was so strong in Kuzaki that these men always dived in the same groups as their wives. Men were surprisingly good divers, often bringing in big catches *(dairyō)*, and they would boast of their prowess as divers. They had long breath *(nagai iki)* and joked that if only the women had the muscle to haul the men back into a boat, they could take up diving as a *funado*. Men, however, never turned their catches into the Cooperative; carrying the abalone to the Kumi-ai for weighing was always done by the female diver of the household.

Mentioned in the previous chapter was the one wet suit per household rule, which was maintained in Kuzaki to discourage divers from spending too long at sea during the summer diving season. When a household had a male diver, he got to wear the wet suit, but in general most women wore wet

Figure 9. A *funado* coming up (D. P. Martinez)

suits if they possibly could (it was a problem if a *yome*'s mother-in-law felt that as a *funado*, she got the wet suit). It was not only wet suits, but all aspects of diving that the Kumi-ai regulated: deciding the beginning and end of diving seasons; whether the weather and sea were safe for diving; and from which beaches the divers should work. Some of the older women resented this control and talked angrily of how they—and only they—had real first-hand experience of the seafloor and knew best, from day to day, where to dive. Nonetheless, the Cooperative consulted women only behind the scenes—but it did not hurt if the Kumi-ai *chō* had a *funado* wife to give him advice.

Wet suits, however, are not part of the image of the sexy, white-clad *ama* associated with the past. In fact, the white suits—*amagi*—that divers did occasionally use if they couldn't wear a wet suit were actually part of the clothing divers traditionally wore to keep warm *after* diving. In the past, as stories and grandmothers would have it, women dived wearing only loin-cloths and a head covering. Since the 1950s, all divers, whether in wet suit or *amagi,* had taken to wearing fins, face masks, and cotton gloves to pro-tect their hands. All women also inserted a type of putty that they called *mimiendo* or *mimidana* into their ears so that when underwater and under increased pressure they did not have to clear their ears. Many women com-plained that despite this precaution, they grew deaf because of diving.

Aside from all this comparatively modern equipment, the divers still used the same *nomi* (literally, "chisel") of various sizes that their ancestors used (see Figure 10). Most *nomi* were meant to last a diver's lifetime and were made in the village by a grandfather who had learned the skill from his father. It was considered bad luck to drop and lose a *nomi* in the sea. Most of the older divers marked their *nomi* with figures designed to ward off evil, and these were the same figures that are carved on the charms that were placed above the entrance to the house. A large *nomi* was also called a *kaki* and was used for chopping seaweed underwater; the smaller version, called a *kaginomi,* was used for prying abalone off the rock shelves. The small hand *konomi* was for the more fragile shells of the sea urchin and sea snails. To carry abalone while diving, *ama* used a small net *(ami)* suspended from a wooden float that was called a *tanpo;* some modern *tanpo* were made of styrofoam. Seaweeds such as *wakame* and *tengusa* were stored in the float-ing half-barrel called *iso-oke.* The seaweed *hijiki* was gathered into sacks by a working couple, and these were left to float until they could be hauled into the boat or pulled ashore.

Summarizing the equipment a diver used also gives a good indication

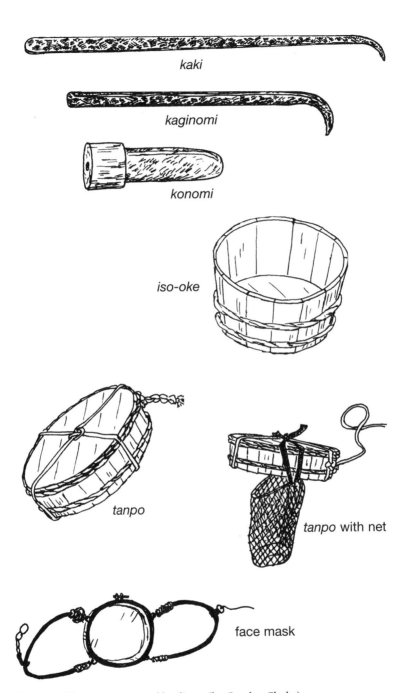

kaki

kaginomi

konomi

iso-oke

tanpo

tanpo with net

face mask

Figure 10. The equipment used by divers (by Carolyn Clarke)

of the catches an *ama* brought up during the diving year. Table 2 lists the time of year, catches, and types of divers who do the work.

After diving, the women normally retired to the *koie* (hut) to rest.[5] Grandmothers explained that in the past, the women built their own *koie* from wood and bamboo, but the four sets of huts found in Kuzaki in 1984–1986 were made of concrete blocks and were constructed for the divers by the Kumi-ai. The basic structure of the *koie* remained the same as in the past: Half the hut was for washing, with running water, and the other half had a hearth in the center where the women sat, warmed themselves, napped, and talked. According to divers in other villages, these *koie* were the center of a diver's life—the real home where one could relax, sing, nap, and exchange, albeit guardedly, information about the day's diving (cf. Tanaka 1983, 40–60).

The *koie* in Kuzaki corresponded to the four village divisions. Yet the diver's use of the huts could be confusing; for example, a woman who lived

Table 2. Diving seasons in Kuzaki

Month	Catch	Frequency and Divers
early April	*hijiki* (brown algae)	1 full day, all women
May–September	abalone	1 hour daily, all divers
late May–June	*tengusa* (agar-agar)	1 hour, 1 day, *fujin-kai* members
August	*arame* (seaweed)	3 full days, all households
September/November	*uni* (sea urchin) *takobushi* (a form of abalone)[i]	1 hour daily, all divers
September only	*kaki* (oysters)	as required, anyone
December	*arame*	3 full days, all divers
(first half)	*sazaya* (sea snail)[ii] *namako* (sea slug)	in good weather, all divers (same as above)
February	nori (laver)[iii]	as required, mostly older women
March–April	*wakame*	10 days, two 1-hour diving sessions daily, all divers

Notes:

i. Plath found that the terms *"tokobusho"* or *"fururame"* were used.

ii. In Ōsatsu and Toba City, the term was *"sazae."*

iii. This seaweed is cultivated in sheltered bays and sold in packages in all supermarkets in Japan. Still, the grandmothers in Kuzaki preferred to wade out and gather their own nori, drying it at home for personal use.

in Satonaka and brought her catch in to be sold at the Kumi-ai when it was Sato-tani's turn might use the Kainaka *koie*. This was because a woman always went to her mother's or mother-in-law's *koie*. Thus a young woman often used a *koie* that was not related to where she lived but to where she had lived as a child or even to where her mother-in-law once lived. After the older woman's retirement from diving, the younger woman might join the *koie* corresponding to the village division in which she lived, especially if there were friends or even matrilineal cousins of the same age as she in that *koie*. A diver might choose to continue to dive with her mother/mother-in-law's *koie* if she had grown comfortable with the women there.

Male divers were never allowed into the *koie* until every woman had showered. Then they were allowed to go into the washing room, which they had to leave immediately after washing. Men had their own fires outside the *koie*, and many would return home to wash rather than wait a turn in the *koie*. Men who did use the *koie* followed their wives to their mothers' *koie*; or, if a wife was not a Kuzaki woman, a man would use his mother's.

When diving far away from the village's central harbors, especially in the warm summer, the women would gather on a beach, build their fires there, and spend as much of the day as possible in the sun (wearing hats and sunblock to protect their skin). The male divers would have their own fire away from the women, but communication between the two groups occurred. Many times I would see a woman warm up a bit of food at her fire and carry it over to her husband in front of his.

Tanaka (1983, 97–113) writes of the *koie* as the base for the groups that the divers form. These groups, or *nakama,* are described as long-term associations, competing with other diving *nakama* and very difficult to enter as a novice.[6] In Kuzaki the *nakama* were surprisingly fluid, changing not only throughout a diver's life cycle but also throughout the diving seasons. In the spring when diving for *wakame,* the women stayed in the huts, which as noted were based both on the village geographical divisions and matrilineal relations. In the summer, a group *dōkyūsei* loosely based on matrilineal kinship might form; that is, cousins of about the same age would share a boat out to a small island where the men and women would share a fire. Or, if the beach was large, the younger women would group around one fire, older women around another, and the men around their own. If the diving took place close to the harbor, the women returned to the *koie* and the men stayed outside.[7] *Funado* almost always returned to the hut; their sense of *nakama,* reinforced by kinship, was strong. *Kachido* would follow any of the patterns described above and sometimes added a visit to the *koie* after hanging around a fire elsewhere. Inside the *koie* the older women showered first, young women would offer the senior divers tidbits from their lunchboxes, and *fujin-kai* business was often discussed.

This tendency to divide into *nakama* based on the matrilineal kin group remained strong despite all the changes in diving patterns in Kuzaki. Diving times might have been shorter, women dived where they were told rather than where they thought best, and male divers had been added to the picture. This tendency was not surprising if one considers the ways in which a young girl learned to dive.

In the 1980s, all of the village children spent the summer playing at diving. All children seemed to own face masks and always took them along when going off to the beach to swim. This diving was true play, for no adults supervised the older children, and the younger children were watched by grandparents who volunteered to act as lifeguards from the shore; there was no formal diving instruction. Only in August, when the sea was at its warmest, would a diver take her adolescent daughter or—more recently—son with her on dives. In the 1980s it was more likely to be a son learning from his mother, since many teenage girls refused to practice diving on the grounds that it would coarsen the skin and ruin their hands. This practice diving was very informal, the child staying out a full hour with the working adult divers and practicing duck diving to reach the seafloor and holding the breath, but again, a child was given no formal instruction.[8]

In 1984–1986, there were no young women in the village who dived regularly; the youngest women diving were in their early thirties. The younger daughters-in-law in their twenties worked in Toba or helped in village inns. No girls above the age of sixteen dived. Since the end of *dekasegi* work in the 1940s, there no longer seemed to be a clear pattern of progression from childish practice diving to becoming more skilled *kachido*. Some women in the 1950s had stayed at home and dived; in the 1960s women did odd part-time jobs and began diving in earnest after marriage. In the 1980s, the most typical pattern I found among the younger divers in the village was that they had hoped to marry outside the diving villages in which they grew up —perhaps to a white-collar worker—and when they married a Kuzaki man instead, they began to dive. Thus, for some of the women, to be an *ama* was to have failed at moving up into the class of stay-at-home housewife. For a few others it was a conscious choice: They married a young man in the village whom they liked and went on to learn to dive. A smaller group of women were city-born wives, who after marrying into the village learned to dive because it was a good way to earn money part-time.

As already mentioned, this truncated pattern of learning to dive meant that fewer women moved into the *funado* category since they were spending less time diving and began to learn about technique later in life. Traditionally, only the best of the young divers worked as *funado,* and other women moved into that class as they grew older and gained competence and experience. The progression was from a shore diver perfecting her skills to a boat diver who was skilled and could rely on her memory of the sea bottom to help her. That is, the diver's accumulated learning over the years gave her a mental map of the seafloor *(iso),*[9] and it was her ability to keep secret her favorite spots from others that would add to her reputation as a skilled diver. Some of this knowledge was learned from one's mother-in-law, but a diver had to keep in mind how the *iso* changed from season to season and year to year and had to be able to adjust her diving accordingly, while also adjusting this knowledge in light of having to dive as ordered by the Cooperative. With the Kumi-ai's control over diving, even a *funado*'s mental picture of an area might be a year old and not very useful. But different catches required different skills, and these still needed to be learned from an older diver.

What were the techniques a diver needed in order to be considered skillful *(jōzu)?* The measuring of another woman's skill was commonplace in Kuzaki and was based on the comments made by those who had dived with a woman and by keeping track of the size of catches a woman brought in. The men who pulled in the barrels of seaweed during *wakame* season would judge as well; since a boat's load of *wakame* was divided evenly between all the women diving from it, noting that one diver or another was benefiting from the hard work of the others was enough to bring sharp comments. "She spends all her time on the surface resting," was one deeply critical statement. Divers were not above comparing their own success or failure with friends, and the village grapevine was extremely quick and accurate. A large catch *(dairyō)* was immediate news throughout the village, and continuous poor catches were also grist for the mill. I learned of the quickness and accuracy of the village grapevine on the day I brought in my first and only abalone: By nightfall, the entire village knew to tease me about my *dairyō.*

Kuzaki divers were quick to volunteer information on why a diver was always successful or not. A good diver was said to have long breath, so that they could stay underwater long enough to locate the abalone or gather lots of seaweed. A poor diver was accused of being fearful; of not wanting to scar her hands by reaching into dark crevices; of having short breath; or of being lazy and resting for too long; in short, a poor diver was not willing to take the risks necessary in order to be successful. Interestingly enough, good divers boasted only of having long breath—never did they say that they were not afraid (nor did they say they *were* afraid). Long breath was not only the ability to stay underwater for thirty seconds to a minute; it also meant the ability to keep diving at a consistent pace and to take as short a break between dives as possible.

Funado divers were almost all described as number one *(ichiban),* and the acknowledged best diver among the *kachido* was a woman of thirty-eight who was also praised for being beautiful, slender, and hard working. This is an important point about the seemingly innocuous term "skillful": Being *jōzu* involved not just having excellent diving skills—it included others' assessments about how well a diver fulfilled her duties as wife, daughter-in-law, and mother. An acknowledged good male diver did not get praised as well for being handsome or slender, but he would also be judged on his ability to work hard at everything, not drink too much, and to fulfill his duties to the *ie* and the village.

Women had not only to be skilled and responsible but also attractive. For example, the worst diver in the village was considered to be cowardly, too fat, lazy, and a woman not worthy of others' trust. Thus, skill and personality were seen to be connected. To be *jōzu* at one thing alone was not possible—it was a moral evaluation of the whole person.

This notion of what it takes to be skilled is not unusual in Japan. To be skillful involves a willingness to learn, to be humble, to work hard and uncomplainingly, to try to be cheerful and supportive of others. This willingness, then, is part of someone's personality and helps in developing diving skills; it cannot be divorced from the self.

With almost a full year's diving, women in Kuzaki had plenty of opportunity to judge each other's skills, as a quick overview of the diving season shows. The measuring of a diver's endurance would begin with a month's diving for *wakame* in April. Divers often worked in water that was 6–8 degrees Celsius (43–46 degrees Fahrenheit) for one hour, twice daily, and not even a wet suit would keep a lazy diver warm for long; constant movement was necessary. So the diver who climbed into the boat before the end of the diving hour because of cold or exhaustion was criticized. The work of *wakame* gathering was not otherwise arduous. A diver would duck-dive to a depth of a meter or meter and a half, then chop at the thick stalks of *wakame* with her *kaki.* When her hands were full, she would surface and load the seaweed into her *iso-oke,* which was attached by a rope called an *isozuna* to her waist. Women who surfaced before their hands were full because they were short of breath were commented on by the men who waited in the boat to collect the *wakame.* The men were supposed to be watching all the women they had brought out, who might number five or six; so if a woman was always too tired to swim her barrel of *wakame* over to the boat and they had to move toward her, this could also be a point of criticism. In contrast, an adventurous diver who had swum far to gather large amounts of seaweed would have her harvest collected without a murmur of complaint.

Preparing the *wakame* for sale was part of the work of the *ie* but was done partly in the public eye. So, when the boat returned from the sea and the seaweed was divided among all the women diving from that boat, all available members of the family would be onshore to collect their share of the harvest. As mentioned, the men doing the dividing sometimes complained if a household got the same as others when they felt that the diver from that *ie* had not really done her share—but it did not change the division of *wakame*. Then the family would set to work as the divers retired to the *koie*. They would cut off the stem *(mekabu)* and the frilly edges of the seaweed called the *kuki* and leave these to dry on the bamboo mats on the beach. The main strand of *wakame* would be hung from nails on poles and left to dry for two days. Once dried, the diver and her mother-in-law would spend a day tying the seaweed into bundles of 5 kilos each. Often an older woman would add the *wakame* that she had collected from the shore and dried, so that even among households that dived together, the amount taken to the Co-op to sell would be different.

Wakame harvesting was altogether different from *hijiki* collecting, which was more the work of couples. *Hijiki* was gathered in one full day in early May, preferably before the start of the abalone season. Some couples would choose a spot to gather the algae off the rocks near the shore; others would take a boat out toward the small islands that dotted the coast a kilometer or so offshore. Competition could be fierce for arriving first in a place and claiming it, but in contrast to the emphasis on matrilineality in *wakame* work, this diving was done by groups of patrilineal kin. In all cases, the technique was the same: The divers, wrapped in layers of clothing or wearing wet suits, would swim in the shallow waters around the rocks looking for patches of *hijiki*. When a good patch was found, divers would remove a gunnysack they had tied to their back and begin to dive (often going down only half a meter) until the patch was harvested or the sack was full. Each sack was marked with the *ie shirushi* and, when full, it was tied shut and left to float on the sea. At the end of the day, the sacks would be loaded into a boat—or if found near shore, into a van—and taken to a beach where the *hijiki* was spread out to dry. After two days the *ie* would take the *hijiki* to the

Co-op, where it was weighed and packaged. The most important skills to have for this sort of gathering were endurance and consistency—filling as many sacks as possible in the one day of permitted gathering.

Another form of seaweed gathering was *arame* harvesting, which occupied two days during the summer, generally in August before Obon, and another two in December. This seaweed could sell for 150 yen a kilo, and in 1986 the summer gathering netted up to 7 metric tons. The Cooperative, as noted in the section on elections, kept all the funds from the summer gathering, and all the work done by the divers was seen to be volunteer. Two members from each village household were expected to come out and help with the *arame* cutting. The women went out in boats—generally two women and two boatmen to a motorboat—and once at a good spot they would leap overboard with a rope tied around their waists. A diver would swim out to a patch of *arame*, dive down about 5 or 6 meters, and begin cutting. The *arame* a diver gathered was put on her back, tucked into the rope around her waist. When she was laden with the seaweed, the boatman would reel her in, literally lift her face downward toward the boat, pull out the *arame* from the rope, and then drop the woman back into the water. Both the ability to swim with the extra weight of seaweed on her back and, at the same time, the ability to go totally limp were important. Most divers found this sort of diving tiring and were glad it lasted only two days.

After the *arame* had been gathered, it needed to be laid out to dry in the sun and, for days on end, Kuzaki beaches looked as if they had turned black with seaweed. When it was dried, the Kumi-ai would once again request two volunteers per household to help weigh and stack the *arame* into piles that resembled black haystacks. The *arame* stayed in the village until the Cooperative found the best buyer for it.

From May until December, diving involved a series of catches: abalone, *takobushi* (a type of small abalone), sea snail, sea urchin, sea slug, and oysters. The diving for these different catches required similar skills, techniques, and equipment. For all this diving, women would use a *tanpo* with its suspended net, which kept the catch in water and alive until the end of the diving period. Only for abalone diving would the women split up into *funado* and *kachido* groups; for all other types of diving included in this category, the women waded in from the shore or went in groups in small motorboats. As previously mentioned, men dived only for abalone.

Diving in the summer was considered to be the safest type of diving possible, yet water temperatures might stay at 12–14 degrees Celsius (54–57 degrees Fahrenheit) until late July when the ocean begins to warm up (compare this with an indoor swimming pool that has an average temperature of 31 degrees [88]). August and September temperatures might reach the 20s (70s). Also, with more frequent days of sunshine, visibility underwater improved to some extent, especially after the harvesting of the various sea-weeds. By summer it was expected that the spring *wakame* diving would have made a woman fit again (many women claimed that they put on up to 10 kilos of weight during the winter break from diving) and that she would be able to dive for longer periods with shorter rests than during the colder season. Even if she found few abalone, a woman would make sure to bring up something else—a sea urchin or sea snail—which, although out of season, was to be taken home to eat. It was important that a diver prove that she was able to find *something* underwater.

The various skills necessary to be a good diver all came together during the summer abalone diving. The speed with which a woman worked, endurance of the cold, long breath, and the need for little rest were all essential. Abalone diving was the real test of that elusive quality that made the best divers: the ability to locate abalone in dark holes or under rocks by touch alone. Compared to abalone, sea snails, sea urchins, oysters, and even sea slugs tend to be easily visible—the first three clinging to the upper surface of underwater rocks, the latter a bright red among the dark seaweed. A diver just needed to find a good spot and fill her net. Abalone, however, is more difficult to locate, and a diver was primarily judged by her success during the abalone season.

Funado excelled at locating abalone, but even they were judged by the size and type of abalone that they brought in. A *dairyō* of large 1-kilo black abalone *(kuroawabi)* was the best, followed by green *(aoawabi)* and white *(shiroawabi)*. Black abalone was considered the most delicious of all and therefore fetched higher prices on the Tokyo market. The major skill here was for the diver to remember from one year to the next what the area had been like where she had dived and where the abalone was most likely to be. Also important was the ability to dive deep; the larger and older the abalone was, the more likely it was to have moved into deeper areas and, for some reason, to be found in groups of two or three. Another important asset for gathering the bigger and stronger abalone (clamped to the rock with all the strength their foot could muster) was to have a strong arm, for prying the creature loose could be hard work. Long breath came into play here: A diver needed to be able to stay under for as long as it took to pry the abalone loose. Divers and husbands alike often summed up these skills, but I personally would add "nerves of steel," or the opposite of what is termed *"kowai"* (fearful). Swimming at such depths, the *funado* had restricted vision and needed to proceed by touch, putting her hand into crevices that might hold an angry biting eel. A diver might follow a crevice along until she was stuck when it narrowed and had to have the presence of mind to back up and swim out without panicking. Women did not often talk about these final skills; interestingly, it would be their boatmen husbands who would tell me of the dangers of being on the seafloor. Perhaps it could be said that the men would worry *for* the women, who could not afford to be beset by fear.

Yet no diver, male or female, took safety for granted. It was not just the boatmen who were important safeguards for a diver, but for *kachido,* all divers relied on each other. When I was allowed only to watch *kachido* diving (in the colder weather), I too was expected to keep track of the number of heads bobbing up and down in the sea. Anyone leaving the ocean earlier than other divers would come sit next to me and keep an eye out as well, asking me if I could spot someone who seemed to have disappeared. No one was ever lost or hurt while I lived in the village, but an older Ōsatsu diver did die in the sea in 1984. This not only increased people's watchfulness but led to a renewal of ritual protection for Kuzaki divers. In fact, ritual protection of divers and their families occupied a large part of daily life in Kuzaki and needs to be examined in some detail.

Diving and Ritual: Women's Work

In previous chapters, I have described three large ceremonial events—two of them religious in nature—in which the men of Kuzaki dominated. This was a marked contrast to the smaller rituals that surrounded both the household and diving for which women were responsible. While it made sense that women should have had charge of the routine maintenance of this part of life as it related to their labor, it is interesting that they were also meant to learn how to care for the household's ancestors as part of their tasks.[10] As Lebra (1984) has noted, the ancestors whom many Japanese women worship daily are their husbands'; there is no bond of blood, yet if the ancestors are not to become hungry ghosts, the woman must remember them. In chapter 7, I describe Obon (the Buddhist festival of the dead) and how the village's older women become involved in maintaining all sorts of boundaries: those between the living and dead, between families, and protecting the village boundaries. The last part of this chapter describes how smaller rituals can be seen as being about the blurring of boundaries. *Ama* were workers who constantly juggled their various roles in life, and their ritual work reflected this. So it was that they worshipped as divers, mothers, wives, daughters, and daughters-in-law. When I asked if men ever were involved in this essential, repetitive, and perhaps mundane type of worship,

I was answered with a laugh: "Men also worship, sometimes"—an interesting way to sum up the public male participation in large ceremonies.

I've already described two large rituals that are associated with the diving season: Hi-matsuri in July and Nifune in November. There was one practice, however, that occurred all throughout the year and was normally done by the female diver in the household. Every twenty-eighth day of the month, the women climbed Sengen-san (Mt. Sengen)[11] to leave offerings for various deities. Only the divers of the household did this, as they were the ones in greatest need of protection and thus responsible for making this important trip. The whole process took little more than an hour and included a rather steep climb to the highest point in the area.

There were two sacred areas on Sengen-san. The first featured a Shinto altar, on top of which was the shrine dedicated either to Sengen itself or to Princess Konohanasakuya.[12] This was a typical closed Shinto shrine facing east and containing the *shintai*. To the right of the shrine as one faced it was a triangular black rock that represented Ryū (the dragon deity of the sea). To the left of the altar there was a vaguely phallic stone that was said to help with infertility, while the pebbles on the altar around this stone were good to take home and rub on a sick child to help cure their illness. Once more, on the right as one faced the shrine, there began a semicircular path on which were set six small torii facing in auspicious directions. No one knew what all the gates were for—one was for safety at sea, another just for boats, one faced Ise Shrine, another the Imperial Palace—but all had offerings left on their little stone altar. The offerings consisted of boiled sweets or individually wrapped biscuits and, as the offerings were left, the women collected some of the sweets left behind by those who had come before them. These offerings were good to take home and put in front of the Buddhist altar, as well as to give to children to eat because the deities had blessed them.[13]

The offerings were made by placing the object first in front of the shrine, perhaps pouring some sake out as well, bowing one's head, clapping twice, and saying a short prayer. Rice and money were also appropriate offerings. If there had been consistent bad luck in fishing, an egg might be left for the dragon, because—as it was explained to me on my first trip up Sengen-san —dragons love eggs. Going around clockwise, offerings were also left at the six torii. I was told that it was all right for *anyone*—even a foreign anthropologist—to leave offerings and pray, but one must not ask for too much from the deities (especially when praying at the torii) because they would punish a greedy person.

Then the women went over the mountaintop westward, down to a sacred area that was essentially Buddhist in nature. There were several Buddhist figures outside a hut that also faced east. The hut housed a figure that some thought was Kojin or Koshi.[14] Offerings in this area were made first to the Buddhist Jizō-sama (the protector of children)[15] on the left-hand side as one faced the hut. Once more the offerings were sweets, biscuits, rice and/or money; incense was sometimes lit as well. Again, beginning at the right-hand side as one faced the statues were two rock formations that were given offerings just because they are oddly shaped and said to be sacred.

The trip back down was less arduous than the climb up, and late worshippers might encounter the woman from the Fujin-kai who had been delegated to go and collect all the offerings still left on the altars at the end of the morning. These were taken home by the officers of the club. As has been noted, this seemingly simple act of worship was delegated to the women in the *ie* who dived; thus occasionally both mother and daughter-in-law would

Figure 11. The altar to Sengen-san (by D. P. Martinez)

climb the mountain. The offerings to the various deities were for the welfare of the children and general safety at sea, for good luck in diving, good crops, and big catches in fishing.

As was noted about Hi-matsuri, all rituals are by nature polysemous, but in this case we see one set of ritual actions at different sites that represent the complexity of Japanese religious life. The worship of Sengen as a mountain might be an ancient pre-Buddhist tradition, but incorporated into this monthly pattern of worship are Taoist, Buddhist, and possibly Confucian elements. The importance of direction is Taoist, the worship of Jizō is Buddhist, the figure in the hut is identified as Confucius flanked by Buddhist guardian demons, and the most important altar is that of a Shinto deity—even if the identity of that deity is ambiguous. While the Meiji Restoration divided the religious traditions of Buddhism and Shintoism that had become assimilated to each other over the centuries, leaving a residue of Taoist and Confucian practices to be labeled as "folk" religion, in this monthly journey up Sengen we get a glimpse of pre-Meiji worship. I use the term "glimpse" purposely, since I do not want to argue that this is what Sengen worship was like for the villagers over a century ago; but certainly the mixture of sacred areas on Sengen is closer to the pre-Meiji situation, when religious practice—with all its strands—was seen to be one system.

I soon learned that modern women had opinions about religion. The

Figure 12. An offering to the sea dragon (D. P. Martinez)

idea that Shinto worship was open to anyone certainly contradicted the pre-war nationalist idea that Shinto was *the* Japanese religion, but many women offered me this bit of information, urging me to pray. In contrast, the offering of eggs to the deity of the sea occasioned a moment of what I came to see as typical pragmatism on one worshipper's part. "Do the eggs get taken home as *naorai?*" I asked. "No, they get eaten," was the reply. For a moment —this in my first month of fieldwork—I was truly awed by this example of belief. "They're eaten by the dragon?" I finally ventured. Laughing, the woman said: "The dragon? No, foxes!"

This capacity both to worship powers that were not verifiable by science and yet to be utterly practical at the same time is an attitude not uncommon in Japan. While westerners seem to demand serious mysticism whenever they encounter nonmainstream religions, the fact remains that most practitioners of other religious traditions just get on with what they do; and, if they pause to reflect, they are quite capable of recognizing logical inconsistencies in what they practice—and even of laughing at themselves. The rationality of religion is not scientific, despite the efforts of social scientists to construct rational explanations for religious practice. In Japan, the inconsistencies are often huge: Deities dwell in *shintai,* on mountains, they *are* mountains, the mountain is a dragon, the dragon is the deity of the sea—but it is foxes that eat its offerings. A deity might dwell in the village shrine, yet need to be invited in and then sent away. Ancestors are worshipped daily as if they were near, but they are summoned during Obon as if they were far away. Deities have been identified with bodhisattva and bodhisattva with Shinto deities. It's not clear whether everyone understands that this mixture of religious systems is the way it used to be. Once a Kuzaki friend took me to the Asama Temple Museum, where we saw a statue of Amaterasu in which she stood with her hands held in Buddhist attitudes, but despite my excitement at this evidence of pre-Meiji assimilation, she had nothing to say. Religious practices such as worshipping Jizō as both a protector of children and an aid to infertility or maintaining village boundaries that acted as protection from ghosts and demons were important even if sometimes described as old-fashioned beliefs that were followed just in case. So too, this held with fishermen, who believed in technology as supremely important in modern fishing but didn't neglect older rituals.

Most important was that everyone took part in worshipping. One wise young woman (Seiko-san) explained village practices to me in this way when discussing her sister-in-law, who lived in Kyoto and was a member of the new religion, Soka Gakkai:

My husband's sister and her family couldn't live here in Kuzaki. You noticed that they belong to Soka Gakkai and they don't believe in any other religion than Soka Gakkai. It's the sort of religion that doesn't allow people to have other beliefs. Here, in the village, we have all sorts of beliefs [*iroirona shinkō ga oru*].[16] We worship the deities of the fields, the deities of the sea, the deities of the mountains; everywhere you turn in Kuzaki there are deities we worship. Then, of course, there are the buddhas. Yes, in Kuzaki we have all sorts of beliefs, and to live here you must worship as everyone does. You can't just follow one religion.

What interested me about this statement was Seiko-san's saying that her husband's kin could not have lived in the village because Kuzaki was a place of various beliefs and practices. These formed part of daily family life and were the basis of community solidarity, and not to take part in the practices of all the village was not to be a member of the village. So it was that even poor divers and "bad" wives were expected to visit Sengen monthly, while even foreigners were allowed to worship; the practices and worship constituted part of the social fabric of Kuzaki. To not take part in them was to isolate oneself from social life. Not everyone, obviously, had to do everything; as in the rest of life, everyone had a role to play.

One male informant tried to generalize about these roles by telling me that "Shinto is a women's thing, Buddhism a men's thing"—a statement that, in terms of participation, made no sense at all, as we shall see. Yet when I tried the idea out on others in the village, no one denied this rather broad dichotomy; one person went so far as to offer me the idea that the sea was female and therefore, of course, it was women's work to worship her. What I did not realize for a long time is that the simple explanation of one thing for men and another for women referred specifically to the situation of men and women in Kuzaki. Buddhism is about the household, the patrilineal; Shintoism is about the worship of external forces: the sun, the sea, the wind, rocks, and so on. The aligning of one sex with each practice acted as a trope for a basic reality: Men were at the center of everything in Kuzaki—both in the household and in village political life, they were the insiders. Women tended to come from outside the household—outside the village even—and had to be taught to dive, to be good daughters-in-law, to worship the ancestors. They were necessary for both biological and social reproduction, they even wielded some economic power, but first they had to be socialized anew into Kuzaki ways. They were outsiders who had to become insiders. To associate women with Shinto—the religion that is seen to be quintessentially

Japanese and is concerned with the worship of powerful external forces that are needed to reanimate the social and yet must be treated with caution because they are dangerous—makes sense. So it was that women's ritual practices took place outside the large rituals of village life. As we have seen, they would light candles in the evening (Nifune) or leave offerings on rocks while men took part in larger rituals; they stayed at home cooking while men dressed in their best and went to the temple or shrine; women worshipped at the household *kamidama* (gods' shelf), leaving the Buddhist altar to the older women and men of the household.

The trip up Sengen was one of two women-only acts of worship within Kuzaki (the other, sutra reciting, is described in chapter 7); it was the only one that was never incorporated into a larger ceremonial where others took different roles as their station in life dictated. And it was an act of worship both essential—you had to do it if you were a diver—and made light of: It was a woman's thing. It had its parallel in the rituals surrounding the launching of a new boat—men's work—but no real opposite. As with the time women spent in the *koie* or in Fujin-kai meetings, it seemed to be about female solidarity but never about feminist rebellion. The *koie* and Sengen represent domains that are female, but with permission, men can enter the *koie*, and the worship on Sengen is for everyone's benefit. Thus even the diver who confesses to going to the sea because she loves it only temporarily escapes everyday reality. In the end, diving and worshipping were both done to benefit the whole and not the individual. Women were only a part of the social whole, and this was made obvious by the rituals that surrounded the beginning of the abalone diving season.

The first of several tasks that had to be accomplished before the start of the diving season was the making of rice cakes *(o-mochi)* on April 6. This day, as previously mentioned, was actually a Buddhist *tendoku* (literally "skipping") day: The village priest and the grandfathers sat in the temple reciting sutras over the books that contained the household family records.[17] The women used this day to make huge batches of *o-mochi*, mostly in modern *mochi*-making machines rather than in the old giant wooden tubs that needed huge pestles to beat the cooked rice into a paste. Enough *mochi* was made to give away the fancier sweet-bean stuffed cakes to family kin—but on this occasion, only to patrilineally related kin. One batch might be given to the wife's mother if she had made enough. Several small plain cakes were made and left at various sacred Shinto areas throughout the village: the shrine on Ijika road and the shrines on Yoroizaki and Yoroizaki Beach. The Buddhist temple got some rice and plain *mochi* as well, but almost as an afterthought. All the leftover rice cakes, plain without sweet filling, were frozen and saved to eat throughout the rest of the diving year. These leftover cakes were toasted in small pieces over the divers' fires and were often eaten with a lump of brown sugar. They were the ultimate high-energy food, loaded with starch and carbohydrates, as well as blessed by having been made on a sacred day.

For the people of Kuzaki, this giving of rice cakes in April was a sort of Chūgen (mid-year giving of gifts to kin and seniors) and was not repeated in July when the rest of the nation was involved in Chūgen gifts. It was during the July nationwide Chūgen that kin from Ijika and Anori who had received *o-mochi* from Kuzaki in April returned the gifts.

On April 7, each household in the village collected their *amacha* from the Buddhist temple. This is a specially blessed tea that the diver had to drink to make her strong.[18] During the following few weeks, whenever there was free time, the diver would check all diving equipment, perhaps purchasing a new facemask or more gloves. If her husband dived as well, the wife also checked his equipment. This was the time when new wet suits were made, old ones repaired, and special protective charms were brought by the Kumi-ai from the nearby mountain temple called Aonomine-san.[19] Each household purchased a number of charms to tie onto the straps of each diver's facemask.

The official start of the abalone diving season was May 15, but the Kumi-ai had the authority to start a day earlier if the weather was good and might not hold, or conversely, a few days later if the weather was bad. Despite the diving throughout March and April, the divers acted as excited and concerned as if they had not been diving at all. When the Kumi-ai announced that diving could begin, a final offering would be made at home to the Shinto deities and the diving equipment given one last check.

On the day that abalone diving started, the village Shinto priest purified the sea. For this the Kumi-ai delegated its beach officer to set up several small altars on Yoroizaki Beach and to make sure that the proper offerings were ready. These included a large cake of *mochi,* fish, *wakame,* rice, salt, sake, oranges, and branches from the *sakaki* tree. The ceremony usually took place after sunrise at 6:30 A.M.

Before going down to the beach for the ceremony, the women divers (never the men) went up to the three shrines on Yoroizaki Cape to leave offerings of rice and bits of *mochi* before the three closed altars of the sea deity, Amaterasu, and Yoroizaki itself. There was a newly cut tree stump by these shrines in 1984–1985, and offerings were left there as well. Then they went down to the beach, where a large flat stone would be chosen and a small offering left on it. These offerings were eventually washed out to sea.

Since the *harai* ceremony took place on the beach, all the women sat there and waited for the Shinto priest to begin the ritual. The only men at this ceremony were the priest, the Kumi-ai *chō,* and one officer to help with the cleaning up afterward. None of the male divers ever attended. Waving a large *sakaki* branch, the priest purified the ocean and the women and presented offerings to the deities. At the end he read a prayer requesting a safe year of diving and bountiful catches for Kuzaki. Then sake was offered to the deities, and the women also came forward to drink a small cup of the rice wine. Everyone took a small handful of the rice that was offered to the deities, and this was saved to use later in the day before the first dive.

This day was the only one in which diving was performed as in the past —that is, divers chose their favorite spot and carried all their equipment to the beach in baskets slung from a pole. The beaches were generally small inaccessible ones that could be reached only by climbing down a cliff. Still the *kachido*—both men and women—made an effort to select what they thought would be the best beach, as a good catch on this day would bring luck for the rest of the year. *Funado* had the easier task of going by boat to an area they might remember as having been especially bountiful the year before. On these tiny beaches, or before climbing into the boat, the women made one last offering to the sea: Selecting a smooth stone, they set some *mochi* and rice out for the deity. This was accompanied by a prayer for safety. The male divers looked on but never participated, even in this last extra rite.

Still to come in this cycle of ritual related to diving and fishing, which includes Hi-matsuri as well as Nifune, is a description of the New Year's and Hachiman festivals—two more occasions where the men took large public roles, while the women remained in the background. These January festivals were seen to be more closely tied to fishing and are described in the next chapter, but it is worth noting here that the cycle of ceremony associated with the sea and the passing of seasons is about many things. One main purpose of these rituals is to mark the proper ordering of the world as seen through the cyclical repetition of the year and the acting out of appropriate roles by each member of the household and village. It would be too simplistic to argue that the rituals are meant to ensure the correct passage of the seasons—winter to spring, spring to summer, summer to fall, fall to winter; they actually both mark and celebrate the correct passage of time rather than attempt to shape it. The playing out of everyone's correct role in village and private ceremonies served a similar function: marking the passage of a person through a predictable life cycle. Yet, unlike the marking of the seasons, these rituals might also be seen to reinforce ideologically the proper ordering of the social world, and thus they are as much about *making* as *becoming*. Women look after the areas that pertain to their labor and their families; men worship in the name of village solidarity. That is the way the world should be. Worshippers were quite aware that the rituals reflected an idealized rather than a lived reality and laughed at my serious questions about meaning and symbolism. But they were also aware that, idealized or not, participating in these rituals demonstrated a commitment to take part in the Kuzaki community life.

These forms of adherence or constraint notwithstanding, the women of Kuzaki as *ama* were, as noted previously, seen as extremely independent women by outsiders. As has been argued, this grew partly out of the representation of *ama* in various media, but there was also a grain of truth to this depiction. While Kuzaki women were not amazons or true matriarchs, the fact is that they spent time largely in the company of other women, many of whom were kin, and this meant that they had networks of kin and friends who supported and helped them. City women who had married into the area often formed their own little subgroup during diving sessions, but they were still a large enough group to be able to rely on each other. This of course meant that women, as a kin group or as an age-grade, could wield power either privately or publicly as shown during the Cooperative elections. And women as a group could exert pressure on other women, for *seken* is made up not just of unknown others—it includes close friends, family, and even oneself. A woman who complained about her husband's drinking or abuse to her female friends was not just letting off steam but appealing for support and making public a situation that could affect her husband's status in village life. The hours of gossip in the *koie* could have important consequences. Conversely, men's drinking sessions could serve similar functions.

Thus adherence to external form was not enough because so much of private life was discussed in public. One of the ways in which I began to be aware of some individuals' isolation from the village was that in conversation with me, people would sometimes parody their behavior. It was not enough to act out the role of good wife, mother, or worshipper—a woman had to be seen to embody the qualities to which her exterior actions pointed. Village society judged not just how one toed the line, it judged a person in reference to what were seen as interior motivations and what was known about private behavior. To pray on Sengen for your children's health when the children were seen to suffer emotionally from a mother's neglect or to give thanks for a husband's good luck in fishing when the husband complained that the work of fishing was the only thing he and his wife ever did together—in both situations, the judgment of others was harsh. No woman could hope to become Fujin-kai *chō* or hope to have her husband become Kumi-ai *chō* if she did not meet the approval of *seken*.

As we shall see in the next chapter, even fishermen's rituals that were celebrated as occasions that benefited the larger community contained a similar element of judging the person. Yet the construction of appropriate masculinity did not necessarily include skill; it was more about being a good person—being able to get along with others outside of the household.

CHAPTER 6

Keeping the *Ie* Afloat
Part 2. Fishing, Tourism, and New Year's Rituals

As previously noted, fishing and running inns or working in the tourist industry were not the only economic strategies open to men in order to help support their households. Yet for many Kuzaki men, the transition from poor fisherman to comparatively rich innkeeper was an important goal, and other jobs—in construction or public service—were considered a poor second. Fishermen and innkeepers were seen to be alike: In both, men felt they were their own bosses, even if they were dependent on the vagaries of the outside world; both were jobs that involved the whole *ie* and not just one member; and both allowed a man to take part in wider village life. The transition from one to the other seemed a natural progression. Thus all nineteen innkeepers in 1984–1986 still did some fishing or owned shares in larger fishing ventures (initially there was only one *oshiki* crew; by the time I left Kuzaki, there were three), and many of the twenty-four full-time fishermen discussed their dreams of opening their own inns.

Fulfilling these dreams was not an easy task. In a place where flat land was at a premium, it meant inheriting or—more difficult—buying a good plot of land that was not too far outside the main village. Since many *ie* appeared to have followed a pattern of inheritance in which boats and equipment were inherited by sons and parcels of land by daughters who married within the village, spare land often belonged to the women. Moreover, this land was often a tiny field tucked away in the mountains and not the best place to start an inn. One solution was to knock down the family house and rebuild it as an inn with separate living quarters, but this required a large investment of cash to start—something most fishermen did not have.

Money earned from fishing and diving had, as mentioned, declined over the years due to overfishing in the 1960s and 1970s. The families who had become rich at that time had promptly built their inns, while other Kuzaki fishermen left fishing or continued, disconsolately, with their traditional mode of livelihood. So it was that fishermen in the village spoke disparagingly of their work: Any idiot could fish, I was told more than once, especially with the advent of technology. Modern boats in Kuzaki had motors and radios, and some had sonar in order to map the seafloor. With the Kumi-ai dictating the fishing seasons and issuing daily permission to take to the sea in order to fish, even the skill associated with being a canny fisherman was seen to have been undermined. A good fisherman could look at the weather, examine the state of the sea, and decide where to fish; fishing in Kuzaki was thought no longer to need those kinds of skills.

This was in sharp contrast to the attitudes held by older men in the village. Among the men in Kuzaki who had been born during the Taishō and Meiji eras, I interviewed only two who had not been fishermen. Figures are not available for the dead members of these generations, but of the living, these two men represented 4 percent of the population, and I suspect that the percentage would be valid for the village as a whole during the early Showa years (1926–1945). Of the grandfathers born during 1913–1926, almost all served as sailors for the Japanese Imperial Navy during the war years.[1] Six of these men were captured, and one, serving in the army rather than the navy, spent time in a prisoner of war camp under the British at the end of the war. After the war, during the 1950s, the traditional pattern of women diving and men fishing held in Kuzaki. There appears to have been a shift during this time of couples separating for their migrant labor— women staying at home to dive, men working on large fishing fleets up and down the Pacific Ocean.

Work outside the village was a good way to gain experience as a fisherman and also to earn extra money toward a boat of one's own. As with diving for women, this outside work also helped toward maintaining a balance in the village. One man per household fished; if his son was old enough to work, he often fished outside the village on the crew of some larger boat. When the elder man decided to retire or decided that he needed more help on the boat, the son would leave the outside work and return to Kuzaki. There is logic to this: In theory, it prevented overfishing and guaranteed an extra income to the household as well. This pattern was based on two important facts: Most Kuzaki fishing, except for the Ise lobster (ebi) fishing of the winter months, was near subsistence fishing; and all fishing was done by the head couple of the household. In the past, when a son took over fishing within village waters, his father would teach him the best spots for fishing—knowledge kept secret within families.

In Kuzaki (as well as in nearby Ōsatsu, Anori, and Ijika), women were allowed on boats. This was unusual in Japan, where other ethnographers have recorded a strong taboo against women on fishing boats.[2] Yet in Kuzaki—or so said my informants—women were never forbidden to fish.

Most of the grandmothers proudly recalled how they worked the oar of the old boats while the men put out the nets. They regarded modern motorboats as a convenient way for their daughters-in-law to do less physical labor than they had in the past.

With the emphasis on income earned from diving and winter lobster fishing, all Kuzaki fishing had been and remained focused on the family as the basic unit of labor. Except for squid, for which traps were put out, all fishing in Kuzaki was done with small nets. It is clear that fishing in the village had not been carried out on a large enough scale to merit big crews or varying technologies for different species, despite the fact that from the 1950s onward, many men returned to the village with the experience of much more varied fishing.

In Kuzaki, as Moeran (1984, 166) has also noted for the potters of Sarayama, the past was recalled with a certain amount of nostalgia and was idealized. In the past, the entire household worked together; in the past, daughters-in-law worked harder. In the past, there was no need to buy any food from outside the village. The *ie*'s fields and rice paddies always yielded enough food, as did fishing and diving; there were more fish in the sea, and it was a pleasure to take the boat out to fish. Confronted with such nostalgic discourses, it is hard to be sure just what fishing was like in the past.

Yet even in the 1980s the village's remaining fishermen would say— after denigrating the skills needed to be a modern fisherman—that fishing was the best way to earn a living. Of the thirty-eight village men in their fifties, five still fished, while eighteen of the men owned inns and still did some fishing. That is, 60 percent of the men in their fifties were still involved with some fishing. In the group of forty-year-olds, nineteen fished and one owned an inn; others worked outside the village. This is a drop to 40 percent, while of the group of men below the age of forty, only 28 percent were involved in fishing. When asked, all these men said that fishing was a good way of life. A man is independent when he fishes; it is wonderful being out at sea; and there is a great deal of excitement, an element of gambling in going after a catch. One innkeeper told me that he hated working in the inn started by his father because he had to be conscious of the guests all the time. Despite similarities between owning an inn and fishing, then, the latter was seen to allow a man more freedom.

The women in fishing households liked the long evenings spent prawn fishing; for them, this time alone with their husbands was seen as a time to be cherished. Both men and women regarded a boat as a peaceful place to spend time. Yet this image of togetherness—nostalgic also—was being replaced by more modern ideas of class and its associated qualities. While all Kuzaki families claimed to be middle-class and owned the status symbols of that class—cars, televisions, air conditioners, private baths, several indoor toilets—some *ie* were deemed to be grander than others. Divisions between "dirty" fishermen and nonfishermen were starting to be felt, and a household balcony filled with drying fishnets was enough to cause some villagers to turn up their noses and complain about the smell. Some signs of this growing schism were seen during the 1985 election, when members of nonfishing households got up to make speeches about what was perceived as the Kumi-ai's overinvolvement with fishing when fewer men in the village were occupied in the job.

The Cooperative and Fishing

In order to fish in Kuzaki, one must, as one of the fishermen told me, "buy nets, have a boat, and have patience." In spite of claims that modern technology made fishing too easy, most men would admit that skill was still needed—skill and luck, the fishermen would say. Beyond that, a man needed the right to fish off the waters of Kuzaki.

As with diving, fishing in Kuzaki was totally controlled by the Kumi-ai. So the waters that until 1903 belonged to the village as a whole were part of the Cooperative estate. It was the Co-op that allowed a fisherman access to this territory. The Co-op could also license a fisherman—that is, it issued a license to conduct a certain type of fishing, providing that the person also had fishing rights. Thus all twenty-four fishing households had the right to fish in Kuzaki waters, but only thirteen of those *ie* had the license to engage in prawn *(kuruma ebi)* fishing. One household, a new one to the village, Ono *ie*, had a fishing license to do big-net fishing, the *oshiki* fishing that was of such concern during the 1985 elections. All villagers, through participation in the Kumi-ai, had a voice in deciding on how the sea as a resource was used. So divers and innkeepers, wanting clean waters for tourists, often sided with fishermen on the main issues raised at Co-op meetings.

In an attempt to prevent overfishing, the Co-op restricted the size of boats and of nets, while making sure that the fishing seasons were adhered to. It also set the fishing times for each day and banned fishing on Fridays. In addition, the Cooperative took a certain percentage from all fish sold since it acted as the wholesaler for all Kuzaki catches.

As in diving, the Kumi-ai phoned the market daily to establish current prices. Most fish was sold within the village to various inns, pubs, and restaurants, but at market prices. Expensive catches such as lobster were auctioned in bins of up to 10 kilos to the highest bidders. No fisherman was supposed to sell directly to an inn or restaurant. All fish still available after these initial sales went to Toba City to be sold there.

The other ways in which the Kumi-ai was important to fishermen have been previously listed, but they are worth reiterating briefly. It took funds from each fishing household for the National Fisherman's Aid and Insurance fund; bought gasoline in bulk to resell to Kuzaki men; and it also bought nets, weights, bins, tackle, and rain gear to sell to the fishermen. It communicated with other villages over fishing territories, settled disputes, and monitored the weather conditions constantly. The Co-op was also central in attempting to bring in new methods to help the fishermen. It participated in an experiment in which abalone were grown in tanks for the early part of their life cycle and then seeded into the sea, the goal of which seemed to be to increase the numbers of abalone in Japanese waters. The Co-op head told me that this did not appear to be working since the main problem was pollution—the seeded abalone survived no better than those naturally reproduced. Another example that illustrates how the Cooperative both controlled fishing and yet tried to innovate was the experiment in prawn fishing, a venture that was continuing while I did my fieldwork.

Prawn Fishing

The fishing of *kuruma ebi,* a large type of prawn (genus *Penaeidae*), was introduced to the village in 1975. Before that, the fishermen said, the boats were too small and the nets not good enough. The Kumi-ai added that during the 1970s, the amount of prawn in that area of Japan naturally increased and that since then, cultivation had been carried out in order to keep up the prawn population. Prawn fishing had become a major source of income for the thirteen Kuzaki households that fished during 1984–1985 (see Table 3).

The prawn season ran from April to October, coinciding with the abalone diving season. With good weather, the boats went out every day but Friday and festival days. Far more arduous than the traditional forms of fishing in Kuzaki, in which nets were set out in the evening and collected at dawn, prawn fishing began at 3 or 4 P.M. and could go on until midnight or longer. It was done farther out at sea than other types of fishing and so took place out of village waters. Thus the boats of several villages might head for the same spot on a given day. To avoid conflict, the Kumi-ai of Anori, Kuzaki, and Ōsatsu cooperated in organizing their prawn fishermen.

The organization required for this new form of fishing in which all three villages participated was rather complicated. On the days when there was to be prawn fishing, the Kumi-ai *chō* spent the afternoon checking the weather by consulting other men, old grandfathers, and even women and the weather station for the area, as well as constantly phoning the heads of the Anori and Ōsatsu Cooperatives. Any fear that the weather might become bad expressed by any one of them could end in the cancellation of the day's fishing. I have seen fishermen wait for an hour or more outside the Kumi-ai because they were sure that the weather would hold, but until the *chō* had convinced the other Co-op heads that this was so, they could not head out. Often prawn fishing was canceled at the very last minute, after the boats had already been loaded with nets.

If it was decided that there would be eight or more hours of calm weather ahead, the boats went out in three groups with four, four, and five boats each. Each group had to rendezvous with the four or five boats from Anori and Ōsatsu to form three flotillas of eleven to fourteen boats each. The area to be fished by each group was decided in advance by the Co-op heads. Once out, waiting for the other boats in the group to make their appearance could take as long as two hours. During this time, the boat radios were in constant use, checking with the Cooperative, with other

Table 3. Average yearly earnings for diving and fishing households in U.S. dollars

Households with one diver and no prawn fishing:	
Diving	6,195
Fishing	22,875
Total	29,070
Households with one diver and prawn fishing:	
Diving	6,195
Fishing	37,476
Total	43,671
Households with couple diving and no prawn fishing:	
Diving (wife, year round)	6,195
Diving (husband, abalone)	293
Fishing	22,875
Total	29,363
Households with couple diving and prawn fishing:	
Diving (total from above)	6,488
Fishing	37,476
Total	43,964

These figures represent the family income before tax. In 1984–1985, annual income tax for a household earning $45,000 a year was 30 percent.

Kuzaki boats, or gossiping with friends who were fishing nearby. The Kuzaki fishermen used the radios as if they were telephones, and much Cooperative politicking was carried out on the evenings spent prawn fishing.

Once all the boats of a group were gathered, lots were drawn in order to determine the order of net laying for the area the group was to fish. The boat drawing number 1 could choose what was essentially the best place to lay their nets, and the other numbers had to lay their nets behind. That is, the number 1 boat's nets from the first line of nets faced the shore (see Figure 13). The number 2 boat was generally assured of a good catch as well, but all other boats had to resign themselves to poor catches. The fishermen were uncharacteristically silent about how this system of lots had been developed, leading me to wonder if early attempts to decide the order of laying out nets had caused much conflict. The typical explanation was simply, "This is how we do it; we leave it to luck."

Fishermen tried to downplay the fact that numbers 1 and 2 were practically guaranteed to do well, arguing that if the first boat chose to put its nets in the wrong place, it might be the third or sixth boat that would be lucky to lay its nets near a large school of prawn. Regardless of this rationalization, the moment of picking a number—from a small net that one boat brought around to the others—was always a tense one. Anything might serve as an excuse for good or bad luck. Once, our boat spotted a dead bird as we waited—a bad sign, I was told. But when I drew the number 1 (for the first time in that year), I was told that it was good luck to counter the bad omen —and consequently, I helped bring in that household's largest prawn haul

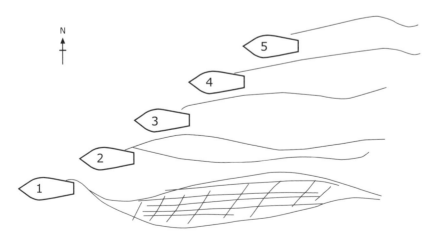

Figure 13. Pattern for net laying (by Carolyn Clarke)

ever. This earned me the nickname "Dairyō kamisama" (for the deity of large catches), and my services for picking numbers were in high demand. At the end of my fieldwork, I still had the nickname because even a diver diving near me would bring in a large catch—or so it was said. This imbuing of strange people or objects with the power of *kami* has a long history in Japan, but it should not be misconstrued to mean that people actually thought I was a deity, since even newly chopped down trees can be *kami*. The power of strangers is a fickle one (Yoshida 1981, 87–99), and some villagers told me that my luck consisted of making a fisherman or diver try harder when I was around.

Lucky or not, after the choosing of numbers the nets were put out. Most villagers used light nylon nets (gill nets) with light weights and small mesh for prawn fishing, and at least twelve nets per boat were used. The nets were tied together before setting out, and the first and last nets had buoys with blinking lights attached so that a boat could find them again in the dark. Once this was done, the waiting began. There was usually a wait from 6 to 9 or 10 P.M., when the prawn came out to feed. During the wait, the couples on the boats would eat an *obentō* dinner, radio their friends again, practice karaoke singing, discuss family business, or nap. One couple insisted that their boat futon was for more interesting things than naps, declaring that the arduous prawn fishing was not going to interfere with their sex life.

As in all fishing, pulling the nets in had become woman's work. In the past, men did this while the wife held the boat steady. When motorboats were introduced, it had become the man's job to handle the boat's engine while the woman used a mechanized pulley to help bring in the nets. First, the buoy was brought aboard and then the net's lead line was wrapped around the pulley, which the woman than cranked in order to haul in the rest of the nets. If there were no prawns, this work was quickly done; however, a large catch required that the woman stop cranking and untangle each prawn from the net. The prawns were then placed in the boat's hull, which was partially full of seawater. A large catch of two to three hundred prawns could take hours to bring in, and in these cases the husband had to leave off the steering and come forward to help with the nets. One man used a pole attached to the tiller in order to keep the boat steady when he went forward to help with the nets.

Despite the fact that a boat skipper did not have much choice in selecting where he could put his nets (unless he picked the number 1), all this hard work was seen as very rewarding. During the year 1984, the thirteen prawn-fishing households brought in 13,610 kilos of prawn for a gross profit of 32,783,875 yen (or U.S. $204,000). Of this amount, the Kumi-ai took 4 percent or 429,913 yen ($2,687), leaving 32,353,963 yen to be shared among the thirteen households. This potential 2,488,766 yen ($15,555) per household is not an accurate estimate for everyone's earnings, and no one was keen to share with me which households had experienced consistent good luck and thus the larger share of the money. Gossip might be that one family had five *dairyō* in a year and another ten, but as independent businessmen, fishermen were not going to give me accurate figures for their *ie*. Yet potentially, prawn fishing was seen as the way for a fishing household to earn money in Kuzaki; the Co-op had done its best to promote it, taking only a small percentage from the sales and reinvesting this money in the purchase of cultivated prawn for the next year.

Despite this success, fishing households continued to decrease in Kuzaki. Two severe winters since 1984–1985 resulted in poor prawn seasons, and fishermen were becoming more and more discouraged. *Kuruma ebi* fishing required large motorboats (about 30 feet long) and a great deal of time. In 1975 it seemed a good idea to invest in these larger, more expensive vessels, but the slumps of 1985–1986 and 1986–1987 discouraged any of the other fishing households from making the investment in larger boats. Also, because the Cooperative so controlled and coordinated prawn fishing, the issue of skill was often mentioned. Prawn fishing required luck, not skill, the men would say. While the Cooperative blamed the winter for poor seasons, the fishermen blamed it on bad luck.

The fishing households often argued that small-scale fishing would die out in Kuzaki and thus they had to earn enough money to start new businesses. The Kumi-ai itself was turning to larger-scale fishing in order to earn money. Until 1985, only the Ono *ie* did this sort of fishing, which involved huge nets, a 30-foot motorboat, and a sizable barge. That year two innkeepers requested fishing licenses to start their own large-net fishing businesses. Although the inns held the license, small crews hired by the inn-owning household did the fishing. Often these crews included young kin of the innkeeper. The innkeepers saw this as a good investment, and it was obviously the direction the Co-op believed fishing in Kuzaki had to take: fewer fishermen doing large-scale fishing. So the number of fishing *ie* in the village continued to decrease, but the Co-op believed that by adapting in this way, fishing in Kuzaki would not die out.

Fishing and Equipment

Luck and skill notwithstanding, the right equipment was also necessary. The replacement and purchasing of new equipment was a continuous drain on *ie* finances. In 1984–1985, one household did invest in a new boat, which can give an idea of the costs involved in full-time fishing. This household had only one son who at thirty-five was still unmarried, and the *ie* had been doing all their fishing in the oldest boat owned by any of the twenty-four fishing households. With a few large catches over the years, they were able to afford a boat with all the latest equipment at a cost of 5,000,000 yen ($31,250). Included in the price were a power engine, sonar equipment for tracking fish underwater, a small refrigerator, and a tiny toilet. When I asked if he really needed all that modern equipment, after having been able to make do without it for so long, the son replied: "No, not for fishing, but for the tourists—yes." He thought that fishing in the village was going to end and that the only money to be made from any sort of fishing would come from taking parties of fishermen or scuba divers out. Thus an ultramodern boat was worth the investment.

A good fishing boat without all the fancy equipment might run about 3,000,000 yen ($18,750), and several households had bought boats at this price in the late 1970s and early 1980s. Almost all households also kept their older, smaller motorboats to use for diving or running errands. All boats in Kuzaki were bought from an Ōsatsu boatmaker whose household had in the past made wooden boats for the area's fishermen as well. Once a boat was purchased, the fisherman became responsible for all the maintenance. There was a Co-op workshop just across the road from the main harbor, and on any rest day one could find all the fishermen in the village there, repairing smaller boats, tinkering with engines, or just gossiping. As many of the men who fished had also served as sailors on larger fishing crews, they had some experience of mechanics and general boat repair; consequently, I only once saw a repairman called in to do some work on an engine that had virtually exploded.

A boat was, of course, the major investment a fishing household made. On top of that, there existed the annual expenses of gasoline and nets. According to the Cooperative where the gasoline was sold and nets were ordered, gasoline consumed in a year by a large boat could cost up to 1,000,000 yen ($6,250). Most families averaged four to six new nets a year, costing 600,000 to 800,000 yen ($3,750 to $5,000). This last figure might be lower for *ie* that did not do prawn fishing because they tended to keep only two sets of nets—about half a dozen heavy nets for lobster fishing and as many again of nylon gill nets for general fishing. For prawn fishing, a household maintained a third set of lighter-weight gill nets. Most households also kept steel traps for squid fishing, but since they last for years, few people were sure of how much they cost.

Nets were also treated with great care, cleaned daily and carefully by hand and repaired as often as possible. Cleaning nets was not just an activity that was necessary for their care—it had social implications as well. As with *wakame* drying, net cleaning was meant to be a household affair that took place in public. All the fishing households would set up wooden horses by their docked boats around the main harbor. The nets would be pulled over these by the fisherman, his wife, his mother, by the children if they could be made to do it, and—during my fieldwork—by the anthropologist. From 6 A.M. onward on the days after fishing, everyone involved would come out to do this work. Dead fish, tangled bits of seaweed, shell, still-poisonous puffer fish, old tin cans, and other debris had to be carefully removed by hand or with the use of a small hooking tool in order not to tear the net. As this work was done, the Co-op would call up the fishermen to have their catches weighed, and all eyes and ears would be on the respective *ie* as they did these tasks. A large catch, then, was always public knowledge and had to be appropriately celebrated. This last was part of the many rituals that surrounded fishing and ensured that luck was not taken for granted.

Fishing and Ritual

Kuzaki fishermen claimed that religion was women's work and that they did not think about such things; yet, as most ethnographies on fishing societies point out, such claims do not necessarily correspond with ritual behavior.[3] The fishermen of Kuzaki were no exception to this. As in diving, the danger of being at the mercy of the sea and weather made the fishermen extremely cautious in their attitude toward the deities—especially Ebisu, the patron god of fishermen and merchants.[4] Thus, although fishermen claimed to rely solely on technology for success in fishing, various aspects of fishing required ritual attention. New boats had to be purified; all boats decorated for a special ritual at New Year's and any large catches had to be marked with a series of offerings to the gods. The new form of prawn fishing involved making a yearly pilgrimage to Kii Peninsula, where there was a shrine associated with it. Close to Kuzaki was the complex of shrines on Aonomine-sama where many fishermen had left photographs of their boats in the shrine especially dedicated to boat safety.

Ritual life and fishing had been even more complicated in the past. Some of the Kuzaki grandfathers could remember that the old wooden boats had eyes painted on them so that they could see. One informant argued that the eyes were painted on in order to make a boat look like a fish and so draw more fish to it. Most people, however, seemed to identify the boat with the female and human, not a fish. So too, a few older men still referred to the bow of the boat as *"atama"*—the word for a person's head.

Younger fishermen used *"omote"* for the bow (meaning the head or face of an object). All villagers used the standard terms *"tomo"* for stern, *"torikaji"* (side for pulling in) for port, and *"omokaji"* for starboard.

Boats were always named with lucky characters, and these were the same stem characters that a household would use in naming children. For example, the Okamoto *ie* boat was named *Gen-maru*, the character for *"gen"* meaning origin or source and *"maru"* meaning boat. The eldest son of the household was named Gen-en, the grandfather was called Genichi, and the household was referred to as Gen-ya (Gen shop). The importance of a boat to a household can be understood from a description of the purification ritual for new boats.

The ritual for purifying new boats was one that villagers claimed had not changed much over the years. First, the new boat had to be decorated with flags that had the characters for *dairyō* printed on them. Ideally, each household that was related to the owners of the new boat had to provide one of these flags. Then the boat was launched from the harbor, and on board there should be as many children as possible, for children bring good luck (so do foreigners, it was said). If possible, I was told, a longhaired woman should also come along to represent the Fukunokami (the kami of good fortune). Also included were friends from the fisherman's *dōkyūsei*. Heading left from the beach toward the open sea, just outside the harbor, the boat should circle around three times to the left—that is, around to the port, the side for pulling in fish. The first turn was for *dairyō*, the second for safety, and the third turn was for the Fukunokami. At the end, offerings of *azuki-gohan* (rice with adzuki beans), *kenchin* salad,[5] which was eaten on various other ritual occasions such as weddings, and sake were made to the god of the sea from the bow. These offerings were made again off the port side and then off the stern. No offerings were made from starboard; the fishermen said that "nothing important happens on that side."

When the boat returned to the harbor, a crowd gathered and the boat owner threw gifts of *sechi mochi*,[6] coins, fruit, and sweets to the waiting villagers. These gifts represent the wealth of a good catch, which must be shared with others. This was explained as follows: "A fisherman has to give in order that the deities reward him with good luck. He must share his luck with others." This is a theme that recurred during the New Year's ceremonies, which I describe below. Then, if the weather was good, the household held a banquet on the harbor by the new boat. Only men were invited to this—male kin of the household and *dōkyūsei* friends of the boat owner. As in diving rituals where even male divers do not participate, women do not partake in the boat purification except that they have to prepare the meal, and one woman is supposed to travel on the boat itself. In 1985, the

a man repair his own engine? Was the boat in good condition? Was a man accurate in his judgment of the weather conditions? Did he take part in village life? Was he financially astute? A successful business venture (such as the free-range egg business of Tamago-ya) was ridiculed a bit, but the failed attempt at pig farming by another household was still the subject of angry comments years later: When the wind blew in the wrong direction, I was told, the smell had been unbearable.

Women, then, were judged mostly on their skills as divers, mothers, wives, and daughters-in-law. Men were judged on their success in business, which required skill, but they were judged on how well they got along with other men. They were also commented on as fathers, sons, and husbands. The link, as with skill in diving and moral worth for women, was clear: A man who could take care of his family was a good man. The best was to be a man who did this independently; as fishing became devalued, innkeepers were held in higher esteem. Working for themselves rather than a boss, they could fulfill all their family, village, and—on retirement—ritual duties.

Yet standards of behavior were more rigid for women than for men. A man's infidelity was common knowledge but was joked about rather than spoken of with censorship. Perhaps this attitude is echoed in the discourse about the person. Women had to be attractive as well as skillful in diving; they were judged on what they brought to the household—be it added income, healthy children, or good fortune. Men worried about luck more than skill and were judged for being a nice or good person—that is, on their ability to get along with others rather than what they brought to the *ie*. As the core of the household and the village, men were secure in the relationships they had built up over their lifetimes. As newcomers to Kuzaki, many of the women had to prove their worth—daily and for years. Women could not rely on luck but had to develop skill. Both the liberty allowed a man and the way in which he was evaluated can be seen if we look at the household's involvement in running an inn, as well as the events of Hachiman-san.

Running an Inn in Kuzaki

Although there were only nineteen such households in Kuzaki, tourism was an indirect source of income for most other households in Kuzaki. As already mentioned, through the Cooperative, the twenty-four fishing *ie* sold their catches mainly within the village and then to the tourist hotels in Toba. The sole restaurant in Kuzaki—Maruichi—catered both to tourists and villagers, and the household that ran the pub called Samantha relied on tourists and young fishermen for its income. If the six households headed by young widows who worked in village inns and the seven one-generation households headed by retired men are subtracted from the 116 Kuzaki *ie,* fifty-two households could be said to have relied for their income on work done outside the village. Of these, two had household heads who worked in Toba City government, one was the Buddhist priest's household (who also worked as a high school teacher), another was the Shinto priest's household (who was also the village milkman), and one was the *ie* of a social service employee. This leaves forty-seven *ie* of which at least four worked part-time running a shop or pub within the village as well as in construction outside Kuzaki. As far as I was able to determine, the other forty-three *ie* were involved in construction work, working for the bus or train service, and working in hotels outside of Kuzaki. All three of these are related to tourism in one way or another.

The fact of tourism was inescapable for the village, and it could be argued that tourism has in effect saved Kuzaki. Thus it is possible to talk of the continuing concept of the traditional *ie,* although as noted earlier, previous work patterns meant that the *ie* in Kuzaki rarely achieved the ideal form.

Tourism for Kuzaki was embedded within the erotic and exotic images surrounding the *ama* that were described in chapter 2, mixed with a construction of traditional Japan. Added to this heady brew was the imagery of the *ama* as pearl divers—something they had never been. The association between divers and pearls is made clear in the Mikimoto Pearl Museum located in Toba City. While the long descriptive pieces on divers explain that the *ama* dived for various things—not just for the pearl oysters that Kokichi Mikimoto would then buy up for his experiments in the creation of the cultured pearl—no tourist, foreign or Japanese, ever seems to take in this fact. Since the perfection of the cultured pearl in 1893, the image of *ama* as pearl diver has developed so forcefully that it is almost impossible to convince people that this is not so.[9]

It was Mikimoto who also designed the "traditional" diving costume that has become associated with the divers. Adapting the *amagi* that the divers wore after diving to keep warm, he created the thin white skirt and blouse that demonstration divers now wear. Mikimoto is said to have done this because he noticed the foreign visitors to the diving demonstration in which the *ama* dived wearing only loincloths were shocked. This information is to be found under one of the photographs in the museum, and again, no visitor ever seems to notice it. This is a sort of symbolic invention of tradition, for the image of white-clad women diving into the deep blue waters in search of luminescent pearls—pearls that glow like the truth (the pun being in the use of the radical *"shin"* in the words for both "truth" and "pearl")—is striking and, obviously, what people remember best from visits to Mikimoto Pearl Island. This triad of Japan, truth/pearls, and divers/tradition is not even an unconscious association: The short promotion video shown every half hour at Mikimoto Pearl Museum makes the point clear in both Japanese and English.

While the cultured pearl industry is important for the inhabitants of Shima Peninsula who have turned from fishing/diving to cultivating pearls for Mikimoto, in Kuzaki it was the resultant tourism that was important. Shima was made a national park as early as 1946 in order to protect both Ise Shrine and the cultured pearl industry—one from the Occupation forces, the other from urbanization and industrialization. The visitors to Shima came for the scenery, to worship at Ise, to eat the local seafood, and to bring home gifts of local produce; many also bought pearls. Thus, following Graburn's analysis of domestic Japanese tourism (1983), Shima National Park offered both types of attraction that the Japanese tourist prefers: cultural, educational, and traditional as well as the more modern sun, sea, and sex.[10] Kuzaki relied on the images of divers as sexy women and the fame of their fresh seafood to bring tourists to the village. It should be noted that in the late 1950s and early 1960s, the first lodge *(minshuku)* and larger inn *(ryokan)* were successful because of the team of anthropologists that came yearly to do research on Kuzaki. The daughter of the man alleged to be the richest in Kuzaki claimed that her father's fortune was built on the summer visits of the Aichi University research team to his inn.

Researchers aside, the main source of tourism for Kuzaki were short-term visitors who came to spend a day or two only in the village as part of a visit to Shima in general. The increase in inns from two to nineteen occurred in 1965, and the number had not changed since 1980. The new places had several stories—the newest had seven and so was called a hotel—and large bath and banquet facilities. The old *minshuku* was but a guesthouse, providing lodging for what had been the occasional visitor.[11]

There was a great deal of competition between *ryokan,* and everyone determined how well a place was doing by its location and the number of rooms the inn had. That is, there were more than enough tourists, so a family that could afford to build and run a large inn was seen to be capable of earning lots of money (but never in specified amounts, in case the anthropologist might somehow spread the information around). One inn did fail during my fieldwork. I was told that this occurred because the daughter-in-law was too inexperienced to run the place alone (she was a widow), and her father-in-law did not help matters by gambling. That inn's clientele seemed to consist mostly of the father-in-law's *yakuza* friends who came in huge American cars from Osaka. Needless to say, the villagers were glad to see it closed down. Within a year, a new inn had opened in the village and was, according to the owner, doing a booming business.

As mentioned, I was never able to get figures either from the villagers or innkeepers as to how much was earned in running a *ryokan*, but the general belief was that they all did well. Any question as to which was the richest household in the village was answered with the name of a *ryokan* owner —not necessarily the same name in each case, but always an innkeeper. If new homes, cars, and big boats could be taken as indicators of wealth, then the various innkeepers in Kuzaki were indeed doing well.

What was considered important, however, was that running an inn was family work, and it kept the *ie* together. In fact, the youngest adopted son-in-law in the village had been adopted into a *ryokan* family, and it was said that a fishing family would never have been able to entice a young man into a marriage. This is a marked change from the past, when marrying an *ama* was considered a lucky thing. The work of running an inn involved all the household members. The eldest man would book guests and bid for fish; his wife would clean rooms and cook; the daughter-in-law was expected to clean, do the bookkeeping, cook, and hire the geisha; the son would purchase food, drive the inn's van, and prepare sashimi; and daughters and sons would clean and also drive the inn's van. This is a very general description, of course, and does not include work in the fields and rice paddies, housework, or diving. All family members would be involved in child rearing, as they were all at home. The extended family was also important, as it was the female *shinseki* who often worked as geisha in these inns. The visitors to an inn wanted to meet real *ama,* and they got real *ama* acting as geisha. The work of a *ryokan* was seen as an extension of the household work in fishing and diving—so much so that some of the inns, like boats, had names that came from the older family shop name.

Attitudes toward tourists were varied (Martinez 1989, 1996), but no one denied the importance of the tourist trade for Kuzaki. Tourism was accepted as long as it kept to the narrow confines of the beach or inn. There remained one particular aspect of village life into which the tourists were never invited: the religious life of Kuzaki. So while the life course of an individual was marked by ritual and larger festival events, this side of village life —although of great interest to any domestic tourist looking for "the real Japan" (cf. Ivy 1995)—was not for commercialization. People could go to Ise or Asama for religion if that is what they wanted, but in Kuzaki, religion was too important to be turned into a tourist event. Thus the most important ritual that a middle-aged man could take part in was, in 1985, attended by villagers only. This ritual was called the Hachiman-san matsuri, and during my fieldwork I saw within the ritual signs of a transition in village political life: The inclusion of an innkeeper's son-in-law in this event was deemed to be a significant change in Kuzaki tradition.

The Hachiman-san Festival

This festival, celebrating the appearance of the deity of war in Kuzaki, is actually part of a longer series of events surrounding the New Year. As with all large village religious occasions, the New Year celebrations were located both within the household and outside it within the village. Leading up to December 31, household members were busy with a series of mundane yet significant tasks. The village grandmothers tidied up the graveyard early in December, and fishing and diving stopped on the fifteenth of the month. The next two weeks were meant to be spent in house as well as boat cleaning and the repairing of boats and any equipment that needed it. On the thirty-first, however, it was not just housework that needed to be done—the remaking of protective amulets for the household was also important. These were called *tsubuki*[12] and were put in various places: over the household's entrance, on the *kamidana,* on the car, on boats, and in fields.

The various ways in which scholarly articles describe and name the amulets attest to the fact that religious traditions in Kuzaki were constantly changing. One example is the *tsubuki* for the main entrance of the house, which was made of sacred rice straw rope on which a wooden plaque was hung; on its front, the following lines were penned:

> Good fortune is life
> The gate of Somen Shōrai's descendants[13]
> Bad fortune is destruction.

On the plaque's back was written, "Long enduring like the ancient laws," with a pentagram drawn on the right. According to the Okamoto family, with whom I celebrated the 1985 New Year, the pentagram had to be drawn without lifting the pen. To the left was drawn a symbol made of five lines down and four across called a *shimehan.* This last is representative of the Kuzaki dialect: The *"shime"* appears to refer to "tying off" or "closing"—thus the word could mean a type of lock. Iwata (1961) writes that charms with these two symbols on them are called *mayoke* and are used to ward off demons. He also claims that in Kuzaki, the star is called a *doman* and the figure made of lines is the *shimehan*. I might well have been given a particular family's interpretation, or perhaps a simplified one—the charm called a *genkan* (the word for what it was set over—*genkan*, the entrance), and both symbols simply termed *shimehan*—but it could also be that villagers once distinguished between the symbols and in 1985 no longer did. People were clear on the fact that the two symbols with their complicated patterns were so complex that a demon would become lost following the lines and would never find its way into the house. Even the way in which the plaque was attached to the rope was complex and meant to confuse demons.

Many household implements got variations on this *tsubuki:* The *kamidana*, the car, boats, and even the fields had protective amulets made. The amulets for the last two were made from plaited straw into cone shapes. These cones were bound together in twos and tied with a ribbon. Inside was an arrangement of *sakaki* and white paper called an *izuriha*, and on top of this was a pair of wooden chopsticks. These *tsubuki* remained in place for the twenty days of the New Year celebrations and were filled daily with *azuki gohan* by the grandmother of the household. Yamaguchi (1991) would argue that these made objects are offerings to the gods, who prefer the made to the natural—a point that is discussed in chapter 7.

Despite the activity that filled the household before and during New Years, however, the public face of the holiday remained largely male. One representative of each household attended the ceremony, held at midnight at the village Shinto shrine. This was generally the eldest man of the household, who made a point of remaining sober until after the shrine rite was complete. The ritual was a complex yet typical one of offerings and purification that ended long after midnight. The end of the shrine ritual marked the start of a series of New Year's visits, which meant that a household stayed up waiting for male kin to drop by and exchange New Year's drinks. Women did their visiting during the day.

The first of January also saw the start of rituals that were clearly related to the life of Kuzaki as a fishing village. While dawn saw women and children on the beach watching the sunrise and praying, 9 A.M. saw the fishermen on their boats and the rest of the village on the docks. The boats had been cleaned and decorated with colorful banners and flags. Then followed a ritual very similar to the boat launching already described.[14]

While the crowd of women and children waited, the boat owner carried a tray with offerings of a large rice cake, a small bowl of uncooked rice, 100 yen in 10 yen coins, and greens onboard. The consistency of Shinto symbolism is seen in these offerings—that is, the *kami* are offered the fruits of the fields and the rice paddy. On the boat, the boat owner poured sake

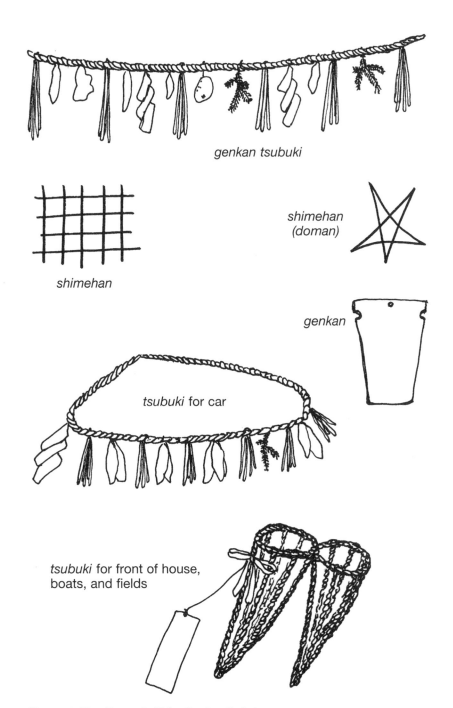

genkan tsubuki

shimehan

shimehan (doman)

genkan

tsubuki for car

tsubuki for front of house, boats, and fields

Figure 14. New Year *tsubuki* (by Carolyn Clarke)

on the prow. Then, from boxes that had been stored on the boat, the man would begin to throw out gifts of oranges, sweets, biscuits, and money wrapped in paper. The first few were thrown out as offerings toward the sea; next everything was tossed out to the waiting crowd. Women would wear the same nets around their waist that a *funado* diver wore, and caught offerings went into the net as if they were produce from the sea. Again, the giving of all these goods was seen by the villagers to be necessary. If a fisherman wanted to have good catches that year, he had to begin the New Year by being generous and sharing with others of the village. For the divers, the more goods one caught, the better the chance of good diving and large catches during the coming year. The object for both was to secure *dairyō* in two different spheres of economic life. The villagers called this mimetic ritual "the boat of large morning catches."

The women and children went from boat to boat and spent the morning cheerfully stocking up on sweets and oranges. After each fisherman finished, however, he left the boat and went to the *koie* where his wife and/or mother sat after diving. This was, as already noted, something never done the rest of the year. Other village men made their way into the *koie*, where a fire would be built and cakes of *mochi* were toasted and eaten along with drinks of beer and sake. Save for the drinking, this was what the women did after diving, and the men made many jokes about being "just like women" as they spent the morning inside what was normally a female sanctuary, doing what the women did: relaxing, eating, and gossiping. When I tried to ask why this was a custom, I was told, "Because it is the only day of the year on which we can do this!" I suspect that after I left the hut into which I had been briefly invited to look, the jokes and drinking went on and on. Both the party in the *koie* and the tossing of agricultural products from the boats are what Yamaguchi (1990), following Bakhtin, would call a moment of pure *asobi* (play)—a reversal of the normal that is ludicrous. What fisherman ever found oranges at the bottom of the sea, and what man, diver or not, would ever dare join women in the *koie*? New Year's day is meant to be a celebration of the world as chaos—a world that, with boats cleaned, houses tidied, ordered, and waiting, will be restored to normal on the day Hachiman visits the village. But first Hachiman must be chosen.

While the village men sat in the *koie* in 1985, the Cooperative executive officers met in the Co-op offices to toast each other with sacred sake brought from Ise Jingu. This was not just an excuse for drinking but an important meeting: They had to choose the man who would become Hachiman-san on January 5. This man had to be worthy of the honor of being possessed by a *kami;* he had to be strong enough to fast and remain celibate for the days leading up to the ritual; he had to be a fisherman (which in 1985 narrowed the pool considerably); and he had to be from the *dōkyūsei* of men in their forties. Two more men were chosen to play the *daimon* (Kuzaki dialect for the feudal lord, *daimyō*) and his attendant. Four responsible teenage boys (about sixteen years old) also had to be chosen.

The *daimon* and his attendant were played by married men from the age-grade of men in their late thirties; in 1985, a village innkeeper's son-in-law was chosen to be the *daimon*. This was talked about for days by other villagers, for the role of *daimon* was seen as a test of a man's dignity and his ability to take part in a complex ritual. A man who has been *daimon* has a good chance of being selected to act as Hachiman a few years later. Choosing an innkeeper seemed an acknowledgment that, eventually, there would be no fishermen to become Hachiman-san, and this role would be taken over by other men in the village. In fact, in 1991, the owner of the free-range egg business in the village, Seiko-san, was chosen for the role of Hachiman —another sign that fishermen no longer dominated life in the village. It was in discussions with Seiko-san that I had confirmed something I had suspected in 1985: Being selected for the role of Hachiman was tantamount to being named as a candidate for Kumi-ai *chō*, although a man would not run for that office until almost a decade later.

Given its significance, the selection of Hachiman-san was not without its problems. Although in 1985 there were still a few men in their forties who were fishermen, the officers worried about selecting a man who would be just right for the role yet who was younger than anyone else who might have recently been Hachiman. Given the small pool of men in their forties (and who fished), as well as the exclusion of men who were judged to be too irresponsible to take part,[15] there were only a handful of men available to be considered. This decision-making process was described by the officers as "selection of fit persons for higher positions" *(jinzai-tōyō)*, and it took all morning. When all the candidates were finally selected, each was telephoned and asked if he would take part. This was done in reverse order: The more lowly attendant to the *daimon* was phoned first, and thus the news began to spread through the village as people calculated who would be chosen next. By noon, the man who was selected for possession was called and asked if he was willing to begin, on the following day, a three-day fast as well as abstaining from sex (a point made much of by everyone) for that time.

The selected candidate in 1985—Matsui-san, the joking PTA head— had to spend the following three days learning the ritual of bow and arrow. As far as I was able to tell, no one turned down the request to be Hachiman, but it was agreed that most candidates asked for a little time to think it over and to discuss it with their *ie*. On January 2, all the selected candidates had to begin the hours of training required for the role.

The most difficult bit of training was for the man who would be possessed by the *kami*. Not only was he fasting during this time (he was allowed only water), but he spent six to eight hours a day for the next three days rehearsing the performance of the ritual. Every step was carefully choreographed and was done over and over for hours on end. The grandfather who taught this in 1985 had done so for every Hachiman since he had performed the ritual himself in the 1950s. His performance had been judged the greatest of his generation, so he went on to train others for the next thirty years. I spent several hours with him during training, waiting for the perfect moment to ask him about the meaning of the ritual and the way in which it had to be performed. He quickly realized that I was waiting to pounce on him with questions, for at the very moment when I turned to him to ask, "What does this mean?" he smiled at me and said: "Don't ask me what the meaning of this is. I don't know. There have been some very wise professors from Japanese universities here to watch this and to watch me making *noshi awabi* with the other grandfathers. I always tell them: 'I don't know the meaning of this. I just do it.'"

This dance (as I found myself thinking of it) parallels the shamanic dance done on the first of July during Hi-matsuri, when the Ise dancer reenacts the first of all shamanic dances to bring Amaterasu to Kuzaki. If, as argued in chapter 4, Nifune could be said to be an interesting opposition to Hi-matsuri (a young male god, the villagers heading out to his terrain, etc.), Hachiman could well be described as the rite that complements Hi-matsuri in more ways than one. Until the Meiji Restoration and his co-opting into an important role as the *kami* worshipped by the Japanese military, Hachiman had been a bodhisattva in the Buddhist tradition.[16] Thus despite the largely Shinto aspect of the New Year's celebrations, before 1868 the Hachiman celebration may well have been an accompanying Buddhist ritual. The inclusion of a feudal lord in the celebrations would be consistent with this Buddhist past, since it is the *daimyō* who is credited with bringing Buddhism to the Mie Peninsula.

But unraveling connections and building neat models is a process that, as the grandfather's reply to me indicates, is never straightforward. The history of Hachiman himself is a good case in point. As with many Japanese deities, this history is complex. He is said to be the Shinto deity who in life had been Emperor Ojin, who reigned from C.E. 270 to 310 (Sansom 1958, 41–42). Ojin was a ruler noted for the peacefulness of his reign, but he was born of Empress Jingū, known for her invasion of the three ancient Korean kingdoms (Herbert 1967, 433). Ojin supposedly spent the campaign within his mother's womb, his birth delayed until the war was over. His main claim to fame was for bringing culture and progress to Japan from Korea. After his death he was worshipped as a *kami*, but some centuries later he became identified with the ancient deity Hime-gami, a female deity sometimes considered to be a single entity and sometimes three deities collectively worshipped as Munakata (Herbert 1967, 426). The Munakata deities were female sea deities called Tagori-hime, Tagitsu-hime, and Ichikishima-hime. The Japanese reading of his name—Yahata or Yawata (literally, "eight flags")—has been seen as a reference to the deity O-wata-tsu-mi-no mikoto, another name for the deity of the sea. Thus, as Herbert notes, in many temples Hachiman was worshipped not as the deity of war but of shipping and seafarers. He was also seen as the protector of Buddhism in his more military aspect, and Kitagawa claims that at Usa, Kyushu, Hachiman was associated with Maitreya, "the Buddha yet to come" (1987, 248). In general, however, Hachiman was most frequently associated with Amida, the Buddha of the Western Paradise.

The people of Kuzaki—even Seiko-san, the amateur folklorist—were not given to outlining such detailed etymologies or to unraveling historical antecedents. True, the worship of Hachiman might have come with the Soto Zen Buddhism that the feudal lord Haku Hatsu brought to the area (the same Haku Hatsu that might be the young deity housed on the island outside the village), and the worship of Hachiman might well have been co-opted by Shintoism during the Meiji Restoration. But in light of the disfavor into which State Shinto had fallen (and with it the furor over the worship of war dead at the Hachiman Shrine in Tokyo), no one was willing to go into any detail about the ritual with me. The fusion between constantly changing symbolic forms (cf. Ohnuki-Tierney 1990) and political expediency has led to an interesting implosion in the anthropological study of Japanese religion: When questioned, informants prefer to give no answer or only functionalist explanations. As a result, anthropologists have been slow to explore beyond the obviously Durkheimian meanings of rituals. True, at one level Hachiman matsuri is yet another festival about village community; but at another it marks a man's success, and at still another it is an interesting construction of ritualized history that makes claim to a unique identity for Kuzaki, as further description of the ritual will make clear.

In 1985 the chosen candidate practiced the dance for three days, and the constant repetition of movement as well as the fasting led to a trance-like state. This state might well be described as an *enstasy* (cf. Zaehner 1961, 128;

Eliade 1958, 171–172)—a calm state often found in much of Japanese ritual. The desired effect was to make the man sensitive to the *kami*. The dance motions consisted of drawing a bow and arrow three times in a set pattern. Hachiman had to approach the target from the right (facing the target), and on his left would be a bow and arrow. He stood in a ballet-like plié with his arms at his side, and then he bowed, pulled up his *hakama*, and skipped to where the bow and arrows were laid. Crouching rather than kneeling, he had to free his right arm in one movement from his sleeve, bring his right hand over his head, take the bow and six arrows—still with the right hand —pivot on his left leg while still crouching, straighten, skip four steps to face the target, and in groups of one, two, and three, shoot all six arrows (see Figure 15). That is, the first time he shot it was with one arrow drawn on the bow, the second with two arrows, and the third with three. I was told that it did not matter whether he hit the target—it was more important that he collect the arrows and draw the bow correctly.

While this training was taking place, the other men were practicing, in a more relaxed manner, the way they would play the *daimon* and his court.

Figure 15. Hachiman-san (D. P. Martinez)

At the same time, the wife of the Kumi-ai *chō* was responsible for making the offering these men had to carry on the day of the ceremony itself: an elaborate rice cake whose symbolism was, as the grandmothers pointed out to me, that of wedding offerings. This cake was called *bokubu mochi* and consisted of five layers of white and pink *mochi* placed atop a tray of uncooked rice. The bottom two layers were white and round in shape and the top three pink and diamond-shaped (called *hishimochi*). This was crowned with a fern that was placed in a persimmon wrapped in paper. On top of this were two shrimp crowned with white paper and tied with silver and gold string; added to this at the very last minute were two sea bream. This fish was the same one used in Kuzaki wedding ceremonies and represents fertility for the couple as well as being associated with Ebisu, the deity of fishermen. Next to this cake were two sake flasks decorated with paper and two lacquered *miki* containers filled with more sake and also decorated with paper. Much of the symbolism here, as in the boat launch, is the same as that associated with any contract in Japan, especially weddings.

On January 5, 1985, just before dawn, Matsui-san got up and ran naked to Yoroizaki Beach. There, he told me, he bathed himself the required three times in the ocean and then ran back to his house, where he waited and prayed. No one is supposed to witness this event, and I was told by several people that I was not to even attempt to peek and photograph the event. Matsui-san joked about my using a telephoto lens and then made me promise not to even try. This was the moment to which all the practice had been leading—the moment when the candidate was fully possessed by the deity. From that moment until the end of the ceremony, Matsui-san moved as if in a trance, his expression both serious and nervous, tranquil but tense. Later in the morning he donned the elaborate outfit that Hachiman-san must wear: the divided skirt called *hakama* and a wide-shouldered upper garment.

At about 11 A.M. on the morning of the fifth, the two men who were to play the courtiers had to prepare four large fish called *bora*. Each fish had to be freshly caught (the Kumi-ai officers having been out fishing for several days in a row to catch the various fish needed for the ceremony) and immediately gutted, cut into six, and carefully sewn back together with loose, easy-to-cut loops. These were then placed into two small barrels and left for later. Then the men returned home to be dressed in kimonos that the Co-op stored from year to year for the ceremony.

At about noon there was a luncheon for the important members of the festival in the town hall: the attendant, Hachiman-san, the *daimon*, the priest, the Kumi-ai *chō*, the *semmu-san*, the four young attendants, and the grandfathers of the village all dressed in their best crested kimonos. The courtiers, priest, and Cooperative executives sat facing the other men in careful order (from left to right): the *daimon*'s attendant, the *semmu-san*, Hachiman-san, priest, Kumi-ai *chō*, and *daimon*. Behind them was the tray with the *bokubu mochi* and Hachiman's bow and arrows.

The food was served by members of the Seinendan, who had spent the morning building the target for Hachiman. The food served was made by the wives' club and had to include the following: two pieces of pickled horseradish; salad made from vegetables, fish, and rice; two adzuki beans and one small fish; two cups of sake; and bamboo. This had to be eaten with wooden chopsticks. Hachiman-san sat impassively through all of this, keeping to his fast.

At the end of the meal, the four young attendants took sake flasks out from behind Hachiman and, kneeling, poured sake for all of Hachiman-san's attendants, while the grandfathers shouted directions to the boys who had not rehearsed this. Then all the grandfathers were served. When everyone's cup was full, the men said, "It is finished," and drank. The courtiers and Hachiman-san stood, gathered the bow and arrows, and left in a group.

A procession was formed with Hachiman-san at its head. He was followed by the *daimon*, the Kumi-ai *chō*, the courtier carrying a tray with the *mochi* cake, two boys carrying jars (I shall refer to these as attendants A), and two boys carrying the barrels with the fish inside (attendants B). All the grandfathers followed; outside villagers waited to watch the procession. It was at this point that some of the watching grandmothers told me that in the past the procession had included seven young village girls dressed as temple maidens following the four boys, and that they too carried offerings. No one could give me a reason why this was stopped.

The procession made its way from the town hall to the Shinto shrine, where the ritual was to take place (the priest had slipped ahead and was waiting). The Seinendan had set up a target on the far end of the green where the memorial to the village war dead stood; the priest had also set up a small altar to the right of the target with an offering of sake already on it. The area was arranged so that everyone from the procession had a designated place to sit. The grandfathers, *semmu-san*, and Kumi-ai *chō* had seats together, facing the target and the tatami run on which Hachiman performed his dance. To the right of this, facing the target, stood the priest, Hachiman-san, the *daimon*, and his attendant. The bow and arrows were placed on the table at the end of the tatami run. The rest of the village crowded around, standing; on one side, one household had set up their brand new video camera to record the occasion.

Once everyone had gathered, the Shinto priest performed a purification ceremony with a *sakaki* branch. Hachiman himself was purified first, then the other participants, and finally the villagers. At this point attendants B entered and placed their barrels in front of the grandfather's seats. They turned, bowed to the priest and Hachiman-san, and then left. Then Hachiman went to the tatami, bowed to the grandfathers, and began his dance.

As a dance, it is different from the shamanic dance performed to call out Amaterasu at Hi-matsuri. There the masked *konju* dancer impersonated the goddess Ame-no-uzume, reenacting a mythic event that lured Amaterasu out, into the here and now, into Kuzaki. Hachiman's dance was an interesting variation on this: The man performing his tranquil dance was already possessed, the *kami* already present, having become manifest at the end of several days' hard work. The moment of possession—the dawn run and swim—was not to be witnessed and yet, by all accounts, it was a real moment of tranformation. The difference between these two events might well grow out of their different roots. Shamanism is associated with Shinto, and the *enstasy* of Hachiman is more reminiscent of esoteric Buddhist rituals that involve fasting and repetitive physical movements (cf. the "marathons" run by the monks of Mt. Hiei in order to become living Buddhas). In the end the ritual itself—the shooting of arrows—was seen as unimportant. It did not matter if the target was hit or not—what brought luck, I was told, was to have pieces of the target. So the village children charged the target at the end of the rite and tore it to bits.

When the children finished destroying the target, the Kumi-ai *chō* and *semmu-san* left their seats, took the four fish out of the barrels, and placed them on two tables that attendants A had brought out. Attendants B returned with knives in their right hands and a pair of chopsticks in their left. At this point, the *daimon* and courtier appeared, carrying two bowls. Kneeling, they used their right hands to take the knives and their left hands to take the chopsticks. Holding the fish in place with the chopsticks, they cut each fish (which they had already prepared) into six, sliding all the pieces, save the heads, into their bowls. As they finished, they bowed and the grandfathers applauded their neat work. Attendants B wrapped two of the fish heads in white paper and presented them to the Kumi-ai *chō* and *semmu-san*. Attendants A brought out trays to put the fish-filled bowls on, and these trays were also passed among the grandfathers, who put offerings of money next to the bowls. Again, attendants B wrapped the last two fish heads in white paper and presented these to the *daimon* and his courtier; upon accepting the gifts, they tucked them into their sleeves. As if at a play, everyone watching applauded.

While the villagers left, attendants B bowed to the grandfathers, took the trays from attendants A, and carried them to the priest's house. Returning, they brought with them two new trays: one with chopsticks and another with a bamboo pen. The tray to the right was carried to the Kumi-ai *chō*, and he took the pen; the tray to the left was taken to the *daimon,* and he took the chopsticks. Attendants A also went to the priest's house and returned with long thin stalks of bamboo with the leaves still on and pitchers full of sake. Dipping the bamboo into the sake, they sprinkled the *daimon* and each took one of the chopsticks from him; again they sprinkled him with sake. Going to the grandfathers, the attendants bowed, receiving applause; then all the men went into the shrine to share sake in *omiki* (a toast or offering). The four boys served more sake and followed it up with gifts of prawns and persimmons for everyone. This marked the end of the festival for most villagers.

At that point Matsui-san, as Hachiman, returned home where his wife and mother had spent the day preparing a feast for his *dokyūsei.* This took place at about 4 P.M. It was a fast-breaking feast, and in 1985 I was allowed as the only woman to attend this party. Matsui-san was interested, at this point, in only two things: drinking and discussing how hard it had been to abstain from sex. He was looking forward, so he said, to sleeping with his wife again. When I asked him about the *matsuri,* he replied: "It brings good fortune to the village and to the man who becomes the *kami.* It is a great honor, you know, and I will have *dairyō* all the rest of the year because of this. That is the importance of Hachiman-san. It brings prosperity to Kuzaki and to the man who becomes Hachiman-san. But it is not easy being the *kami*—it was very hard this dawn to get up and run naked to the ocean to purify myself in the sea. You [the anthropologist] couldn't have done it, could you? But it was then that I felt the *kami* in me. It was then that I became Hachiman-san."

Matsui-san grew very merry with his drinking and fell asleep while his guests continued to enjoy the feast. One man irreverently put a ribbon in the former deity's hair and made me photograph the moment for posterity. "There," he said. "You can add that to the other pictures of him you took today."

Trying to Understand Hachiman-san Matsuri

In chapter 1 I argued that understanding fieldwork data could include work done long after fieldwork, especially in the case of Japan where reading on religion, history, and other ethnographic works could occupy years. Much of my understanding of rituals in Kuzaki grew out of this sort of research, for I found that explanations by Kuzaki's ritual specialists were often lacking or tended to be extremely functional. It is tempting to fall back on the sort of phenomenological explanations Jeremy and Robinson (1987) give —that the rituals of everyday life in village Japan are not performed for their meanings but are part of the daily flow and not closely examined. I agree that, as with religious practices in most societies, rituals in Kuzaki were not discussed in terms of meanings but only in terms of what they *did* (hence Reader and Tanabe's pun on Japanese religion in their 1998 title, *Practically Religious*): They brought luck, health, safety, and so forth. The symbolism of rituals is often described as being about the balance between forces, movements to the right or the left, offerings of correct foodstuffs, or purifying people, places, and things.

Yet given Japan's long and scholarly history and its centuries of producing religious specialists, it seems odd that rituals are so hard to unravel. The problem, I have argued, is precisely that the weight of politics over the years has made people leery of trying to ascribe fixed meanings to ritual events beyond the purely functionalist. Also, it is obvious that these events have acquired various meanings over time; a one-to-one correlation does not tell us enough about the rituals in Kuzaki.[17] This, I think, must certainly be the case for Hachiman, a bodhisattva who became an important Shinto deity in State Shintoism. As the deity of war, defender of Japan, and the *kami* worshipped by soldiers during the Second World War, he remains something of a contested figure. Not surprisingly, then, the Aichi report on Hachiman matsuri reads simply: "January 1st, selection of man for Hachiman; January 11th, Hachiman matsuri" (1965, 63).

Of course, it is striking to note that the festival has changed even over twenty years: What took ten days in the 1950s and 1960s took only four in 1985. People were clear on this: Working at jobs in the city meant that, although fishermen could take the whole of January as holiday, most villagers could not. They had to be back at work with the rest of the nation. The ritual, then, had been chopped to fit into most villagers' work schedules. If religion in Kuzaki is seen to be a part of everyday life, then when life changes, it is no surprise that ritual does as well. So much of village life revolved around work that was considered sacred—purification rites, diving for Ise's abalone, the making of *noshi awabi,* the prayers for the dead, and so on—that the villagers were quite at ease with sacredness. The serious attitude that secularized modern people associate with ritual was not totally missing, but it was subsumed under the attitude that what they were doing was natural. Sharp divisions between the sacred and profane were not made in Kuzaki. Thus when I tried to ask about the creation of sacred space, I was met with puzzled looks; sacredness is inherently everywhere. In the end I decided that sacred space was not being made in the sense of *tsukuru* (see chapter 8) but was only being marked out for the occasion. Since all space was sacred, different bits of it needed to be partitioned off at appropriate moments in time.

It might well be a mere semantic distinction to say that sacredness is not being made, just marked out; is not the end result the same? Asquith and Kalland (1997) argue that the experience of nature in Japan is on a continuum, ranging from what is ignored and/or feared to that which is tamed and/or safe. Perhaps it should be argued that the very creation of the social and what is safe within the wild constitutes a meaningful action—an expression of power that is what *kami* and the sacred are all about in Japan. The creation of sacred space is, then, something that took place in the mythic past; ritual actions in the present might well mimic this creation, and as Taussig (1993) would say, create current social reality. Thus it is the mimetic act that becomes important for anthropological analysis; the marking of the space in and of itself is only part of a larger process.

A similar argument could be made about the process of becoming a temporary *kami*: Any man might be worthy of the honor, but first others must assess him. Equally as important as the fact that most village men might well become Hachiman for a day is the reality of being judged worthy of the experience of possession. Who will be marked out in any given year depends on the choices a man has made as well as on how others see him. This assessment of a man is a never-ending process, and becoming *(naru)* a deity parallels lived experience, which could be said to be about making: to become, one must make (in fact, one of the meanings of *naru* is also "to make"). This involves hard, repetitive work in which the needs of others are more important than the benefits to the individual. As in the case of judging a good woman, getting the form correct is important, but having a good heart/spirit *(kokoro)* is also essential. Hachiman involves choosing a man who is deemed to be the latter and works on teaching him the former: The man has made himself in relation to others, and now he can become. Not only must he make/become, but this must be seen. It is no coincidence that—like a Japanese theater performance or the *bōsōzoku* (motorcycle gangs) spectacle (cf. Standish 1998)—the concept of *mitate* (looking at to compare or form an opinion) is essential here. Writing of the importance of made offerings, Yamaguchi (1991) links *tsukuri* to *mitate*. The making must be must be seen, witnessed, and assessed by others.

Thus, as with all other villagewide rites, the ceremony is about family and community. This approach is not new: Morioka (1968) has noted how in Japanese villages much religious behavior is dependent on the person's position in the household. If the *ie* is extended to the village *dokyūsei,* then, as in Nifune, Hachiman gives us a picture of how the whole village works during the New Year celebration at large and small tasks that aim to recharge the village as a whole and the household in particular. The *ie* is not only the basic unit of production, it is one of the basic units of ritual activity—so much so that Plath has noted that in Japan the "family is the family of god" (1964). An analysis of different actors' roles might tell us, once again, about the importance of gender and age in the hierarchy of village life, but it tells us little about Hachiman matsuri as an event in and of itself.

At the level of mimesis that creates the social, the central theme of Hachiman was one that everyone pointed to by telling me how particular symbolic objects were used in other situations. It is the sealing of a contract, or perhaps the sealing of two contracts: one between Hachiman and the villagers and the other between the villagers and the political powers that had been. Whether in the past the *daimon* himself actually came to the village or just sent his representatives, the villagers could not tell me. I would doubt that elite members of the court actually came yearly to confirm the continuance of Kuzaki's role as Ise *kambe* and as provider of sailors for the local coast guard. Yet the theme of the ritual as a sealing of a contract is clear: The symbolism of the rice cake, the *tai* on the cake, the drinking of sake, and the giving of gifts can be found, as already noted, in other parts of Japanese society. The emphasis on village solidarity—everyone playing their role—constitutes a sealing of the contract that includes the whole village, not just its leaders. The significance of both the feudal lord and the *kami* being present points to a true historical relationship: It was in feudal Japan that religion was consolidated, and during this time the state gained authority over both local and religious practices.

The performance of the handing over of the fish and pens as some sort of reconstruction of history could well be labeled pure symbolic invention, but this part of the ceremony also corresponds to a certain modern attitude most villagers expressed. They were a special village, a place of momentous past events, and they deserved to be more important and richer than the village next door. This was not the political reality they lived in, but Hachiman-san matsuri, as with the Hi-matsuri, was seen as a cogent expression of Kuzaki's specialness. As another ritual that was the yin to Hi-matsuri's yang (as is also Nifune matsuri), all the obvious complements are there (see

Table 4. Comparing Hi-matsuri and Hachiman-san

Hachiman / Nifune:	Hi-matsuri
male:	female
winter:	summer
fishermen:	divers
the political order:	the mythic order

Table 4). Villagers would be dismayed if I labeled these purely *symbolic* oppositions, à la Lévi-Strauss. Rather, they are *necessities:* Each is needed for the continuity of life itself.

The Kumi-ai *chō* showed me the records of the names of the main actors in past Hachiman-san festivals; they went back only to the beginning of the Showa era (1926). What happened before this is not clear. Perhaps the ceremony was more Buddhist in nature and very differently organized, with other villagers taking part—it is hard to be sure. What is clear from looking at this festival is that despite the public and communal nature of this ritual, it can also have a deeply personal meaning for individuals. Men recalled when they were Hachiman, others looked forward to it, and apparently being chosen for the role corresponded to other sorts of ambitions. As a polysemous event, the ritual is about larger social realities; it is also a dialogic ritual that reaffirms a man's place within village life, marking a progression through what might be called a certain construction of masculinity: the *ii hito*. The *ii hito* is one who is able to lead and follow, to balance his own ambitions with the needs of others, to be cheerful, friendly, and responsible. Possession by the *kami* might well be symbolic of this: It is brought about by the individual's own hard work, but once it occurs, he is at the mercy of the possession. This sounds like something a Cooperative head once told me—that to be Kumi-ai *chō* was a great honor, but it was hard work to be the representative of the village, at the service of others. In the end, this statement might well sum up life for the people of Kuzaki: Very few responsible men or women escaped service to others. As villagers grew older, their roles in important rituals grew more prominent, as a look at the making of *noshi awabi* and the rites surrounding Obon will show.

CHAPTER 7

Elders and Ancestors

Making and Becoming

This is a good point to review some facts about the concepts of making and becoming. In Japanese, the use of the verb "to become" *(naru)* as an auxiliary verb in the infinitive is quite common: It is *becoming* spring *(haru natte imasu);* a person is in the process of *becoming* an adult *(otona natte imasu);* one has *become* nothing—a polite euphemism for being dead *(naku narimashita).* The verb is both a polite way of making statements about states of reality and/or being—rather than the harsher phrase formation that indicates something or someone *is* something *(desu* or *iru* or *aru,* which are used also)—and perhaps a way of indicating that life is about a continuous process.

In talking about differences in Japanese and Western attitudes toward the dead, I have heard various Japanese friends and students argue that it is this notion of process—of becoming—that is a key difference between Japan and an undifferentiated West.[1] While this approach ignores the vast array of practices to do with the dead in the West, there might well be a kernel of truth in relation to an idea of self. As much of Western discourse talks of the adult self as a fully formed entity, then it is this self that endures (or not) after death in heaven, hell, or purgatory. In Japan, the self is always in the process of becoming, and this process continues after death. This is not the paradox it might seem, for in many uses of the verb *"naru"* there is the implication that the process is brought about through action either of the self or something or someone else. To have become angry often implies that a person was made angry. In relation, then, to human life (and death), "to become" is often part and parcel of having been made *(tsukuru).*[2] Living humans are not passive in this process; they have agency. The dead, however, must be helped to become nothing.

Important to understand, as I have suggested in relation to skill in women and being an *ii hito* for men, is that making *(tsukuru)* is both an act and being acted on—very much a part of *naru.* A social person is made

167

through the actions of others (parents for children, the superiors in the work environment for adults, elders for the dead) and oneself. It is not that women just *become* good divers and mothers because that is what they are taught. They must work at it by making conscious efforts to enact the role of a good daughter-in-law, a hard worker, and a good parent. Also, it is possible to be someone who won't or can't meet social expectations. Yet social expectations, the gaze of others *(seken),* acts as a constraint while allowing leeway. Matsui-san, who was Hachiman in 1985, was still teased about the failure of his attempt to raise pigs commercially, and some people were still truly angry about the whole business, but in the end it was not held against him. There were women who worked as geisha in the inns who were forgiven the possible excesses of this job because they were so well liked in other respects. It was well accepted that life was about making decisions and choices. Parents spent hours of conversation worrying about what their children had chosen to do or would do in life. Nostalgia for the old days, when everyone had done what was expected of them, could be contrasted with the nostalgia both men and women expressed for life on the move, on boats, as part of a crew or as part of a husband and wife team, when they were truly free. *Seken* then is not just the panoptic community but also an acknowledgement of the fact that people are accorded autonomy within the community that makes them accountable for their actions.

In contrast, the dead are "made" by others. Kuzaki dead might well be on the path of "becoming" a bodhisattva *(hotoke),* but this was not possible without the work of their families, priests, and the village as a whole. In fact, this making was largely the work of village elders who, as many said, had the time to do it but who also occupied a liminal and mediating position between the living and dead. In terms of their life cycles, they had moved on from being young, parents, or politicians and now were *rōjin.* The term *"rōjin"* is properly glossed as elder, but in Kuzaki to be an elder without being a grandparent was unthinkable. It was the old people of the village who were charged with some of the most important ritual work, as was seen in the example of Nifune matsuri. And among these people were many who performed small ritual tasks—such as remembering holidays that were no longer celebrated by others or places of worship no longer used—and who would take it upon themselves to pray or make offerings as was appropriate.

As with so many aspects of life in Kuzaki, this work was often gendered: Men made *noshi awabi* out of the abalone for which the women dived; women prayed for the village dead at Obon, special anniversaries, and the equinoxes. The division between female/Shinto and male/Buddhism discussed in chapter 5 is clearly challenged by this ritual division of labor, a paradox to which I will return. This chapter on making and becoming begins by describing the work of making *noshi awabi.* It is in this act of transforming something natural into something purely cultural—food for the *kami*—that some important issues are raised, particularly in relation to the ideas of male continuity, offerings, and sacrifice.

Noshi Awabi

As described in chapter 3, Kuzaki was still a *kambe* of Ise Shrine and provided the dried strips of abalone that were offered to the *kami* at Ise daily. Three times a year the village men made these offerings, which involved a long process of boiling, cutting, and drying. The process began with the Kuzaki *ama* diving in Yoroizaki Bay for the abalone. Diving was rarely permitted there; it was one of the sacred areas of the village (although boats did dock there and there were some women's diving huts just at the top of the bay), and only women who were not in a state of pollution could dive for the Ise abalone. This meant that a woman could not be menstruating and must not have had a recent death in her family.

According to the tales of the origin of *noshi awabi,* the diving, making, and offering of the abalone should take place in April, August, and November. Most villagers told me, however, that they did the work generally in June, November, and December because those were often slack periods in the fishing/diving year. I first watched the making of *noshi awabi* at the end of May 1984. The villagers were being punctilious in following the rules, as an Ise priest and an NHK camera crew had come especially to watch and film the process for a documentary on Ise *kambe.*[3] I was able to watch the other *noshi awabi*–making sessions later in the year and was thus able to form a good idea of the difference between the expected way of performing this ritual task and the more relaxed way it tended to get done on other occasions.

It should be noted that almost every villager I ever encountered in Kuzaki told me that the best way to eat abalone was raw, straight from the sea, and preferably still wriggling. Generally, small *awabi* were cooked in hot fires after diving and eaten in a semi-charcoaled state; this was the preferred method of preparing abalone that was not totally fresh. Most people felt compelled to ask me to notice the shape of the abalone itself when alive, moving and folding in on itself. Its resemblance to the vulva of a woman was remarkable, and on this basis I was told it was good for everything from longevity to fertility in women and virility in men. Large abalone shells with their mother-of-pearl interiors were also prized and often left as offerings to Shinto *kami*. The scarcity of the abalone, the skill needed in diving deep for the large *awabi*, and the difficulty of prying the abalone from its rocky perches all made it a prized catch. Abalone fetched good market prices in Tokyo and beyond. As an offering, past and present, to Ise, abalone was clearly charged with symbolic meaning. It was a luxury item; giving it away was a real financial sacrifice on the part of divers; and it also represented something inexorably female being offered to the supreme female *kami*, the ancestress of all Japan, and her companion *kami* at Ise. Yet abalone was not offered in its raw form, but—like something out of Lévi-Strauss—it had to be cooked, both literally and metaphorically. Not only that, prepared sea snails were also sent as a companion offering. These, as was frequently pointed out to me, once pried out of their shells, resembled tiny penises. But when I tried to find out why such gendered offerings were made, the answer was simply, "This is what we do."

So what was done? The abalone from Yoroizaki Bay were collected the day before the making of the *noshi awabi* took place. They were kept alive in tubs of saltwater overnight and, after dawn of the designated day, the eldest grandfathers of the village (those in a state of purity, with no recent death in the family) would gather on Yoroizaki Beach to be purified by the Shinto priest. For this purification ceremony they wore the white clothing of Shinto lay ritual specialists, which—except on a day when NHK did some filming—was removed after the ceremony to reveal comfortable everyday clothing. From the beach the men would troop up to the small hut at the top of the bay that marked where the Shinto shrine had been before its rebuilding on the Sengen side of the village. Next to the hut was a fenced-off area, like a corral, that was cleaned twice a year by the elderly men only. Farther on from the corral was the stone that marked the place where Princess Yamato is said to have sat and tasted her first abalone. In short, it was very sacred terrain.

Outside the hut was the sacred well in whose water the abalone and sea snails had to be soaked as part of their preparation. After soaking, the abalone then had to be carefully pried away from its shell. This was the task of the Kumi-ai *chō* and the *semmu-san*, who at some point in the day left the task to their wives to complete. Once the abalone was out of the shell, the tiny body of the animal was cut off and the large foot, oval in shape, had to be cleaned with a small scrub brush. The abalone from Yoroizaki were huge, since they were dived for only three times a year and conserved in that sacred space the rest of the time. This meant that they were literally giants; the collection I saw at these sessions was uniformly large.

Prepared abalone were laid on bamboo racks in front of the grandfathers, who had arranged themselves around the racks in order by age. The eldest grandfather, who was about eighty, sat at the top of the racks, with the next oldest to his right and the other men around the space until the youngest man (in his sixties) was found seated at his left. The men were meant to do their work kneeling, but—complaining of arthritis in their knees—they sat tailor fashion instead. As well as the racks of drying *awabi*, there were three buckets of abalone soaking in water; these were judged to be too tough to work with immediately.

The making, as with certain forms of Japanese cooking or food processing, involved cutting. The oval foot was cut into a more rounded form and all the small shavings saved, with a little of the foot's black frill left on. The knives used bore the Shrine's name, and these sickle-shaped blades were used to further cut away two small strips from the main body; these were not entirely cut off but used as guides for the knife's continuous circling of the *awabi*. The end result, if a man's hand did not slip, was a long strip of abalone with a sort of knob left in the center—all that was left of the main foot of the abalone. Finished strips were hung over the tops of buckets until there were enough collected to tie up with the sacred rope made from rice straw. A large *awabi* might yield three strips, but a skilled man was expected to cut a smaller abalone into one continuous strip. Strips that somehow were judged to be too small were tacked together with a bit of rice straw inserted through the two ends of the abalone.

Bundles of strips were finally carried off to the back of the hut to be hung from two bamboo poles. They were covered with burlap bags and kept constantly wet so that, in the hanging, the strips would lengthen. The strips dripped into buckets below, from which the water was taken and reladled onto the abalone. Two space heaters were also used to help the process of lengthening, and when judged long enough, the strips were taken outside to dry in the corral, hung from the bamboo poles that filled the center of the sacred space.

Some small *awabi* were cooked as food to be sent to Ise priests and stored separately while the longer process of making *noshi awabi* occurred. This cooked *awabi* was prepared by women. These very sacred tasks were done with lots of cheerful gossip and joking, eating of small bits of abalone, and more jokes about revitalized libidos. The breaks for tea, lunch, more tea, and just to rest aching bones were numerous, yet lots of work did get done.

More solitary was the work of preparing the sea snails a few days later. This was the work of the wives of the Co-op head and his assistant. In this process, the snails were boiled, and I was allowed to help (not an option for the *noshi awabi* making). The snail, once cooked, had to be removed from its shell and have its intestines removed, leaving only the small, dark, edible bit of the snail, which had to have its skin removed as well. These cooked bits of snail were also left on bamboo racks to dry in the sun.

Two weeks later or so, the drying process was completed. Then the second bout of *noshi awabi* making would begin at about 6 A.M. and involved the grandfathers as well as the *semmu-san*. In the year I observed the process, two men (including the *semmu-san*) sat apart from the other men, cutting long stalks of rice straw (77 cm). The main group of workers sat around a long, low table set up in the *noshi awabi* hut and rolled the strips of abalone flat. This involved the use of a cylinder *(noshiki)*.[4] The abalone was wrapped around the cylinder, which was then rolled on the table; after this the strip was pulled off. Other men were matching up flattened strips of abalone for width and then cutting the strips to set lengths as measured out on a *sunpo*. Two sizes of *noshi awabi* came off the *sunpo*: 25 cm pieces and 13 cm pieces. The longer pieces were made into an Omidori and the smaller into the Komidori; very tiny bits were also cut for the making of a Tamanuki (see Figure 16). All this work was done almost as if on a production line, the sequence being:

1. Abalone rolled
2. Given to men at left to measure
3. Once measured, the pieces were cut
4. The larger pieces of cut abalone were folded in half, and all the pieces sorted into groups according to width
5. The smallest bits were taken to a heater where they dried until rubberlike in texture

Again the men sat in order of age and hence experience. This time the eldest man sat at the head of the table, with the next oldest man to his left, all the way around to the youngest at his right. The men constantly consulted, and I noted in my field notes that "knowledge was clearly being passed down the line." This process took a large part of the morning until a food break at 10 A.M. After the break, work began on making the Omidori, Komidori, and Tamanuki offerings. For the first, the folded pieces of abalone were pierced and arranged in groups of five. On some of the lengths of straw that had been cut earlier, five of these groups were strung together; on others, seven sets of five were strung. Then two of these decorated lengths of straw would be joined, end to end, and a third piece of plain straw would be added. The straw would then be rolled, by hand, until it was ropelike in texture, with five sets of five pieces of abalone hanging from each end of the rope. I was told that the total number of abalone groups strung onto the Omidori should come to twelve (seven and five) to represent the months of the year. I found myself noting that many Omidori had just ten sets of five, but I was not sure what to make of this. Komidori were similar, save that the smaller pieces of abalone were used to make them and were ordered into groups of two sets of five and three sets of five that were tied together.

Tamanuki were more difficult to make, and it is more difficult to describe the making of them. A thick bundle of straw would be rolled into a rope, which would be twisted into a circular shape. The circle would be twisted around itself until it formed one thick length of rope. Then four stalks of straw would be knotted together with twelve tiny pieces of *awabi* woven into them in such a way that they joined the thick, twisted straw rope to the thinner abalone-studded straw. Two such sets of straw would be matched for evenness of the spacing of abalone and tied together as had been the Omidori.

The Omidori were bundled into groups of ten, and 112 groups of ten were needed (the groups were called *den*). Komidori were also bundled into groups of twenty, and 237 *den* of these were needed. Tamanuki were also grouped by tens, but these were hung to dry yet again on bamboo poles rather then being placed in further groups. In the afternoon, dried whole

Figure 16. Completed Ise offerings (D. P. Martinez)

abalone (234 in number) and the sea snail (930) were brought out, laid carefully on trays, and placed also on the bamboo poles next to the drying Tamanuki. If thought about, these numbers are large and a waste of profitable abalone—a fact which no one appeared to mind at all.

I was told repeatedly that the three types of *noshi awabi* were offerings of thanks that had to be given to the *kami*. These were offered daily at Ise and, I gathered, the different types were offered on the altars of different shrines. I got the impression that the whole abalone and sea snails were given to Ise priests for their consumption, but I was never able to confirm this.

At the time of my fieldwork, I was haunted by the nagging sensation that all this cutting, drying, more cutting, and more drying was all too like the processes described in structuralist analyses and had to mean something about the dichotomy of the raw and cooked, the male and female. Perhaps a purely structural analysis is called for here, but more interesting for me is the fact that this processing of food to be offered to the *kami* was seen as practical: Shinto deities are meant to be offered fresh produce and Buddhist deities are meant to be offered cooked food (cf. Cobbi 1995). Yet abalone is not available all year, nor could Kuzaki villagers make *noshi awabi* every day and send it to Ise. In the past, it was pointed out to me, the trip to Ise took three days on foot and the abalone and sea snail would be rotten by then. So the food had to be prepared but not cooked. Thus the distinction between what was offered in Shinto and Buddhism was maintained, despite the fact that all the drying might well be analogous to a form of cooking (drying through heat is, after all, just another form of putting something on the fire). There is another way in which this event could be looked at: Yamaguchi argues that the gods prefer made objects and that "*Tsukuri* is a device used to associate something in immediate view with the primordial things of distant [past]" (1991, 64). I will return to this point later, but I should note that this was not an explanation offered to me by the villagers.

In fact, I found that even at the time of writing the notes about *noshi awabi* making, I had become more interested in another question altogether: Why was it that only thirteen of the village grandfathers had taken part in this ritual labor? These were many of the same men I would meet later doing the ritual work for Nifune matsuri and a slightly smaller group of men than those who would take part in Hachiman matsuri or in several of the Buddhist rites. Some absences were explained by telling me that some men were in a state of *kegare* (not *hare*, not pure) because of deaths in their households. Yet the total of men involved was not as large as there were elder men in the village. I was told that some men were also too old to take part in ritual labor, and some old men were as yet too young and inexperienced. What I observed, however, was that a man had to be active in the Ryōjin-kai and to express a real interest in doing ritual labor. An old man who felt too ill, couldn't be bothered, or perhaps liked his drink a bit more than doing even the occasional communal work at the grandparents' club seemed to rule himself out. Again, a process of self-selection seemed to be going on. In contrast, the work of the Nembutsu-bāsan (sutra-reciting grandmothers) seemed to be organized on different principles. Larger groups of women took part in this (almost all the eligible village women), and the process of belonging to this group was more clearly articulated.

From Offerings to the *Kami* to Caring for the Dead: Women's Work

Working with *noshi awabi* was to work in a state of purity with once living or fresh objects from a sacred area that were being preserved, albeit in a changed form, in order to offer them to the *kami*. Dealing with the dead is another activity altogether, yet with interesting parallels. While memory is being preserved, perhaps, nothing else about the dead remains the same—not their state of being, nor their name, and not even their personality. There are two issues in dealing with the dead that must be taken into account when discussing practices of ancestor worship: the pollution of death and dying itself and the hard ritual work involved in worshipping ancestors. It is perhaps no small matter that it is the women who do the bulk of this work in Kuzaki. The concept of pollution is the stuff of religious studies with various wide-sweeping debates, but I would like to sum up some points here as they will help form a historical framework for the description of practices in Kuzaki. The second topic, ancestor worship, I will address in the next section.

The fact of death's terrible pollution is evident from Japan's earliest recorded myths. The creation story that tells of the founder deities Izanami no mikoto and Izanagi no mikoto is an important example of early Japanese attitudes toward death, but it is also, as Ebersole (1989) notes, an example of how death is also seen as a creative moment. Izanami no mikoto dies while giving birth to the fire *kami,* and in extremis yet more deities are born. From her vomit come two deities, from her feces two more, and from her urine yet another pair. As a mythic representation of death, this is graphic stuff. Interestingly enough, when her spouse Izanami begins his rituals of grieving and purification, yet more deities are born. From his tears come one *kami,* and, after Izanami's journey to the land of death to visit his spouse, a whole slew of deities are born from his purification rites. As Ebersole (1989, 88) notes:

> In these myths death itself is not conceived as merely the absence of life: rather, death in one physical or phenomenal form yields new life in another. But following the creation of a break: a radical disjunction between the realm of the dead and that of the living; the metamorphosis is now accomplished through ritual means. In the myth Izanami's entry into Yomi and her 'death' are not viewed as permanent until Izanagi breaks the taboo of entering the burial hall and views the corpse. The significance of this point has not, I think, been sufficiently appreciated. The finality of death is a result of the actions of the living.

For Ebersole, this realization is the foundation of the rest of his book about politics in early Japan. Barley argues that we should take "death as evidence for the importance of the collective over the individual" (1995, 159). In understanding this point, Barley argues that better context must be given when it comes to describing death and its rituals; in the Japanese case, this is possible and many anthropologists concerned themselves with this wider context from the 1950s onward (cf. Smith 1974).

Before the advent of Buddhism in the sixth to eighth centuries, death and its associated rituals were about pollution, cleansing, and most probably, more about the collective than about individuals' grief—a bold statement since we have little evidence other than the myths with which Ebersole works. It seems clear that the dead—at least the important dead—became *kami* after dying.

With the arrival of Buddhism and its accretion with Shintoism, it seems whatever Shinto rituals for the dead that may have existed were taken over by Buddhism. Thus the two religious systems came to rather neatly cover a person's whole life: Shinto rituals dominated birth, life, and marriage; Buddhist rituals came to dominate funerals and the mourning or anniversary rites celebrated in the years after death. Ooms (1976), following various Japanese anthropologists, made a very neat structuralist diagram out of this fact, showing how rituals held for the dead mirror the life cycle rituals of the living. Anthropologist Ohnuki-Tierney (1987) argues that this transition led to an eventual fixing of the status of the Shinto death specialists, who centuries later became outcastes in the medieval caste system of Japan. In fact, death specialists seemed to have served aristocratic families. In ordinary families, until the latter part of the twentieth century, the preparation of the dead for burial and more recently cremation had been women's work. Washing, dressing the body, weeping the night through next to the body—

this has long been the domain of women. Nowadays a whole funeral industry has sprung up, but some of the first rituals to do with the corpse are still held to be women's work.

To return to the idea of the collective and individual, however, what Buddhism seems to have offered Japan was the idea of named dead who could be remembered individually rather than as diffuse *kami*. And the concept of reincarnation was never a strong one in Japan, so the dead journey toward Buddhahood in a carefully monitored cycle of anniversaries during which their families have much ritual work to do. The final outcome of this journey, it is hoped, is becoming "nothing"—but as Smith (1974) has noted, this is a recent belief. In many parts of Japan, he records, the Buddhist memorial tablets were moved from the Buddhist altar in the house *(butsu-dan)* to the Shinto altar *(kamidana)* on the thirty-third or fiftieth anniversary after death (in some places earlier). But by the mid-twentieth century, only a few places in Japan still held what had once been a more common belief: That after an appropriate amount of time, the dead went from being a bodhisattva to becoming a *kami*. Hendry has argued that in some parts of Japan the belief was that the dead became *kami,* then returned to an undifferentiated sort of pool whence new individuals were born—not exactly reincarnated but reconstituted, as it were (personal communication).

How widespread and uniform these beliefs were is not always clear. While during the Tokugawa era much of Japanese religion was systematized and administered by the government, various ideas about the dead continued to be found throughout Japan. In fact, Japanese ethnographers such as Takeda Akira (1995) and Tanaka Hisao (1991) have spent years collecting what are seen to be rapidly disappearing beliefs about the dead and ancestors throughout Japan. The variety and complexity of these are sometimes overwhelming: The dead live on mountains, across the sea, in hells, paradises, haunting local areas—albeit greatly changed in form—and so on (see also Picone 1984). Thus to argue that there exists one coherently held belief that all lay people in Japan share about the dead would be incorrect. Included among the many categories of dead are the hungry ghosts, whose families did not or could not care for them after death, and so they are doomed to haunt and harm the living. This last idea is often used by various Japanese new religions as a way of diagnosing what is wrong with a person's life (Davis 1980; Reader 1990; McVeigh 1997). Ritual specialists and mediums—often females dressed as Shinto shamans—are sometimes consulted by families to make sure the dead person is happy with their funeral and other recently completed rites in order to avoid the creation of a vengeful spirit.

As with ancestor worship in many places—especially in China, whose Confucian principles underlie Japanese notions of ancestors—in Japan the ancestors are patrilineal, and the family that is the family of god is patrilineal/patriarchal. This holds true even in places like Kuzaki, where women are far more independent than other Japanese wives. Importantly, however, mothers—women who have married in—are the only female ancestors worshipped. Daughters are meant to move out, so the ancestresses are of the household—but only by dint of hard work and a lifetime of learning to belong. This is a gendered aspect of becoming/making that must be kept in mind.

Women and Ancestor Worship in Japan

There are two sides to ancestor worship in Japan: the public and communal side, which includes extended family, friends, and neighbors (and more recently, employers); and the personal side, which takes place daily, within the household, and is often women's work. The public side covers the time of the funeral and the yearly celebration of the return of the dead to visit their household, Obon, which Smith (1974) argues was already an important, heavily symbolic, and syncretic event mentioned in the earliest records on ancestor worship. In Japan, as in much of the West, funerals have become the work of a huge commercialized industry, but even in urban areas some of this communal flavor remains. It is still a common practice in Japan to give gifts to the family of the dead. In Kuzaki this gift giving was geared toward helping the family during the busy time of the funeral and included food, drink, sweets, and—especially from relatives—money to help with the expenses of the funeral and the related feasts that are held at the time. Female relatives, as Bachnik (1995) has described, come to help with the cooking and feeding of the male relatives and guests. The celebrations during Obon mirror this arrangement, especially if it is one of the special anniversary dates for a dead family member (seventh, forty-ninth, and hundredth day; first, third, seventh, thirteenth, seventeenth, twenty-third, and thirty-third years). These gifts are often returned in kind when a death or anniversary occurs in other village households, but the modern urban equivalent calls for return gifts, worth half the cost of the original gift, to be made soon after the funeral.[5]

One simple generalization that can be made is that the large celebrations to do with the dead are often dominated by the public presence of men, although they are not possible without the work of women. This is what Hendry might call the "wrapping"—the exterior or *soto*—of ancestor worship. Since the dead are seen as belonging to a patrilineal household, it is the men who dominate public worship and feasts. Thus during Obon in the village, middle-aged men visited kin and feasted together, young men organized the dancing (odori) that all villagers took part in, and older men sang the old folk songs to which we danced. In this respect, the festival of Obon seems to me clearly linked with other village festivals, most of these Shinto in character, where men represent their households and women occupy the background, leaving offerings at more personal altars, preparing food, and, if celebrating themselves, doing it separately from the men and less elaborately. In fact, the yearly cycle of events I saw during my fieldwork in 1984–1985 and on return visits seems to fall neatly into the category of events that Bernier has called "creating the cosmic circle"—rituals that are meant to re-create and maintain the social, as well as literally shoring up the physical boundaries of place—protecting what is uchi, the village, against the uncertainty of the outside world, of traveling deities, of natural disasters (not necessarily different from the power of deities). Obon, with its careful inviting in and then sending away of the village dead, is a controlled visit home by the spirits of people who are deemed to be on a journey away from the physicality of place and yet, paradoxically, who are near enough that they could wreak havoc if not cared for.

This work of creating the social has a parallel set of tasks, as I have mentioned, in the more personal maintenance of bonds with the dead that are most often carried out on a daily basis by women. This is not to say that men are never involved in lighting incense and saying prayers in front of the butsudan, but that in my experience it was the women who cleaned the Buddhist altar, made and left offerings of rice in the morning, and added small gifts of flowers and sweets (any gift given to the household was often set before the ancestors for a day or so before being opened), as well as praying. That being said, it was assumed that the eldest woman in the household would do these daily tasks and that younger, newly married women would be more responsible for the kamidana, the care of the household Shinto deities.

The anthropologist Lebra (1983) noted the tendency of older women to worship at the shrines of their husbands' ancestors and asked women about it in her research for her book on Japanese women. She reports that women found comfort in communing with the dead whom they were soon to join. Often they felt they could make peace with demanding in-laws who were transformed by death into kinder beings; Smith (1974) also notes how ancestors are seen to be nicer beings after death than they might have been in life. Lebra argues that this is a looking forward to a woman's final incorporation as part of the household into which she has married. This last refers to the idea that a daughter-in-law is never completely part of the household until death. Marriage rituals, as Hendry (1981) has noted, were often protracted events that covered years of exchanges before the marriage was seen to be complete. In many places it was only the birth of the first child or first male child that completed marriage, but the position of the daughter-in-law was always perilous, and she could be divorced and sent away while her children remained behind. A woman felt more secure when she took over the running of the household from her mother-in-law (in some parts of Japan this included a brief ceremony) and even more secure—psychologically, it seems—when her mother-in-law died. The marriage of her son and the appearance of her own daughter-in-law to boss around was another milestone on a woman's incorporation into a household, and death was not quite the final step, since you needed to be worshipped in order to complete the process.

In Kuzaki there was an added way that women were publicly celebrated as being more of the *uchi* (the inside) of both the village and household, and that is when at the age of sixty she joined the sutra-reciting *(nembutsu)* group of village women. This village practice, common in the sect of Amida Buddhism, laid emphasis on the importance of prayers to help the dead become Buddhas. The women practiced alone or in smaller groups at home and on the spring and autumn equinoxes visited all village households to pray for their death. During Obon, they were the only women who performed a public ritual, and this is fascinating for what it involves. However, becoming a member of the Nembutsu-bāsan, as it was termed, was a family event—a clearly marked ritual transition that could be contrasted with the more implicit inclusion of men in sacred work, where it was said that "any man who wants to could do this."

Becoming a Nembutsu-bāsan

Women were supposed to be practicing the invocations that are part of *nembutsu* beginning in their forty-first year, when they were sometimes referred to as *chū-bāsan* (literally, "middle-grandmothers"). But these monthly practice sessions rarely took place, and it seemed that a grandmother began practicing in earnest only in the year before she turned sixty. At this time, she had not only to be sponsored by the other *nembutsu* grandmothers in her geographical section, who practiced at home with her, but the grandmother also had to make her own handwritten copy of the sutras.

Often the grandmothers felt insecure about their ability to write and had other members of the family do this. Whoever did it, the *nembutsu* were generally written in hiragana only, so that the women could read them without any problems. This meant, however, that the women often had no idea what the *nembutsu* meant. They were aware that the term itself meant "hail to Buddha" but had no knowledge of the original Sanskrit phrase. For the grandmothers, like the men in ritual practices, the meaning was not important, nor was understanding; what mattered was that they repeat the sutra often and with faith. The most important *nembutsu* they recited was one to Amida that began, "Butsu namu Amida Butsu" (Buddha, hail Amida Buddha). The grandfathers also recited this *nembutsu*, the "Sasa Nembutsu," on the fourteenth of August. By the time of their sixtieth birthday, a grandmother should have memorized all the appropriate invocations and purchased a bell to use in some sutras, a set of prayer beads, one new, dark kimono, and several sashes (obi) worn according to the season and occasion. She could not practice as a sutra reciter until she was initiated into the Nembutsu kai.

On the fifteenth of February (the lunar New Year in 1985), I watched that year's women being initiated into the *nembutsu* group. The number of grandmothers entering the group varied from year to year. Each geographical section of the village had its own set of Nembutsu-bāsan who helped with the first part of the initiation. In 1985 I watched the Kainaka group initiate a woman who was kin to the household in which I lived.

The day began at 6 A.M., when the grandmothers who were already members of the group met in the town hall to count the number of good-luck cakes and 1,000-yen notes they had received from local households. I was told that there should be one cake and one note from each household in their section. The counting took about an hour, a time full of eating, gossiping, and tea drinking. The grandmothers enjoyed the *nembutsu* group because they still worked so hard at home and in the fields; this was a time to both relax and socialize. For many women, the time spent chatting before, between, and after reciting sutras reminded them of the cozy times in the *koie* after diving, and I often learned more about diving in the past during these sessions than at any other time.

After 7 A.M., the grandmothers went to the households of the women being initiated. In 1985 there were two Kainaka candidates, and the main Kainaka group split into two and separated. I was told that the household of the initiate should have been cleaned and made ready to receive the *nembutsu* grandmothers, and several snacks should also be ready and waiting to be served. On arrival, the grandmothers prayed before the household *butsudan,* and the new grandmother was allowed only to watch the two-hour session of prayer. There were three breaks in the two hours when the women had a drink, ate a sweet, and then returned to praying. At the end of the session, the household served all the women a meal.

This was, in fact, a rehearsal of the twice-yearly visits that the sutra group made to each village household during the vernal and autumnal equinoxes. On these occasions, the women also prayed for two hours with three breaks and were fed afterward. In each case, the meals had to consist of soup, sashimi, salad, meats, vegetables, rice cakes, rice, oranges, and sake to drink. The grandmothers rarely ate all of this, and the leftover food was then packed for them to take home. They were also given bags of white sugar. One woman told me that this was because in the past this was good payment for their work; sugar was rare and expensive. In symbolic terms, it is similar to the white substance so important in Shinto—salt—but opposed to it as well: sweet to the salt's sharpness (cf. Cobbi 1995).

During the February initiation, all the women rested for a short time after their two hours of prayer, waiting while the initiate finally donned her new kimono. At 11 A.M., all the *nembutsu* grandmothers and initiates met at the village temple. The first stop before entering the temple was at the statue of Amida, housed in a small altar just to the left of the main temple. The grandmothers left some money and uncooked rice before the image of the Buddha and said a silent prayer. Inside the main temple, the altar had been set up with seven offerings: incense, two trays of pink and white *mochi,* and four trays of plain white *mochi,* with an offering of money on top as well as the names of the initiates written on slips of paper. In front of the altar the priest's mat, drum, and bell were set up.[6]

Seated in order by age, the grandmothers waited for the arrival of the priest. The four new women, on this occasion only, sat at the very front of the group; later, as the group's newest members, they would sit at the rear. Since there was no school holiday, the priest was not available, and it was his wife who led the ceremony. She entered the temple from the right-hand side of the altar and welcomed all the women—especially the new women. After saying six prayers with the grandmothers, the priest's wife left them to the hour-and-a-half session of sutra recitation. At the end of this time, the women divided back up into their geographical groups and returned to the houses of the initiated women. There the family had to put on a banquet to mark the grandmother's successful entry into the Nembutsu-bāsan.

This was a time of great celebration, not only for the grandmother but for her entire household. The husband of the grandmother whose celebration I attended kept telling me how wonderful it all was: "Isn't she incredible? Doesn't even look sixty yet!" All the women's children and grandchildren were there, and the eldest son of the household made a speech thanking all the guests. In the case I saw, the son cried with the emotion of it all, especially as he told of how hard his mother had worked to learn all the sutras. The grandmothers, who had had a long day by this time, enjoyed the banquet the most. Although they ate very little, they set themselves to entertaining the others. At the banquet in 1985, the singing began with "Sakura" (Cherry Blossom) but soon proceeded to the truly old and traditional folk songs that tend to be full of puns and sexual innuendo. Eventually, the young women were made to sing. One *yome* covered herself in glory when she sang the well-known song "Musumeyo" and improvised new lyrics, which began, "When I entered as a *yome* to a *ryokan* family," to the glee of all the visitors, for the initiated grandmother was from an inn-owning family. When the women thought they had had enough, one of the grandmothers sang a good-bye song as a hint for the hosts to serve the rice and let them go.

The initiation of the grandmothers into the *nembutsu* group might not seem very elaborate, but it is important to note how it fits in with other types of rites of passage in Kuzaki. In general, the villagers follow the model so often given by ethnographers of Japan: Shinto is the source of all life-cycle rites, and Buddhism is for the dead (cf. Newell 1976). The initiation of the grandmothers into the group, however, is definitely a Buddhist ritual, yet it can only be compared to Shinto rituals held within the village. There is a period of liminality when a woman is no longer active in the Fujin-kai, marked by the category of *chū-bāsan,* which lasts about ten years. In her fifties, then, a woman is no longer a real member of any village group. As I noted, the middle-grandmothers do not really meet; in fact, women in this age bracket continued to attend wives' club meetings but were not allowed to play an active role in this group. Then, in their fifty-ninth year, the preparations for joining the sutra group began, including saving for the clothes, implements, and feast and the learning of the sutras. Still, it was not every woman who was sponsored to join the group; although it was not clear to me why not, some women hinted that if a family could not afford the special kimono, then the grandmother would not join. These few women progressed to the Rōjin-kai but not to the *nembutsu* group as well. All the work of being a proper *yome,* wife, and mother was evaluated at this point; the invitation to join was a seal of approval for a life properly lived.

The ceremony that incorporates the women into the group is a life-cycle ritual, but it elucidates a crucial point: In Kuzaki, caring for the well-being of the dead is seen as so important and so sacred that the women who do it must undergo rigorous training. It is also a marker that the woman has finally been completely accepted into the patriarchal group. She is now fully of the family—something other women don't achieve until their death. The grandfathers who pray at the temple during the vernal and autumnal equinoxes and who do the *nembutsu* at Obon must be in a state of purity, but they require no initiation. The fact that the women must be past the age of menstruation, a form of pollution, is not as important as the fact that they have reached an age when they should have handed on the reins of the household to their daughters-in-law and be in the process of thinking of their own death. The women are now identifying more closely with those ancestors—not theirs by blood, since they have married in—who they will be joining.

Men also feel closer to the household ancestors as they grow older, yet they do not spend as much time involved in the care of the dead as do the women, nor are they organized into a group whose main concern is the well-being of the ancestors. While men have to be purified for anything they do in a Shinto ritual, they do not need such purification for Buddhist rites. Women, on the other hand, must be changed in some way before assuming their place in the sutra group. I have already mentioned that in Shinto, women assume the role of caring for the family deities, and their worship is often in the form of prayer for individual needs; this work is related to their roles as wives and mothers. Men's involvement with Shinto in the large, public festivals was about protecting the village as a whole. This essential dichotomy can be seen in Buddhist ritual work as well: The care of the dead as newly formed/being formed beings was in the hands of the women. In both cases, women were responsible for socializing new beings and making new persons; the dead are like children.

If it can be postulated that most Shinto festivals were about protection for the village, this explains the large role of men in these ceremonies. Men were the protectors of the community. Where Shinto is concerned with individuals, women did the rites. Buddhism is, in general, more about the individual, with each of the dead making their way into the Pure Land. It is only logical that this ritual work was also in the hands of the women. Lebra refers to this when describing the role of women at a funeral: "Observation confirmed the assumption that women perform a primary role in the maintaining and reactivating the human, emotional bond of worship; they see a more social and emotional than ritual and obligatory function in the ceremonial rite" (1984, 268). Women in Kuzaki were clearly seen as the main actors in rites that involve family deities, the individuals within the family, and the household ancestors; in doing this, they enacted the social part of their biological roles—they were reproducing part of the social. Men, as I have already argued, did this for the whole group during other festivals. The work of both, the women and the men, was essential to maintaining continuity in village life. Ties with the past—with historical and political truths, with other places and generations—were all upheld, reaffirmed, re-created, and revitalized on these occasions. And Obon was the most complete example of this.

Obon

Obon, the Buddhist feast of the dead, takes place all over Japan. On the lunar calendar its date varied, but since the introduction of the Gregorian calendar year, most parts of Japan celebrate it during August 12 through 15. During the three days of the thirteenth, fourteenth, and fifteenth, the dead visit their old households and the Japanese celebrate these returns with food, prayers, and dancing. Kuzaki was not very different from the rest of Japan in its celebration of Obon. At least, given the brief descriptions generally found in the standard ethnographies of Japan, Obon in Kuzaki seems to resemble Obon in other places.[7] All Obon celebrations seem to include the cleaning of graves, prayers at the *butsudan,* and three nights of dancing in the temple courtyard. What appears to be unusual about the celebrations I witnessed in 1984, 1985, and 1986 was that they were longer, following a more traditional pattern of rituals for the returning dead than those found in most of Japan.

August 6–11

On the evening of the sixth, the households that have had members die in the past year (these are called *hatsu-bon* households) must build a *tōrō* from rice straw and decorate it with ribbons and flowers; some people even put a light in it. The *tōrō* is a sort of sign to the newly dead (called the *nyugeshi*). It is placed outside the house's main entrance so that the dead spirit can recognize the place as his or her former home. One of the grandmothers told me that the *nyugeshi* have not made the trip before and so need the *tōrō* to help show them the way. Another explained that these dead also do not have as far to travel as some of the people who died long ago, so they begin returning to the village earlier than the spirits of the older dead. Thus, the Nembutsu-bāsan must begin praying early for the recent dead to help see them safely to Kuzaki. Also, some of the grandmothers thought that their praying was also to make sure that other dead—the unclaimed dead whose families did not pray for them and had become hungry ghosts *(gyoji)* —did not try to enter Kuzaki where they might harm the villagers.[8]

All this praying took place on Yoroizaki Bay facing east,[9] on the flat area facing the old Shinto shrine. Early on the morning of August 7, the *hatsu-bon* households erected a makeshift torii for this area called a *chaya*, marking it off as a sacred space where the grandmothers would pray. While this was being done, the grandmothers began Obon at the temple, saying prayers at 6 A.M. with the priest.

A little later in the morning, all village households took the time to visit the household grave. This was generally the work of the wife of the household head and her daughter-in-law; they tidied up, left offerings of water and flowers, and burned incense. At about 4:30 in the afternoon, the grandmothers gathered at Yoroizaki and began the first day of prayers for the returning ancestors. They built a small altar on which they burned leaves called *shihibi*, which are poisonous and good for warding off evil. Offerings of flowers and uncooked rice were also made; weak tea, donated by the *hatsu-bon* households, was poured over the fire from time to time.

On this first day, the prayers lasted only an hour and consisted of general prayers for all the village dead, especially for those ancestors whose anniversary it was: the third, seventh, thirteenth, up to the thirty-third year since the person's death. It was only on August 11 that prayers for the *nyu-geshi* were said. If there were four dead in a year, the grandmothers performed four sets of prayers; between each set they poured tea from the dead's household over the fire.

All this is hard work, and the grandmothers were grateful when the hour was over and they were served fruit drinks and sweets. The cost of these refreshments was divided up by the number of households who were *hatsu-bon* and by the number of households whose ancestors had an anniversary. The daily cost of these *nembutsu* sessions was about 300–400 yen ($1.90–2.25) per grandmother. In the years I watched, there were about thirty-three grandmothers in the *nembutsu* group who required refreshments over seventeen days of praying. The estimated cost of refreshments to be shared amongst the various villages' households came to a total cost of about 170,000 yen ($1,062) for the entire period of Obon.

This pattern of afternoon prayers continued until August 11, and the other villagers during this time would continue to tidy up their household graves and leave offerings. The Seinendan prepared the gifts and prizes that were given away during the three nights of Obon dancing. They earned money for this by cleaning the village roads and taking donations from all the village households. In the evenings, the grandfathers rehearsed the "Sasa Nembutsu," which they had to perform on the fourteenth.

August 12

On the twelfth, new offerings had to be made at all the village graves. The women took sweets and flowers, poured water over the memorials, and lit new incense. Offerings were left at the memorial to the war dead, as well as to the six bodhisattvas on the road next to the village's second graveyard. At home there were several preparations that had to take place. Each household must have made and taken to the temple a flag made of two bamboo sticks wrapped with white, green, and red paper and tied together. The colors of the paper are meant to represent the sky, earth, and fire. Hanging from these sticks would be the name of the family drawn on a banner of blue, red, yellow, green, and white paper. Although some villagers said that these are the colors of the Five Buddhas (who are identified with the elements), I was told also that the colors on the banners were not very important; every household used different colors in different orders, and it was only the colors used on the sticks that had meaning. The children then took these, with an offering of rice, to the temple. At some point, the family memorial tables (*ihai*) were also taken from the *butsudan* to the temple.

In the *hatsu-bon* households, gifts of money would begin to arrive. Everyone in the village should have given up to 3,000 yen ($18.75) to the *hatsu-bon* families. Patrilineal kin to the family should have given 10,000 yen ($63.00) and a case of beer worth about 6,000 yen ($37.50).

August 13

At 11 A.M. on the thirteenth occurred the first ceremony for the entire village, which was held at the temple. Everyone came dressed in their kimonos, and the men carried branches called *kobana* over their shoulders. While waiting for the ritual to begin, the men would leave the smaller branches from the *kobana* as offerings in various places in the temple courtyard (one informant said these branches were offered like incense): before the Amida, by two *hotoke-sama* (no one was sure of their names), and at the entrance to the temple itself. Since the temple was so small, only the village dignitaries got seats inside; the other villagers waited outside. Inside, the grandfathers, Cooperative executives, *nembutsu* grandmothers, and other village men were seated with the first two groups on the left (facing the altar) and the other two on the right.

At the entrance to the temple, a second altar had been built. On it were offerings of watermelon, incense, and three shallow bowls full of water, as well as the villagers' *ihai*. Inside, on the left of this altar, the following offerings for the *nyugeshi* were placed: soft drinks, grapes, peaches and pears, watermelon, and sugar. On a second small table next to this altar were trays prepared by the *hatsu-bon* households; these trays contained cooked rice, a bowl of cooked vegetables, a bowl of string beans, and water. The third table contained memorial tablets for the households of the dead with new Buddhist names for the *nyugeshi*.

The ceremony on the thirteenth, called the Taisegaki-kai (the mass for the dead), required three priests, and the village priest, Suidani-san, was helped by priests from the neighboring villages (he left immediately after the service to officiate at their villages). The three priests then purified the worshippers with a stick reminiscent of the Shinto *gohei*, lit incense, and began to pray. This involved a long series of prayers never explained to me, and the villagers themselves weren't sure what was going on. But at the end, they all rushed out of the temple, stopping only to dip their *kobana* into the water on the exterior altar, which they then sprinkled over the offerings on that altar. Leaving the *kobana* behind but taking the now-blessed memorial tablets (the *hatsu-bon* households must leave their *ihai* for a few days yet) and the banners they made earlier, the villagers went home, while the grandfathers got treated to lunch in the temple.

At this time, the households made special offerings on their *butsudan*. For each of the ancestors who had not yet reached their ninety-ninth anniversary, there were two plates of offerings. On the first day of Obon, these should consist of cucumber and *mochi*. Chopsticks had to be left out for each of these ancestors. The banners, now blessed by having been in the temple, were put on the *butsudan* at this point as well.

Also on this day, the grandmothers of the household made what they called the small *tōrō*, which were placed on the Buddhist altar in the house to call the spirits of the ancestors to the right altar. These consisted of four squares of white paper suspended from a bamboo stick. Outside the house, by the main entrance, the household would leave a tray of offerings for the hungry ghosts who might be wandering around the village, since they had no households to return to. These offerings included *mochi*, uncooked rice, and flowers set on rocks.

On the afternoon of this day, the priest visited the households whose ancestor's anniversary it was. He said a short prayer in front of the *butsudan* and then stopped to chat with the family about prayers for the dead. Had daily prayers and offerings been made? The answer was invariably yes, and the priest quickly moved on to the next household.

In the evening, the *hatsu-bon* households had to entertain their *shinseki* with a banquet. Everyone would come when they could (some people had more than one banquet to attend that evening), and often a house would be filled with patrilineal kin who had come from out of town to celebrate the *hatsu-bon* with their families. All guests who entered the house went to the *butsudan,* lit two sticks of incense, and sprinkled a little water on the new *ihai.* Then a brief prayer would be said. Food was served continuously and the kimonoed guests came and went from the dancing, which took place in the temple courtyard.

While the other adults were visiting with kin, the children and grandparents dressed in costumes and performed the village Obon dance in the Buddhist temple's courtyard. Like all Japanese folk dancing, this was done in a circle, with everyone making the same gesture at the same time. The traditional Kuzaki song and dance, I was told, meant: "We are glad to have you visiting ancestors, but now that you have visited, have a safe trip back" (a rather liberal interpretation, I suspect). Two of the village grandfathers sat in the center of the courtyard, singing into a microphone, while members of the Seinendan beat the drum in front of the grandfathers' platform to give the dancers their rhythm.

The Seinendan were also responsible for giving prizes to the best dancers and costumes (over the next three nights, everyone got one) and for teaching the young children—as well as foreign anthropologists—the steps of the dance. Children tended to come dressed in kimonos, but adults (especially the grandmothers) came in all sorts of costumes: as pirates, men as women, women as men, as Chinese, and as warriors. This Halloween-like atmosphere continued until midnight, when the singing grandfathers retired and the Seinendan put rock-and-roll tapes on; then the young people of the village took over. Still dancing in a circle, they performed the latest popular dances until dawn.

August 14

At 6 A.M. on the fourteenth, every household went to the graveyard with the following offerings: incense, water, rice, and eggplant. On the tray with the offerings was a bell and the household *tōrō.* The visiting dead—for by now they had arrived—must be fed: hence the offerings of food and water. Offerings were made both at home (at the *butsudan*) and at the graveyard. One of the *tōrō* was burned at the grave while the woman of the household recited a short *nembutsu;* then the other three *tōrō* were taken down to Yoroizaki Beach, where they too were burned while a *nembutsu* was recited. The dead having arrived, the small signs to them were no longer needed. The *tōrō* burned at the grave was to call the spirit's attention to their remains (to remind them that they were dead) and the rest on the beach to indicate the direction in which they had to eventually return: east.

On the afternoon of this day, the *hatsu-bon* households were visited by a group of the *nembutsu* grandmothers. The group would count the *hatsu-bon* households and divide their numbers among them. If they were kin to a particular household, they would include themselves in that *ie*'s group; if not, they would be included in the group on the basis of the village geographical divisions. Thus the groups were of about ten to fourteen grandmothers, depending on the household. The *nembutsu* took two hours, with the usual three breaks for drinks; afterward, the family served the grandmothers a meal. At some point during these prayers, the priest arrived and performed his prayers for the *nyugeshi*. The grandmothers were given gifts of sugar and a package from their leftover meals to take home.

Again in the evening, the *hatsu-bon* households had their close kin over (no elaborate banquets this time), and everyone went dancing in the temple courtyard.

August 15

On the morning of the fifteenth, the eldest male grandchild in each of the *hatsu-bon* households helped with the making of the gate *(mon)* for the last part of the festivities. This gate was made of two long bamboo poles wrapped in white cloth and was carried by two of the children later in the afternoon.

The same morning, the younger men from the *hatsu-bon* households made the *kasabuki*. This group was from the generation of parents and could include married as well as unmarried men—men who had already become household head, as well as those who had not succeeded yet (thus they came from the *dōkyūsei* of twenties to forties). The *kasabuki* is an umbrella covered with flowers, stars, and moons and hung with objects that represent the possessions of the *nyugeshi*. Among the objects hung were paper cutouts of grapes, tomatoes, eggplant, green peppers, melon, squash, cucumber, and corn. These represented the crops that (in the past) were harvested at Obon.[10] The objects that represented the dead included the following: a lamp, a man's black obi, a woman's obi, a vase of flowers, hair, a box of money, scissors, a mirror, prayer beads, a bell, tobacco, a lighter, and a scroll with all the names of the dead on it. The *kasabuki* was made in the household of the first person who died during the year, and that family had to serve the makers of the *kasabuki* a meal after their work.

The final ceremony at the temple would take place any time between 3:00 and 4:30 in the afternoon. Before going to the temple, the *nembutsu* grandmothers met and prayed on Yoroizaki. Present were the young men of the *hatsu-bon* households who had brought the *kasabuki* and the white poles for the gate. These were placed before the altar, and the Cooperative head began the ceremony by offering rice and tea over the leaves on the fire. Each young man from the *hatsu-bon* households did the same, and then the grandmothers began their *nembutsu*. This was a summoning of the *nyugeshi* to Yoroizaki and to the *kasabuki* in order that they be ready for the second part of the ceremony to be held at the temple. At the end of the grand-mother's invocations, the *kasabuki* was taken to sit in front of the Rōjin-kai, and the white poles were left against the temple gates.

Fourteen of the village grandfathers began to arrive at the temple, where they changed into the yellow and green kimonos worn for the "Dainem-butsu" (the "Sasa Nembutsu"). Two of the older grandfathers remained in their formal black kimonos and waited in the temple to give advice to the young men from the *hatsu-bon* households. They were supposed to come and ask advice from the older men about their sorrow. The grandfathers seemed to reply in a formulaic way, saying that all was well, not to grieve.

The villagers gathered outside the Rōjin-kai, dressed in their best clothes—often a kimono—and the men carried *kobana* again. One or two men from the *dōkyūsei* of fifty-year-old men invariably would beat on the large drum set up in the courtyard of the Rōjin-kai. This was mostly to entertain the waiting crowd. Then, finally, the grandfathers appeared car-rying bamboo stalks, wearing their prayer beads around their necks, and chanting the *nembutsu*. One of the younger men beat the drum to keep them in rhythm, while the grandfathers made a circle next to the *kasabuki*, pointed their bamboo poles toward the center, and recited the very long "Sasa Nembutsu." As they sang, the grandmothers around them fanned the men to keep them cool (see Figure 17). At the end of the prayer, the young man who had carried the *kasabuki* (usually the youngest of the group of *hatsu-bon* households) picked up the umbrella and went running toward the temple.

The villagers followed the grandfathers into the temple courtyard through the back, while the *kasabuki* carrier and his followers circled around to the front entrance. Then the umbrella had to circle around the temple courtyard—with all the dead person's kin following—three times clockwise. The *kasabuki* stopped before the temple entrance where the priest waited, standing before the exterior altar, which had been filled with offerings for the entire village dead. Here he prayed for the dead, giving them new Buddhist names.

At a signal toward the end of his prayer, the lamp in the *kasabuki* was lit and the carrier then ran out of the courtyard with the umbrella, thus tak-ing the dead with him. Actually, the *kasabuki* was returned to the house in which it had been made and carefully taken apart so it could be used again the next year. The *hatsu-bon* families finally took their *ihai* home, for their ancestors had been properly incorporated and were no longer dangerous or liminal. They were truly on their way to becoming *hotoke-sama*.

The *nembutsu* grandmothers remained behind in the courtyard and, while the grandfathers ate and drank with the priest inside the temple, the grandmothers danced their Obon *odori*. This was the same dance that all the villagers had danced for two nights, but done, as one young *yome-san* said, with flavor. The grandmothers took turns singing the song from the platform and beating out the rhythm on the drum (which one of the men had carried over from the Rōjin-kai), while they danced the dance that told the dead it was time to return—that their visit was appreciated, but it was now over.

At the houses of the *hatsu-bon*, there was another feast for the kin of the household. Again there was dancing at the temple courtyard until dawn. At midnight, the *yome-san* of the household had to go to Yoroizaki Beach and send a candle floating on a makeshift boat east into the ocean, to send the dead back on their way.

Figure 17. The grandfathers reciting the "Dainembutsu" (D. P. Martinez)

August 16

At 11 A.M. on the morning of the sixteenth, the concluding ceremony for Obon was held on Ōtsu Beach (Yoroizaki is too small). One man from each household was present, dressed in their kimonos and carrying the flags that the children had made on the twelfth. Leaving the flags to one side so that they lined the cliff wall facing the beach, the men sat in two rows, facing each other. They sat according to two major geographical divisions of the village. At one end of these two rows were the Kumi-ai *chō* and the *semmu-san;* at the other end were trays set with a broth made of sake and *wakame,* along with bottles of sake. Then the men (again, from the *dōkyūsei* of twenties to forties) from the *hatsu-bon* households carried these trays to the Cooperative executives and offered them the food and drink. Bowing, they drank a tiny amount of sake. Then the young men from the *hatsu-bon* families split into two groups and went down the row of villagers, offering them *wakame* and sake, most of the people taking but a drop of sake. Once everyone had been offered some food and drink, the Cooperative executives were once again given the *wakame* and sake. A bow marked the end of this ceremony, which was supposed to be an offering of thanks from the *hatsu-bon* families to everyone in the village, for the entire village was involved in helping with the first Obon for their *nyugeshi.*

The grandmothers began their "Urabon Nembutsu" on this afternoon and continued until August 24. These *nembutsu* were for the salvation of all the living members of the village.[11]

Conclusion: Obon and the Villagers

The descriptions I have given of Obon have been brief, but even so it is clear that, as with all Kuzaki rites, the rituals surrounding the Kuzaki feast of the dead are complex and loaded with many meanings. It is useful to review quickly the aspects of ritual that I have mentioned above and relate them to Obon. Many village rituals involve the work of the entire family. This is as true of Obon as it was of the New Year. Thus, the duties of a household are as follows:

1. The grandmothers and wives of the household make all the food for visitors, who include the *nembutsu* grandmothers and the village priest; they prepare all the offerings for the *butsudan;* clean and make offerings at the household's grave; they say *nembutsu* at home and at the graves; the *yome-san* will send the dead back toward the east on the sixteenth. If the household is a *hatsu-bon ie,*

then the women are responsible for visiting kin and for several large feasts as well.

2. The grandfathers and the men of the households do little but represent the household at all the major ceremonies of Obon. In the *hatsu-bon* households, the younger men must make the *kasabuki* and the eldest grandson must help make the *mon*.

3. The children enjoy themselves at this time; their only duty is to help make the family banner for the temple.

If we look at the wider roles, the roles of the *dōkyūsei* during Obon, we find that once again, every member of the village is involved through their age-grades:

1. The grandmothers pray throughout Obon for the safe arrival of the dead, for the safety of the village, for the progress of the ancestors toward the Pure Land, and for the departure of the dead.

2. The grandfathers, too, have their *nembutsu*, which is to bring the *nyugeshi* to the temple.

3. The *dōkyūsei* of men in their 40s and 50s have the task of representing their households at the banquets held by kin, as well as at all the ceremonies.

4. The firemen act as policemen during the Obon dancing.

5. The Seinendan organize the dancing.

The young women and daughters-in-law (the Fujin-kai) are the two age-grades missing here, but as is so often the case, the work of Obon keeps these two groups busy at home (see the first list).

Of all the work done during Obon, the grandmothers' *nembutsu* is the most important. In their role of Nembutsu-bāsan, they are not only invoking the dead, they are trying to protect the village from the uninvited dead. They are also the ones who help send the dead back east as well as the women who pray for the salvation of all souls—living and dead—in the village. Again, we see that if the work of the men in Shinto rituals is to see to the protection and safeguarding of the village, then the women during Obon see to the protection and safeguarding of the individuals within the village, of households, and of the ancestors who are returning.

To describe Buddhism with its emphasis on the salvation of the dead as otherworldly and Shintoism with its concern for the well-being of the entire living village as this-worldly would be to repeat a truism that holds for Buddhism in other parts of the world. What is most interesting about Shinto and Buddhist ritual in Kuzaki is that there exists a structural similarity in the roles of men and women in both religions. Thus, whether their role is to ensure the well-being of the living or the dead, the women in both cases are concerned with the welfare of the *individual*. Men's participation in ritual is, on the other hand (save for boat launchings), in the interest of the *village as a whole*. Thus, as described above, even when men recite sutras for the ancestors, it is for all the ancestors of the village—an undifferentiated and potentially infinite group. The prayers of the grandmothers are for named individuals. Table 5 makes this point clearer.

The opposition perceived by the villagers themselves that Shintoism is for women and Buddhism is for men does not seem to hold at all. An interesting aspect of this is that the religion associated with the female—Shinto —relies on the men to act in the central roles of village safekeeping, while the women are responsible for the individual households. Buddhism— supposedly the men's religion—is totally dependent on women for the

Table 5. Ritual participation by sex

Rite	Main Actors
Caring for the household Shinto deities	women (daughters-in-law)
Caring for the household's ancestors	women (grandmothers)
Worship of the sea deities for safety diving, fishing, and in thanks for *dairyō*	women (all divers)
Worship of field deities	women
Worship of Jizō-sama	mothers
Thrice yearly prayers for the new dead and ancestors who have anniversaries in individual village households	women (grandmothers)
Setting up and enacting Hachiman	men (including grandfathers, *matsuri* Cooperative executives, household heads, young men's club)
Setting up and enacting Nifune matsuri	men (same as above)
Prayers for all the village ancestors during the spring and autumnal equinoxes	men (grandfathers)
Making *noshi awabi* [i]	men (grandfathers)

i. I include this here because the making of *noshi awabi* and its continual presentation to Ise Shrine as tribute from Kuzaki are meant to ensure that the village receives special privileges, such as the ritual done in Ise for Nifune matsuri.

safety of both the village's living and dead. It is possible to explain the paradox structurally by pointing out that, in each case, the men and women act as mediators for potentially dangerous powers. The women's role seems to be to mediate for the household with the *kami* and ancestors. The men mediate for the village with the *kami* and ancestors. In a structural analysis, it is only fitting that these categories be mediated by those who are not generally associated with that religion—that is, the male religion by women and the female religion by men. One problem with this analysis is that the villagers never gave me any hint that this is the way they thought of the roles of individuals in Shinto or Buddhism, so it can only be advanced tentatively. Yet the symbolic importance of male and female roles still holds when we concentrate on the more obvious aspect of Kuzaki ritual as a way in which the ideal community is depicted.

What is interesting about the role of the age-grades is that it shows how persistently the ideal of Kuzaki as a community is upheld in ritual. Individual households each have their duty, with members of the household each given a role. Outside the household, the age-grades work together for the benefit of the entire village. It is no accident that the roles of the age-grades can be compared to the various roles of each generation within the household. As I mentioned in chapter 3, the village could be depicted as one large kin group, all descended from the Shinto deity Amaterasu. Whether the ceremony is Shinto or Buddhist in nature, the working out of the roles is similar.

None of this means that Obon is entirely like the Shinto rituals previously described. There are elements that are similar and importantly so: the making of the *tōrō* and *kasabuki* and the aspect of public performance both echo the notions of *tsukuri* and *mitate* found in the making of *noshi awabi*. However, the opposition between the collective group and the individual is a key difference between, on the one hand, the Shinto Nifune and Hachiman-san matsuri, which are held mainly to benefit the village as a whole, and Obon on the other, which involves the entire village yet is concerned with the well-being of the members of the individual households. I only want to stress the fact that these ceremonies, so different in character, are founded on the same premise: that the villagers must cooperate in order to achieve anything, and they must be seen to be working together. This premise is the same for economic and political village life as it is for social and religious life. That is not to say that there was no conflict in Kuzaki—there was—but the ideal was harmony, and both the households and the villagers strove to work together in a harmonious manner.

That ritual in Kuzaki was geared toward presenting this ideal community is not an unusual point to make about Japan. Many anthropologists of Japan have noted the working of ritual in this way. In her study of a Japanese mountain village, Moon notes that the village's most important festival, Saruoi-matsuri, has a message that "is straightforward enough: that the god of the village ensures the prosperity of its residents, and that they should live in harmony and should cooperate with each other" (1989, 350–351). Ashkenazi tells us that all Japanese festivals and festival rituals are "also social affairs" with the opportunity to "exhibit matters of social importance" (1983, 19). Bestor points out that even in urban Japan, *matsuri* management and activities "reflect rigid sexual and age-graded divisions of labor" (1985, 131) and Davis' analysis of fishermen's ritual calls such sexual and age-graded divisions of labor a "mythical charter" (1977, 26). Plath, it seems to me, described it best when he noted (1964) that if we accept the household as the basic social unit in Japan, then ancestor worship could be seen as the family, in a sense, worshipping itself as part of the family of god. This analogy could be pushed further to state that village festivals can be seen as the villagers worshipping the village's own structural principles.

Durkheimian as this is, it is the most obvious aspect of Japanese ritual. It leads on to one further set of questions about this worship of structural principles: If the sexual division of labor in Kuzaki ritual expresses the fact that men should be responsible for the well-being of the community while the women should be responsible for the individuals within the community, what does this tell us about the structure of the Kuzaki household and the structure of the village? How are these seen to be made? And, if we look outside of the village to urban, industrialized Japan, how does this relate to issues of gender? Finally, to return to the central question of this book: Who are the *ama* that the Japanese see them as independent women, and what does this tell us about Japanese women in general?

CHAPTER 8

Ritual, Gender, and Identity

She turned a page at random. "It would, however, be dangerous at this stage to embark on any extensive analysis . . .", she read. "Oh, what cowards scholars are! When you think how poets and novelists rush in with *their* analyses of human heart and mind and soul of which they often have far less knowledge than darling Tom has of his tribe. And why do they find it so difficult to begin or start anything—they must always *commence*—have you noticed?"
—Barbara Pym, *Less than Angels*

The last chapter ended with what was a deceptively neat model: the ways in which the different and complementary abilities of men and women are used in Japanese ritual. Women can deal with the wild, the unfettered; after all, they socialize children. Men maintain the boundaries between the wild and the social. Women can cross these boundaries, calling the dead in, for example, or moving from being an outsider to an insider in the household, in a way that most men don't have to. Men are, despite their prominence in the public outside, *of* the inside, of the patriline. This is not necessarily a new observation about women in Japan; they are after all polluted creatures, menstruation being an old and powerful source of pollution in Japan. And Buddhism was no kinder to women in this regard than Shintoism or Confucianism, although Shintoism appears to have respected women for the power that the ability to pollute conferred on them. It is probably no coincidence that women become more important in public ritual, in the household care of the dead, long after they cease being fertile. What I would like to add to the analysis offered in the last chapter is that while the model about men's and women's complementary roles is very neat and rather Durkheimian, as well as amenable to structuralist analysis, it ignores the fact that people can be unpredictable.

Women may not be able to or want to have children, and men may not want to marry and take part in the household business or in community life. While both men and women (and their children) are necessary to the continuity of social life, they can also forgo their duties. One of the arguments about the concept of the household in Japan speaks to this paradox. Maintaining the household—or in this case the community—is what matters, and the roles people play in its maintenance are crucial; thus it is filling the roles that is important. The strategies for how this is done are governed by ideas of relatedness and the ideals of the patriline, but they are strategies and they are negotiable (Bachnik 1983). There are, however, limits to what and how much can be negotiated for individuals, as the examples of two people I knew in the village demonstrate.

Being in Conflict

I made two friends in the village who, I came to realize as time passed, were both marginalized—and for different reasons. The first was a woman whom I encountered frequently when I did participant observation work in the Kuzaki inns and who was part of the *shinseki* of the household in which I lived, so that I also saw her diving and fishing. Y-chan, as I shall call her,[1] was dynamic, hardworking, and full of fun and humor. She was in frequent demand to do geisha or hostessing work in the village inns, and she worked hard to perfect her skills at this. Singing was one of her great hobbies, and it was she who made me work on the karaoke songs I was asked to sing on every social occasion in the village. Y-chan had a fisherman husband, two children, and only one in-law to look after, and it seemed to me that everything she did, she did with enthusiasm. This was also the impression of a Western friend, another woman, who came to visit me in the field: "This woman is really something."

And yet my friendship with Y-chan was the source of tension within the village. People, male and female, young and old, warned me about doing things with her; the lecture I described being given in chapter 1 about my nights out drinking is only one example of the veiled references made to this woman. I was also told that she was a poor diver (in fact, her catches were average), a lazy diver, and slow to take part in village tasks. It was only toward the end of fieldwork that people spoke to me more straightforwardly about Y-chan: Did I not understand that she had a bad heart *(warui kokoro)?* All she wanted to do was to earn lots of money to start her own inn. When I would point out that this seemed the goal of many people in Kuzaki, I was told that Y-chan was different, for she ignored her husband and children to pursue this aim. It was not that she ignored her husband's wishes that was the worst part—many women did that from time to time—but that she would not even sleep in the same room as him. Did I not know that? The picture continued to blacken. Even the village priest pointed out to me that her children suffered because of her lack of attention to them; did I not realize how much time he had spent trying to help this family?

I tried to understand this different evaluation of what constituted a good person by talking to my other close friend in the village, a young unmarried man whom I shall call M-chan, and I was surprised by his response. "Was it that one way Y-chan seemed to earn extra money was by sleeping with tourists that led to this negative view of her by others?" I asked. "It is none of your business," he said. "You could not prove one way or another that she has sex with tourists," he added, "and you should not pursue that line of discussion. But," M-chan went on, "you should realize that villagers do not care if a woman earns extra money from tourists through sex. If a woman's children are grown up, if her husband does not suffer because of it, it is her business and hers alone. It is wrong if other people were hurt by it, and that is that."

This discussion had interesting ramifications as well. The fact that I had arranged to spend a day out with M-chan visiting old Buddhist pilgrimage sites around Mie so that I could have this private conversation with him became a scandal of its own. Okamoto-san, my host, called in his cousin as head of the *dōzoku,* and he proceeded to lecture me on my day out. Did I not realize, I was told, that there was something wrong about M-chan? There he was, a young man with a good business, an only son with his own successful business, and he was not married—wasn't this odd? He was already old for marriage. His *kokoro* could not be good if he could not find a wife, and I should not be spending time with someone like that. It was their duty to warn me and my responsibility to them (the first time anyone had ever used the terms *"on"* and *"giri"* to me) not to get mixed up with a bad sort like that.

While ethnographically interesting, this conversation left me confused and shaken. If there was something wrong with M-chan, as implied—perhaps a lack of desire to marry through sexuality or just choosiness—what did my friendship with him imperil? Did villagers suspect that I had had an affair with him? How did this disapproval tally with the fact that people of all ages were always inviting me to have an affair or two because I was married and being celibate must be hard for me? While I did not voice these questions, I did inform my hosts that we had only been to see a few temples and that we had actually run into another foreign anthropologist doing the same thing; perhaps they would like to check this fact with *his* village?

The issue was actually similar to the point M-chan had made himself about Y-chan. No one would have minded what I did as long as I did not hurt others. Everyone knew I could not marry M-chan and I should not raise the possibility of a romance with him when it was his duty to find a wife and give his parents grandchildren. If he had a crush on me, and as time went on it seemed that he did, this would only stand in the way of his doing his duty. In such a situation, it is easy to see how others would believe that it had been wrong of me to encourage M-chan by spending too much time with him.

Yet underlying this was the sense that M-chan was perhaps even more different than having affection for a foreign woman might indicate. Despite his status as a fairly rich young man, he was still unmarried in 1991, when he must have been in his late thirties. It was not for lack of possible candidates, I was told—he just did not seem interested. "What was wrong with his *kokoro?*" I tried asking. No one knew. He was in many ways a nice guy —very responsible, very hard working—but he did not marry. This was a wrong in and of itself, and the only saving grace of our friendship appears to be that a small romance had grown up about his not marrying: People hinted that M-chan had not married because it was me he would have liked. I suspect the truth is that M-chan just did not want a wife, and my friendship provided a convenient cover for his bachelorhood. Still, an unmarried only child who chose to remain single was unforgivable in Kuzaki and contrasted with the other unmarried men who dutifully attended arranged interviews *(omiai)* with young women but were turned down because no one wanted to be a fisherman's wife. Such men were to be pitied, not censored.

If these examples seem to fit the well-known aphorism that Japan is a society where "the nail that sticks out must be hammered down," then I have made the point too simplistically. In fact, an unmarried younger brother caused no great comment if his older brother was successfully married with children. Thus the village eccentric, who had spent many years abroad and had returned to Japan somewhat odd, was never criticized. In fact, it might have been a bad thing if such an odd man had married, people implied, but as long as his brother carried on with the inn and his children did as well, it was all right. So too it was with the village socialist, whose free-range egg business was the butt of many jokes, but who had a loving wife, three happy children, and who found lots of time to give to village life. He headed the Kambe-kai, took part in village tasks, was a dutiful son, and, if he refused to learn the innkeeping business—well, his divorced sister and her children had come back to Kuzaki to help his parents with that, so it was all right. And there were one or two women whose lives resembled Y-chan's, but with grown children and husbands who did not complain of being ignored, as Y-chan's did, whatever they did in the inns was accepted as well. In short, it is the nail that sticks out *and causes injury to others* that must be hammered down—and that is an important distinction.

There is a cost, of course, in needing to always be aware of the feelings of others. People coped with the stress mainly through joking and, from my point of view, a lot of male drinking. The wife who said, "Take my husband, please, Lola-chan—all he wants is sex, and I am too tired to do it all the time," caused much hilarity with this offer, but she was making a real point: Her husband both drank and womanized too much and then came home to bother her. She was tired and at her tether's end, and making jokes about it seemed to be the best way of coping. The grandfather who talked of how his wife no longer interested him in bed "because she was so big" was also joking, yet everyone knew that he was bullied by his very tall and large wife, and joking about her saved face, as it were. Neither of these people would think of ignoring their responsibilities to their families or to the wider community, and so they won the attention and support of their friends. Y-chan, on the other hand, had little support from anyone; and M-chan had older people concerned, while the people of his own generation spoke of him in more sympathetic terms.

The Self in Context

How, then, are we to understand the relationship between the way village life was organized and the ways in which people lived within what appears to be a highly structured and even rigid society? Several approaches have dominated the anthropology of Japan almost from its very beginning, yet they often seem contradictory and beg various questions. Is Japan a shame culture in which the embarrassment of being caught out is greater than any possibly internalized guilt—where duty and indebtedness are more important than honor or individual action (Benedict 1974)? Is Japan such a hierarchical society that belonging to the right group matters more than anything (Nakane 1970) and not belonging leads to marginalization (Valentine 1990)? Is it a situational society where the fluidity of inside and outside (Hendry 1995, Bachnik 1994) also allows for a fluidity of self, the movement back and forth between different situations forming a web of relationships that creates a multiple sense of self (Kondo 1990; Rosenberger 1992)? All these have been offered as interpretations for what it means to be a person living within a society that seems best represented through Durkheimian functionalism rather than postmodernist theories.

All these models of the Japanese self need to be understood within a historical context. Mentioned previously was the fact that Kuzaki could only resemble the ideal hometown (*furusato*) because of modern economics. Migrant labor was no longer viable, while commuting to jobs in the city was; diving remained lucrative, but fishing was dying out as a way of life; and tourism filled the economic gaps for a population that was less mobile than in the past. Postwar Kuzaki was a place where all the generations appeared to live together. Because of domestic tourism it still had young people in the village (while other rural areas are largely depopulated, cf. Moon 1989), and for these reasons village households were generally cohabiting economic units of production and reproduction. The village had enough people of all age groups to fill each and every role that the *ie*-like age-grade system required, but this was not the case in the past when young men and women left the village for long periods of time, and even middle-aged men might continue to live and work outside of Kuzaki until retirement age. What the strategies of inheritance and fulfilling ritual and social duties were before the 1950s was hard to discern, for the people who would have known were dead and gone and the oldest villagers were full of stories of what they had done as migrant divers and fishermen. Occasionally I would be told that "my grandmother told me it was like that," but these tales only filled some gaps. We can glean, from the accounts of the first westerners to travel in Japan in the nineteenth century, that initially the peasantry's behavior did not fit the more middle-class model that came to dominate the twentieth century. Embree's account of Suye (1946) shows a much looser sense of village *seken* in prewar Japan.

Yet even the supposed contemporary dominance of middle-class culture must be approached with caution. Kelly (1992) has argued that the middle-class model that the Japanese farmers he studied tried to fit into was less a straitjacket than a guide or loose set of rules. The same might be said of Kuzaki, where, for the first time in generations, the people were able to try and follow the rules more completely than in the past. It might be said, then, that we could think of the social model as one that constrains (cf. Lebra 1984) and that can lead some individuals to feel unhappy and unfulfilled. On the other hand, the model, with its built-in logic of progress, also allowed many people to feel that they were doing the right things at the right times—that they had some control over the unfolding of their lives. Thus, joining the Seinendan, rowing at Nifune, perhaps becoming Seinendan *chō*, and playing a large political as well as ritual role might well allow a young man to plan on becoming Kumi-ai *chō* one day. A young married woman might plan that, when her generation became dominant in the

Fujin-kai, the club money would be spent differently. All *yome-san* dreamed of the day they would be running the household without having to defer to their mothers-in-law, and the fact that some families had adhered to the pattern of owning another house where the old folk would live apart from the younger couple meant that the dream did not involve hoping for an early death in the family.

Thus the constraints of society also could be seen as guiding principles that could lead to a contented old age in which a person still has duties and responsibilities, but where there is also the freedom of the old to say and do pretty much what they want. While it was considered worrying if young women spent too much time together gossiping or a young man spent every night out with his friends, old men and women might well gather daily for little chats as they walked grandchildren or came and went from the fields. Frequent naps, snacking on sweets, and control of the television during the day were also the prerogative of the grandparents in the household. There was also the prestige of the ritual work of the old.

There is something clearly Confucian about this model in which the social contract is seen to be more important than selfish individual wants and the happiness of being old is that the tension between what the self desires and what society demands is seen to be resolved. It also echoes the Buddhist notion that the self is an illusion and thus its desires are illusory as well. In Kuzaki, as in much of Japan, doing the right thing might well be difficult, but the moral evaluation made of a person was based precisely on their ability to sacrifice their selfish desires to the greater good. As an insightful essay by Kuwayama (1990) indicates, the village could be described as a panoptic society where all persons are constantly being watched and assessed. The harmonious ideal, the *tatemae,* masks relationships of power that are constantly being renegotiated (the *honne*).

Thus the selection of a man as Kumi-ai *chō* in his fifties, as described in chapter 4, is the culmination of a series of observations made by his peers and elders throughout his life in the village, as well as the end result of choices that he has also made. Most important to keep in mind is that none of this occurs without constant negotiation. Given two or three possible candidates, all sorts of factors must be weighed and discussed, and anyone with an opinion should be heard. Also, as in the ritual of Nifune, nothing can ever happen without involving the effort and cooperation of practically everyone in the village.

To argue this is to argue for a reassessment of current theories that postulate a multiple sense of self in Japan. As Lebra suggests (1984), the conflict between the self and social demands is probably the same in Japan as in the United States; it is the ideology that lends moral value to this conflict that is different. The difference is one of "the cultural coding of experience, not necessarily in the experience as such" (296). The spread of the cult of individualism (a term that masks different concepts even in the West; see Lukes 1973) in places like the United States means that, perhaps, more people feel able to articulate their sense of constraint and feelings of opposition to the status quo than in collectivist societies. It does not mean, however, as my examples have shown, that Japanese individuals do not feel constrained or that they do not have agency.

Rosenberger (1992) concedes that the Japanese "sense of self" might not be very different from a Western one. That in fact we need to reassess the lived reality of the Western self and see the relationship between Japan's "dividuals" (to borrow from a similar discourse on India that has been extended to the Pacific) and Western *individuals* as different points on a continuum. I would suggest that there is no such monolith as the "Western self," and that the situational self that feminists and phenomenologists propose as the experience of all selves is a generalization anthropologists might allow themselves to accept. In fact, as Mauss (1985) argued in his seminal work on the self, the difference exists not in the lack of a notion of a unitary sense of self in some societies but rather in the social expectations about the roles the self is allowed to play. In some Western societies—the United States being the most obvious—the self is meant to dominate, so that there is no *apparent* conflict between actions and desires; in other societies, the socially constituted person is more important.

I am arguing, then, for a sense of self that is socially constructed (cf. Hendry 1986), but if this is true of Japan, it is also true of the United States. In the United States, people who feel that they are not being true to themselves—that they are constrained and unhappy—might go into therapy to try and fix this. In Japan, the person who says the same thing might well sigh and note that this is the way life is (cf. Plath 1980). As one woman, not from Kuzaki, once told me, "I had to learn to give in." The experience of constraint is not different, but what one does about it is. Self-sacrifice is highly valued in Japan; in the United States, this is seen to be a weakness.[2] But an odd thing happened with the return to analyses of personality in the 1990s: Societies were once again being analyzed and summed up with a terminology that smacked of psychoanalysis. A multiple sense of self might be every human's experience of life, but in using this term about the Japanese we are reminded that a nonunitary self is seen to be one of the symptoms of schizophrenia. The unintended implication is that there is something wrong with the Japanese—that they are not like us, whoever we are.

The Japanese self—if there is a single experience of self in Japan—is best described as a sense of self that is constantly embedded within its relationships, responsibilities, and negotiations with others. Certainly this is what Rosenberger (1992) and others have attempted to describe, although they appear to have trouble making the leap to the notion that all social beings are so embedded. The Japanese self must present itself differently, appropriately, in various situations. There is an assumption that the U.S. self is somehow expected to present itself in much the same way in all situations, and yet there are expectations of difference in relation to roles; an employer should not act like a lover, for example. This different weighting of such social expectations can be difficult to appreciate until experienced (cf. Kondo 1990), and certainly can feel like a burden to the ethnographer.

In Kuzaki, the constant awareness of what others were supposed to need was a social duty for all concerned, although it seemed to me that women bore the brunt of being sensitive to others' (for which read children's and men's) needs. An ambitious or hard-drinking, womanizing man who ignored or somehow abused his family was never going to be Kumi-ai chō, but no one ever lectured me about their kokoro. Men were, after all, men, as the women would laugh. The point is that with everyone trying to be sensitive to others' needs, two things can be said to happen: Some space is left for the self to develop, and a person is judged by how well she or he manages the conflict between selfish desires and social expectations. There is no end product, only a continuous process of becoming in which people attempt to orchestrate a variety of social roles (woman, mother, diver, grandmother, villager, ritual specialist, Japanese, etc.) into a coherent whole, into a person who fills all the necessary roles well. Above the personal, there exists group identity—the person as part of a diving nakama; belonging to an age-grade, to the village, to Kansai, to Japan. And even "identity," as descriptive of group sameness, should be seen as a term that describes processes of identification. Depending on circumstances, one could present oneself as an ama, proudly from Kuzaki or from Kansai, or as a Japanese.

In Kuzaki it was the successful bringing together of all the roles a self had to play that mattered. Kondo (1990) is correct to use the term "crafting" to describe the work people put into playing their social roles, but these must be balanced—centered, as it were—by the self. As I've noted, the relationship is dialogic: A good person tries hard, and trying hard creates a good person. So being called a skilled diver or a nice guy implied a whole moral package—trying one's best and valued for one's efforts. No one, it was clear, got it right all the time: Matsui-san got to be Hachiman, but everyone still remembered his pig-farming fiasco. The closest to perfection one could get was old age, and only the dead had the opportunity to be perfect. In fact, in all of this, the dead—the ancestors—serve as a reminder of life's goals, as well as an obligation: They must have descendants to ensure their afterlife, and to understand this we need to think once more about rituals.

The Dead

It is a truism perhaps that rituals to do with the dead are really for and about the living. I mentioned that Barley (1995) was critical of how this approach meant that researchers often assumed that it was enough to state that the organization of rituals for the dead mirrored what it was the living were supposed to be going through. In Japan it has been argued that rituals for the dead mirror the life cycle of the living, that death must be managed and marked with the same sort of events that mark life: the first visit to the Shinto shrine, celebration of the ages of three, five, seven, nineteen, and forty-two, as well as marriage. Kato (forthcoming), a Japanese doctor, notes that there is a continuum between the living and dead that makes it difficult to draw clear lines. When is a person truly dead?[3] We must add, in a traditional setting such as Kuzaki, a further notion: Such public events also reiterate the sense of community for the living as well as acknowledging the continued near presence of the dead.

Burying and worshipping the dead are arduous and expensive processes; both involve the entertaining of family members, while both kin and neighbors are meant to help with the necessary work. In some ways, this is also a tautology: Since kin and neighbors must be entertained, kin and neighbors must help with the preparations for funerals and anniversaries. Since the dead must be properly worshipped to avoid becoming dangerous hungry ghosts that threaten the living, kin and neighbors help each other with this in order not to be bothered by such creatures. But the situation, as should be obvious from my all-too-brief description in the last chapter, is slightly more complex than that (or perhaps I should say, more *simple*). Male kin and male neighbors must be entertained, and so it is female kin and neighbors who pitch in with the labor. As gifts of money, drink, and food come from other households, women do the work, and this includes decorating altars, making food, preparing return gifts, preparing the corpse (men in Kuzaki dug the graves), and organizing the gifts for the sutra-reciting grandmothers and the payment for the priest who must visit the household on these occasions. In the world of the living, the women of the household do the practical day-to-day work, and these women might include the husband's sister who returns for the event, but their main body is composed of women who have married in. The division of labor was one I saw in all ritual performance in Kuzaki: men in the center, women on the periphery. At the level of the village, as I have argued, these rituals are often about the making and shoring up of village boundaries, reaffirming a sense of place, a sense of *uchi* as opposed to *soto;* but for funerals and anniversaries, the protection of the village against stray dead is left to the women. When the ritual is, we might say, more about the family than the village as a whole, then men remain in the public eye, but women take on the burden of work in a more public way with the very obvious presence of the grandmothers, who pray daily at the temporary gates.

One way in which I tried to understand this in the past was to think about how women are seen to be able to better deal with the outside world, being both metaphorically and literally more of the outside (see also Napier 1998 and Stefánsson 1998). In Kuzaki, this became obvious when I was taken in July to worship the ancestors of the women of Kuzaki in a graveyard on Mount Asama, a famous pilgrimage area where many households had erected stupas (*sutoba* or *toba* in Kuzaki dialect) to their matrilineal ancestors. Come August, these same dead would be worshipped in villages around Mount Asama by the women who had married into their households, but in July it was the daughters, granddaughters, and/or sisters who went to worship *their* dead separately in this sacred place. This pilgrimage to a mountain mirrored the monthly visit Kuzaki women made to Mount Sengen (chapter 4). When I asked about this additional form of worship (additional to the daily prayers in the household), I was told that this was what women did: worship. What struck me was that women were more likely to worship in out-of-the-way places than men—the places some older villagers told me were dangerous (in some traditions, mountains were held to be too sacred for women to even set foot on). When I asked what men did, I was told that they worshipped the *kami* as well—sometimes. Part of belonging in Kuzaki, as already mentioned, was to take part in all public acts of worship, even if you did not bother with prayers much at home. You could not live in the village if you did not take part in village ritual, since to reject this was to reject village social life. For women, then, before they turned sixty and became experts in helping the dead become nothing, years were spent becoming something themselves, as well as literally creating *(tsukuru)* life. It is not just their biological powers that are needed—they certainly make life—but they must also maintain social life at a level we might call infrastructural, while attempting to fit in, to belong themselves. At all levels, age and gender are important: Without women, men would be able to accomplish nothing. And in Kuzaki this sense carried over into worship of her kin even after a woman had married out.[4] Thus large public events that reaffirmed village solidarity and that created village identity were one thing, but women believed that they maintained the family, and it was from the family that the village was built.

What is clear from considering the variety of ritual life in Kuzaki is that rituals *must be* understood as polysemous. They can be very personal, about individual hopes and desires; they are also about the roles each person plays, as well as being about larger identities such as that of the household, the village, the region, and even the nation. At the core are clear ideas about gender and patriarchy. The sacrificial but bloodless offerings are the way in which men make the social and claim reproduction for themselves; it is a way of making descent between sons and fathers.[5] Although women maintain ties with their families, this is, as I have mentioned, at the margins. The symbolic violence of such rituals (Bloch 1992) is that they create the collective to which the individual must in part give in. This might be clearer if we use Taoist ideas of yin and yang, which so many informants liked to tell me were essential to understanding Japanese society. Japanese rituals and the rites of creating and becoming acknowledge the role of both the male and female; there is meant to be a balance and symmetry, as well as notions of superiority and inferiority. In Kuzaki women made life, literally; they also made the dead, metaphorically. Men as part of the patriline were the center, and they made the social; in minor ways, they also dealt with the dead, generally chasing the dead away once they had been named—that is, socialized. This socialization, by the village priest, is perhaps a mimetic event mirroring the socialization of the living by women, and if we follow Taussig (1993), it is the sort of event through which social reality is generated. And if in life it is men who maintain the boundaries of the social and keep the community intact and safe, in death it is the women who maintain the boundaries between the living and dead as fluid—and yet they must also keep the community safe. This inversion matches the myth Ebersole (1992) found so important: Myths about the dead and death in early Japan reaffirmed the importance of the male in social reproduction, despite women's role in biological reproduction. Ritual was the way in which men reproduced the social; women, through their affinity with the outside, their identification with all the untamed powers of the outside, ended up in the kingdom of the dead. In Japanese life, they have been relegated to caring for the ancestors, who must be remembered and worshipped and whose worship is yet another way of reaffirming the social relations of the living.

In a sense, as I have described, all ritual work is work that keeps the living safe. The minor rituals that are performed by women—daily, monthly, or on the margins of the larger rituals dominated by men—are just as important as the more complex *matsuri*. Moreover, large ritual occasions can be imbued with personal meaning, albeit in different ways from the smaller rites that often seem to be intensely personal; both are thus dialogic. As previously noted, women pray for themselves and their family, they give thanks and make offerings for safety at sea and for good health, they might pray to Jizō-sama for a child, or they take care of the offerings in thanksgiving for a *dairyō*. Men tend to take part in ceremonies that are clearly about the social whole but that can mark a man's success in village life or bring the hope of acquiring a wife for an unmarried man. Both types of worship might well be described as a way of focusing or channeling power correctly; both types of ritual use clapping at the start and end of prayers precisely to make the deities pay attention. And both types of rituals have a pragmatic side to them: the symbolism of the contract, which, as discussed in chapters 6 and 7, is obvious and important. We also have to understand that larger rituals are about creating large identities. Generally, the focus is on community identity, but also—as the Meiji government so well understood—national identity is created. Thus, while Japanese claim not to be religious, rituals have not disappeared but have been relegated to the arena of culture: We do this because we are Japanese.

All of these points apply to rituals that have to do with the dead as well. But the relationship between the living and the dead is made more complex by the fact that while *kami* are a form of power made manifest, the dead are in the process of becoming *(naru)*. As noted above, in popular parlance they are "becoming nothing" or have "become not" *(naku narimashita)*, a polite euphemism often used to indicate that someone has died. This term has, to my mind, strong Buddhist overtones. To become nothing is, of course, the end process of many rebirths and of working toward transcendence, which involves realizing that the self is but a powerful illusion. In Japan as in other Buddhist societies, this journey is—among ordinary people—not one made solely by an individual striving to become one with the Buddha, but it is a path that requires the work, the making by the living, particularly of one's descendants. As with the possession by Hachiman-san, it is both a becoming and a making; however, the making that is in one's own hands during life becomes the work of the collective, of others, in death.

The Dead as Other

The structuralist parallels still stand that Ooms (1976), among others, has pointed to in the relationship between rites that mark a person's passage through life and those that mark the dead's journey toward paradise or nothingness, kami-hood or rebirth. Yet there are significant differences. The life-cycle rituals of being presented at the Shinto shrine at birth, at age three, five, seven, nineteen, and forty-two, with their accompanying rites of purification, only mark a person's passage through life. They represent the process but do not necessarily make the person; as rites of passage, they are very schematic. Despite the care with which a child is socialized in Japan (cf. Hendry 1986), parents and others note personality differences, varying abilities, and character traits that are seen to be individual and not a result of upbringing. The making/becoming of a person, a never-ending process from a Japanese point of view, is not just in the hands of parents or society but also the result of what a person is willing or able to do. The dead, in contrast, are at the mercy of their kin. Without the correct rituals, offerings, celebrations, and daily worship, the dead can be doomed to hell or to an existence as ghosts.

Even in postmodern Japan, where so many people respond to surveys about religious belief or practice with a resounding no, the fact remains that most dead are seen off with Buddhist funerals. And young people who say they do not believe in an afterlife often, on the death of a parent, buy a household butsudan and use it to pray for their recent dead. The rebellion against religion seems to be a battle fought against religious institutions and priests who charge so much money for their services. More than one young Japanese has told me that when the time comes, they will pray to and for their parents on their own. Despite claiming not to believe in Buddhist ideas about death and the afterlife, more than one middle-aged Japanese has admitted to going into debt for a parent's funeral, because the rituals, feasts, and buying of a Buddhist name for the dead are expected and cannot be neglected for the sake of seken. If we think of seken as the awareness of others—people both known and unknown who judge and constrain—we find ourselves close to the concept of "habitus" (Bourdieu 1977). However, the element of judgment also speaks to Yamaguchi's (1991) ideas on *mitate* (the ability to compare and criticize). Thus an important part of *seken* is the idea of being *seen* by others; all of life becomes a performance, something that Goffman (1971) noted was in fact fundamental in Western everyday life as well.

Although the weight of *seken* can cause people to act, it is only the dead who should be seen as a total social fact. While it can be argued that the living can never, if taken individually, embody the culture as a whole because they are the sites of so much contestation—between the self and others, between different age groups, between what is male or female, between a local and national identity, between a national and global identity—the dead, as long as they are worshipped, are wholly Japanese. Take the stereotypic and orientalist depictions of the Japanese: hard-working; no sense of an individualized self; responding to particular contexts as needed rather than to some internal moral guide; apt to be friendly yet also prone to great violence, which is only understandable on their terms, not ours (whoever *we* might be); given to odd perversities; depending on silent communication, on rigid routines, and fixed social hierarchies—all of these apply to the dead far more than they do to any individual living Japanese. The ancestor who is worshipped daily and correctly, in a routine and rigid way, will act as guardian, silently communicating comfort and advice, responding as needed, and seemingly acquires a generalized rather than a specific character. If not worshipped, this same ancestor will visit bad luck, disease, and death on its descendants. The dead clearly are *the* Others, who in Simmel's (1964) sense are near yet far and embody qualities that are ours, mirroring the human while apparently transgressing what is human. It is no surprise, then, that in the past it was thought that the dead—even those cared for as good Buddhists—became *kami*. "*Kami*" has many meanings, but Kami as a deity with a possibly human form (rather than a location, a rock, or mountain) is both Japanese and from somewhere other than Japan. The point made by Yoshida (1983) that "stranger deities" *(marebito)* correspond very well to Simmel's description of the Stranger, or the Other, acquires particular force in this case. Even if many modern Japanese reject active belief in *kami* as superstitious (and any comparison with the rites of urbanized Japan will show how much the rituals related to these beliefs have declined, while rituals about the community have increased), it is still impossible to ignore the dead.

In a more metaphoric sense, and certainly at the level of my own analysis, the dead represent the Japanese as they know others—particularly westerners—see them: somehow liminal. They are like us (because modern and capitalists), yet not like us (because operating within a social framework that is so unique and unlike ours that they are more alien than not). The dead, always moving toward something—paradise—but needing the help of the living, are on a journey that could be compared to Japan's postwar development: moving toward a just democratic society but with the help and constant input of the West. The relationship is never equal, but it is strangely symbiotic: Without the living, the dead would never achieve paradise; without the help of the dead, the living might go through life unprotected against other powerful beings. So Japan and the Japanese will never achieve their aim of equality—economic or otherwise—without the West, but Japan also stands as a bulwark, an outpost, of democracy that the West needs in the Pacific. I don't believe that this metaphoric similarity is ever articulated by Japanese; I never heard anyone say such a thing, but the resemblances can best be summed up as a relationship of "Othering." At this basic level of generalization, then, both the Japanese as an object of study and discourse and the West as its structural Other mutually constitute each other. There is no such place as the Japan of stereotypic representations—not even the representations made by the Japanese themselves—although there is a country called Japan by English speakers. Conversely, there is no West as it is imagined by the Japanese, who describe that place usually by referring to simple binary oppositions (individualistic; all *honne* no *tatemae;* a loose social structure in which elders are not respected and all rules about social behavior are so vague as to be nonexistent).

This last stands as a critique of dead and gone anthropological approaches. Or does it? In chapter 1 I argued that studies on Japan have been far more nuanced than they might be represented, yet they have not debunked the image of Japan as a hierarchical society. Augé might call this part of anthropological "place making," where

> the fantasy of a founded ceaselessly re-founding place is only half fantasy. For a start, it works well—or rather, it has worked well: land has been cultivated, nature domesticated reproduction of the generations ensured; in this sense the gods of the soil have looked after it well. . . .
>
> It is also a semi-fantasy because, although nobody doubts the reality of the place held in common and the powers that threaten or protect it, nobody is unaware—nobody has ever been unaware—of the reality of other groups . . . and thus also of other gods; or of the need to trade and marry outside. There is nothing to suggest that, yesterday or today, the image of a closed and self-sufficient world could ever—even to those who diffuse it and therefore identify with it—be anything other than a useful and necessary image: not a lie

but a myth, roughly inscribed on the soil, fragile as the territory whose singularity it founds, subject (as frontiers are) to possible readjustment. (1995, 46–47)

If, as I have suggested, anthropology has not always fallen far into this trap, then whose is the fantasy, whose place making is it? In this ethnography, the work and mythologizing of the place called Kuzaki is that of the people of Kuzaki—but operating within the larger place making of the nation-state. Because the discourse of the Japanese nation-state is about blood, the land, identity, and pride in a different social structure, the people of Kuzaki continue to remake their place in the image of this ideology. They do this both despite and because of the ways in which they could easily be seen *not* to fit the dominant ideology. Rebellious subjects in the historical documents, marginal within feudal and even modern society—the people of Kuzaki strive to be Japanese because they could easily be accused of not being really Japanese. They might be Korean, or just outsiders to the place that is Japan—and yet, through their worship of Amaterasu, they place themselves firmly in the center of all things Japanese. This is not a form of mythmaking that is false, it is a response to the increased homogenization of the discourse of what it means to be Japanese. Ivy (1995) might well label it a discourse of the vanishing, which in this case is even more poignant because, by adhering to all things Japanese (rigid hierarchies—for example, the multigenerational *ie*), the people of Kuzaki might also be seen as in danger of becoming nothing more than images caught up in a production of nostalgia for a Japan that never was nor could be.[6]

But to consign the people of Kuzaki to such object making on my part would be to rob them of the characteristics that made others murmur that they were not quite Japanese: their strong women, a social organization that was more horizontal than hierarchical, a love of the sea, and a tolerance for difference despite their constant assessment of what constituted appropriate behavior. That is the bane of writing as an anthropologist and not as a novelist—the threat of creating a model that appears to explain all, to leave out individual agency. While this is not necessarily an ignored theme in the anthropology of Japan, it often seems to be the perceived representation of Japan: a society where structure is more important than individual wants or desires. What I hope to have achieved through the detailed description of rituals as performed by people is to show the interplay between structure and individuals.

In many ways, the emphasis on structure is a convenient depiction of Japan. As a nation-state, it has achieved a high level of homogeneous mythmaking, or what Yoshino (1992) would call "cultural nationalism." The violence of representation (Derrida 1976) is not just practiced by outside observers but by the Japanese representing themselves to outsiders. The strength of this discourse about blood, place, and identity is rarely worked out as completely in Japan as it seems to have been in Kuzaki. In fact, it might be said that such discourses in urban Japan depend not only on the mythology of place making—the *furusato,* as Robertson has argued (1991) —but also on the fact that some places can be pointed to and even visited as the representatives of this older, truer, more real Japan (Martinez 1989). Thus the perceived continuities with the hoary and ancient past, *mukashi, mukashi* (long ago, long ago, or once upon a time), acquire more force when academic tomes and articles can be produced attesting to the lived reality of such places. Yet as I have noted more than once, Kuzaki can represent this Japan only because of historical circumstances—because of radical changes to a fishing community's lifestyle and because of the opportunities for work in nearby Toba and Ise. If we ask, "What's in it for the people of Kuzaki?" one possible answer is acceptance as Japanese. The totalizing discourse of the nation-state makes for marginality (Yamaguchi 1977), and many modern Japanese attempts to buy the lifestyle of the middle classes (Clammer 1997) are about being just as Japanese as the next person. In the 1980s, the people of Kuzaki could buy the lifestyle but not erase the suspicion that they were still somehow different, so what better claim to Japaneseness than to assert very ancient roots?

This is not to say that this was all fantasy on the part of the people of Kuzaki. Historically, their rituals, beliefs, and practices were old and certainly more detailed and complete than the ritual practices of many other Japanese. It is the choice involved in continuing or not with these practices that becomes important. Bestor (1988) has argued that this way of making identity by giving emphasis to continuity with the past is "traditionalism" as opposed to an "invention of tradition." By bringing the past into the present (cf. Peel 1984; Sahlins 1985), a symbolic representation was being *made:* Kuzaki *was* Japan, even if the rest of Japan appeared to have lost this quality. For the people of Kuzaki, the becoming was in the making.

Notes

Chapter 1. On the Anthropologist and Her Subject

1. Long before any economic slump, my mother predicted that the middle-class upward mobility trend could not continue in the United States and that the class system would become more rigid in time. As an observer of the American way of life, she could well have tried her hand at ethnography.

2. Although how typical Nakane Chie was of other Japanese women could be debated; according to Kelsky (2001), she was a product of a very progressive university, modeled on North American feminist ideals.

3. See chapter 2 for an overview of these fishing ethnographies.

4. Kuzaki, where I did my fieldwork, was no longer officially a village, but a ward *(chō)* of Toba City in Mie Prefecture Japan (see Figure 2); however, it was geographically separated from the city, had a long history as a village, and still regarded itself as somewhat autonomous. All these issues will be considered in chapter 3.

5. This notion of time away linked to older conceptions of pilgrimage is often applied to the tourist in tourism studies (cf. Graburn 1983).

6. Or wasn't. Some shrines house empty inner shrines; that is, they do not contain a symbolic object such as a mirror, stone, or jewel to represent the *kami*. For this reason, Hendry (1993) argues that the wrapping (or construction of the shrine) is more important than the content.

7. Such an argument can be seen as anti-Heideggerian, where the thingness of objects is somehow inherent within them—a sort of authenticity.

Chapter 2. Japan and the *Ama*

1. Yanagita's books *Kaisan seikatsu no kenkyū* ([1950] 1981) and (edited with Hika) *Shima, Shōwa go nen zenki* (1931) were key texts for me.

2. As an elder statesperson, Takie Lebra stands out as a Japanese anthropologist married to an American anthropologist who has often prefaced her work with some placing of herself (cf. 1995). Marilyn Ivy (1995) has explicitly rejected this trend of revealing all (if only this were true) about the narrator and has argued for the structure of her narrative as an implicit revelation of her position.

3. The word *"ama"* can also mean a Buddhist nun, but it is written with different characters.

4. Pierson (1966) translates many such poems from the *Manyōshū;* see especially Book 7/85 and Book 13/23 (pages 9 and 13).

5. This opposition was pointed out to me by David Plath, and I have discussed it in "Tourism and the *Ama*" (1989).

6. Tanabe Satoru published two books in the 1990s on the *ama,* both rather broad overviews: *Nihon ama dentō no kenkyū* (1990) and *Ama* (1993).

7. See, for example, Bernstein 1983; Dalby 1983; DuFoureq 1969; Lebra et al. 1978; T. Lebra 1979, 1981, 1984; Pharr 1976, 1981; Salamon 1973.

8. For examples of classic works that might be described as having a male bias see: Beardsley et al. 1959; Benedict 1974; Befu 1971; Blood 1967; Brameld 1968; Dore 1958, 1978; Glacken 1955; Moeran 1984; Nakane 1967, 1970; Norbeck 1954, 1965; Smith 1978; Vogel 1963.

9. See especially Kondo 1990; Imamura 1996; Hunter 1992; Edwards 1989; and Hamabata 1990. For interesting examples of analyses of both masculinity and femininity, see Allison (1994) and, especially, Robertson on the Takarazuka (1992, 1998).

10. Blacker (1975, 27–28) discusses the "superior and powerful" figure of shamanic women in prehistoric Japan. Such charismatic women seem, however, to have held power as mediators between the spirit and the real world; this does not mean that every woman was considered superior and powerful nor that the status of ordinary women was higher then men's. It could well have been that they seemed to have higher status than women in other parts of Asia, and this impressed Chinese observers who called Japan "Queen's Country" (cf. Kidder 1956, 81–82). In an interesting modern analogy, Moon (1992) argues that if you compare the influence of Confucianism on Korean and Japanese farm women, Japanese women seem much more independent and the impact of the ideology appears much weaker. This of course is in marked contrast to the way a westerner might view the role of Japanese farm wives.

11. DeVos and Wagatsuma (1961) make a similar point in their article, which compares farmers' and fishermen's wives.

Chapter 3. Kuzaki: Making Place and Identity

1. In 1946, Shima Peninsula was one of the first areas after the Second World War to be declared a national park (Graburn 1983, 36). This was part of an attempt to protect the countryside around Ise Shrine, the great Shinto shrine of Japan that had been so implicated in State Shintoism. It was also aimed at keeping industrial pollution from harming the area's lucrative cultured pearl industry.

2. Amaterasu-o-mi-kami (Heaven-shining great august *kami*) was born from the left eye of Izanagi while he was washing his body. Together with her brother Take-haya-susano-wo-no-mikoto (His brave swift impetuous male augustness), born from Izanagi's nose, they form the most important pairing in the Shinto pantheon. They are an "antagonistic" pair—heaven and earth—whose joint action brings the world into being (cf. Herbert 1967, 283–285).

3. Dried and cut strips of abalone or ear shell.

4. The villagers now say that *noshi awabi* should be made in June, November, and December.

5. This probably refers to the festival on July 1 that the Ise priests come to Kuzaki to perform in thanks to the villagers, described later.

6. Kurata's written version bears no resemblance to the village dialect in which I was told various shorter versions of the story. Clearly, honorifics and polite language have been added, but this version is not as elaborated (in terms of language used) as Iwata's (1961, 86–90) versions of the same story. Despite adding the correct language for referring to royalty, Kurata's version appears to have stuck to a more confused narrative; it appears more authentic.

7. I will discuss the symbolism of abalone in chapter 7.

8. It is not clear whether or not this area, Ōtsu, is the same place where Kuzaki's neighbor village Ōtsu stood before the villages were joined in the fourteenth century. Villagers claimed no knowledge of why the areas were divided and named as they are, and the village history gives no information on the subject. It should be noted, however, that Japanese villages are often divided into two parts—not four— and that this might be an indication of two villages with their subdivisions having been joined together.

9. Many specialists on Japanese folk religion have described similar village organization in terms of, for example, "left" and "right" (Matsunaga 1998), or in terms of needing two halves in order to reenact cosmic battles between deities in rituals (Yamaguchi 1998).

10. The folklorist Hori sees elements of Altaic, Southeast Asian, and Polynesian religion in Shinto and its worship of *kami* (1968, 5), while Kato Genchi compares it to the early polytheism of the Egyptians, Babylonians, and Greeks ([1936] 1971). Herbert tries to relate the concept to the Avatars of Vishnu (1967).

11. One informant insisted that in the past, the entire festival was arranged and performed by the villagers themselves. This might well be true, as the *konju* dancer performs dances that belong to the tradition of *bugaku*—court dances and songs originally imported from China that have little to do with diving or the making of *noshi awabi* (Jingū 1986, 85–87).

12. There are several versions as to why Amaterasu took to a cave, the darkness that followed, and the strategies used by various *kami* to try to lure her out (including setting birds to sing and roosters to crow; offering *sakaki*, cloth, and jewels; constructing a mirror; and reciting prayers). Herbert (1967, 284–311) is a good source for the different versions. The list of what was offered to Amaterasu has obvious parallels to all modern Shinto ceremonies.

13. This had changed by 1991 when the village priest retired. Since he had no heir, a priest had to come to Kuzaki from outside to perform most of the major Shinto ceremonies, but the less important purification ceremonies were taken over by the villagers themselves—something that some of the older grandmothers claimed had always been so in the past anyway.

14. This is rather reminiscent of Prachett's Granny Weatherwax, who, when asked by a missionary if she is a believer, answers: "I know a few gods in these parts, if that's what you mean" (1998, 211).

15. In this I tend to agree with Rhum (1993), who argues that we need a better analysis of belief rather than more anthropology that problematizes Western non-belief with others' belief.

16. In contrast, Boyer (1994) has tried to argue for a cognitive human capacity for believing the unbelievable (an oxymoron if there ever was one), but I do not want to go so far as to think of this capacity as somehow hardwired into the human brain.

17. For a discussion of this, see Asad's (1993) critique of Geertz's (1973) definition of how to understand religion.

18. Meiji's raising of Shinto to the state religion was part of a long history of politicized religion in Japan. The early state that is identified with Japan was ruled by a shaman queen; the introduction of Buddhism led to the establishment of monasteries that eventually allied themselves with feudal lords vying for political domination, while Tokugawa's breaking up of these powerful monasteries served to bring religion further under the bureaucracy of the centralized state.

Chapter 4. Organizing the Village

1. From the 1960s there has been a concern in much of the literature on the family in Japan that the traditional household (ie) no longer exists (cf. Okada 1982). Japan is seen to be suffering from a Western problem—the prevalence of the isolated nuclear family. Hendry (1981) discusses how difficult it is to assess the number of three-generation and nuclear or two-generation (i.e., parents and children) families there are in Japan. Given the way the Japanese census data is structured, it is difficult to determine how many two-generation families might be what she terms "succeeded families": families that, having inherited from now-deceased parents, might go on to becoming three-generation families in time. In urban areas, the closeness of the wife's or husband's parents (dwelling on the same street, in the same building, or general area) allows for the ie to continue functioning even though its members do not share the same physical space.

2. Goldstein-Gidoni (1997) and Hamabata (1990) have written excellent ethnographies that depict the continued importance of the ie postwar business.

3. Moon (1986, 187) points out that although primogeniture is practiced in Japan, the highest value is attached to preserving the household so that even in villages with rapidly changing economic structures, such as the ski-resort village she studied, various strategies are employed to keep the ie intact. These strategies, such as son-in-law adoption or inheritance by the second or third son, are not new in rural Japan.

4. This echoes the point Nakane (1967, 121) makes about the system: "An effective dōzoku has been less easily developed in a fishing or horticultural village, both closely connected with commerce and where the economy might be rather

unstable. In such circumstances, the economic standing of an individual household tends to be changeable, so that it is difficult to create, or to maintain, the effective organization of a *dōzoku* over generations."

5. They have been described by other anthropologists such as Beardsley (1959, 248), Dore (1978, 197) and Hendry (1981, 68), among others, as *kōjū, kumi,* or *kō.*

6. The older people in the village did not use the term *"dōkyūsei"* with its connotation that the person referred to was once a school classmate; they said *"hōbai,"* which means "friend." Both terms, however, refer to people in the same age group with whom one goes through the life cycle. The replacement of *hōbai* with classmate points to the persistence of the importance of age-grading in Japan. In 1953, the American anthropologist Edward Norbeck claimed: "Clearly defined age-class systems covering the whole life span of individuals appear to have become relatively rare by the end of the nineteenth century" (373). From my fieldwork and from Bestor's work on urban Japan (1985), I would argue that the older system is now replaced by a similar system based on school classmates.

7. It was precisely this sort of organization, external to the household yet resembling it, that was so useful for the ideological organization of prewar Japan into one "family"; and it is aspects of this type of organization in which a vertical hierarchy is based upon horizontal groups that allowed Nakane (1971) to argue that Japanese companies resembled the *ie.* To be more accurate, it could be argued that in its organization, a Japanese company resembles older village forms in which everyone within the village is aware that cooperation is necessary for both the economic and social well-being of the whole. But while "the company as family" idea was strongly gendered and might well be on its way out, village age-grade organization, at least in Kuzaki, was more strongly based upon the cooperation of both men and women —and even the possible substitution of men by women in certain situations.

8. The word *"rōjin"* is properly translated as "elder"; for the villagers, however, any person over sixty was not only an elder but should have been a grandparent. To reach that age without children or grandchildren was considered a tragedy. I never met anyone in this position in Kuzaki. Thus, for the villagers, the Rōjin-kai was understood to be the grandparents' club.

9. Here the group is deliberately using the term *"kambe"* to recall the village's long and rich association with Ise Shrine. The members of this group want to keep alive Kuzaki's fame as a special village with unique traditions as well as to promote relations with the outside world—notably, with foreign countries.

10. MacDonald (1985, 20) describes these cooperative functions for the village Choshi Togawa near Nagasaki and notes that there are "at least 2000 such cooperatives in Japan, and all of them work on similar principles."

11. The term *"semmu"* is best translated as "executive," but villagers explained the position as being like that of the vice president of the United States.

12. Davis (1977, 26) discusses a similar festival in Wakayama Prefecture called Mifune matsuri (three-boat festival) and notes: "In short, according to legend and custom the original meaning of the festival was to celebrate the Koza fisherman as

warrior. . . . This is not surprising since the culture of the warrior class also deeply colored the parish guilds of the agrarian village. . . . In both the fishing and agricultural village the medieval warrior tradition provided a mythical charter for the enactment of ritual and social status."

13. In his warlike aspect and representing a feudal lord, there seem to be important connections between this young deity and Hachiman-san, which I will discuss later.

14. Most people are never let past the first set of gates, and only the high priest of Ise and the emperor can enter beyond the second.

15. The closest to *shige* that I can find in the dictionaries is *shigedō,* as in *shigedō no ya,* meaning a "rattan-striped bow."

16. Although there are only twenty-four full-time fishing families, many villagers owned boats and they too were represented during Nifune.

17. There seemed to be more than one opinion on this. The next day, a grandfather told me that if the Sato-naka boat had landed first, the next year would be a good one for *bora* catches; if the Kainaka boat landed first, it would mean good sardine catches. This is another interesting hint of a connection between the Wakai kami-sama and Hachiman-san, for *bora* is the fish that must also be offered during the Hachiman festival. In the years when there is bad weather, the grandfather continued, the Sato-naka boat carrying the offerings still had to row out to Kaminoshima, although the Kainaka boat would stay in the village.

Chapter 5. Keeping the *Ie* Afloat: Part 1

1. This is not very unusual in *ama* villages it seems. When I was asked, to my surprise, to give a lecture on my research to the nurses at Shima Prefectural Hospital, I found that most of the women in the audience were daughters of diving women from various parts of Shima.

2. Some men in the current generation of grandfathers found outside employment much more lucrative than fishing and returned to live in the village after a lifetime of work as, for example, a clerk for the railroads. The pattern here was that the wife dived and lived in the household with the man's parents, and the husband might visit on alternate weekends.

3. There are many regional variations on the terms applied to diving women in Japan. Nukada (1965, 32–33) gives us *nakaisodo* for the young women who dive in shallow waters just offshore and also adds *funedo, funado, okazuki, okiama,* and *funekazuki.* For women who dive from boats to deeper depths he gives us *ooisodo, okiama, ooama, oakazuki, funa-ama,* and *funado.* Kita (1965, 41) adds *kachiama* for shore divers. Plath reports that in Fuseda, a village not far from Kuzaki, the terms are *oyogioo* for divers who swim out from the shore and *okedo* for divers who dive in teams from boats (personal communication).

4. Kuzaki men have been diving regularly for abalone since the introduction of the wet suit in the late 1950s or 1960s (various villagers gave different dates).

5. *"Koie"* is made up of the characters for "little" and "house," which are more properly read as *"koya."* The second character of the word I have translated as "house" has the *on* reading *"oku"* and the *kun* reading *"ya."* It is the character's *on* reading that means "house," while the *kun* reading, *"ya,"* is more correctly translated as "shop, store, seller, dealer," or "business." While the latter translation does make clear the fact that diving is a business taken seriously by the divers, the former translation (house) is closer to the way divers view the *koie:* It is a "home away from home." The fact that Kuzaki divers do not use the pronunciation *"koya,"* which is found throughout Japan, but insist on using *"ie,"* which is the word for the household and the lineal descent group, is very telling of their attitude toward these huts.

6. Plath found these divisions to still be important in the village of Fuseda, where he did his fieldwork (personal communication).

7. Even these divisions must be seen as subject to change. A new set of *koie* built outside the main harbor was used sometimes in the summer by couples who dived together as *kachido.*

8. I thought that this was due to parents discouraging the next generation from becoming *ama,* and this was indeed the answer given when I asked why instruction was so informal. But in his interviews with Fuseda divers, David Plath also found this pattern; there the women claim that diving skills are best learned on one's own, and any refinement of one's skills is taught by one's mother-in-law. A mother, it seems, regards her own daughter as a competitor and refuses to teach her the best spots for diving and so on. A woman's knowledge of good diving areas thus stays within an *ie.* The practice of not instructing one's daughter remains in Kuzaki, although having one's own favorite diving areas is no longer possible for *kachido* due to the Cooperative's control over diving areas.

9. The word *"iso"* generally means rocky beach or shore, but the divers of Kuzaki use the word in a variety of ways. *"Iso"* for them could be the seafloor, defined as if it were a continuation of the beach itself—an underwater topography similar to dry land. It could also be combined with seasons to mean the diving season within the annual cycle, thus: *fuyu-iso* (winter diving).

10. In most of Japan, this relationship between women and household gods was important; it was Miyata (1983) who collected the most diverse data on this relationship in his *Onna no reiryoku to ie no kami* (Women's spiritual powers and the household gods).

11. The Chinese characters that make up Sengen can be read as *sen* or *asa(i)* for shallow or superficial, short (time), slight (connection), or pale or light (color); and *ken, kan,* or *ma* for interval, space, between, among, discord, favorable opportunity. Both *sen* and *ken* are the *on* readings for the characters. No one in Kuzaki was able to tell me what Sengen meant, considering it to be the name of a Shinto deity, and they seemed unconcerned that a Chinese reading for a Shinto deity's name might be a bit unusual. Also, the villagers rarely used the kanji for Sengen,

stating that the use of hiragana or katakana helped to distinguish their Mt. Sengen from all the Sengen Shinto shrines that were part of the cult of another deity and that can be found on the slopes of Mt. Fuji (cf. *Nihon Minzoku Jiten* 1971, 388).

There is also a Sengen Shrine on the nearby mountain Asama (which is spelled with the characters for morning, *"asa,"* and bear, *"ma"*—a very unusual reading for the character *"yū"* or *"kuma"*). Interesting to note is that the *kun* or Japanese reading for the characters that make up Sengen could be Asama, and Herbert (1967, 474–475) suggests that *asama* actually comes from the Ainu for volcano. The people of Kuzaki claimed that Sengen was both a dormant volcano and a deity that was close kin to Fuji-san. It seems possible that the Chinese readings were used for the characters of Sengen in order not to confuse the Kuzaki mountain with the nearby mountain Asama. The use of phonetic characters to write Sengen is seen as necessary to ensure that people did not confuse the local deity Sengen with the Asama Sengen cult. As Plath notes, Japanese folklorists have yet to sort out all the problems of the various Sengen cults, but he believes that "in Fuseda Sengen-san is clearly the most important single god for the *ama* today." Since the Fuseda Sengen-san is right above the beach, the divers there worship the deity every day, not once a month as Kuzaki *ama* do (Plath, personal communication).

12. I note both possible deities here because most people in Kuzaki seemed sure that Sengen was a deity and not a cult for the worship of Princess Konohana-sakuya (Princess Blossoming Brilliantly Like Flowers of the Trees). The distinction between deity and cult is not as clear-cut as they represent it, however; one informant insisted that, like other Sengen shrines in Japan, the one in Kuzaki housed the princess. She is the daughter of O-yama-tsu-mi-kami (Kami Great mountain possessor), the deity of mountains, and the wife of Prince Ninigi, the divine grandson of Amaterasu. The princess is thus one of the ancestors of the Japanese race and the imperial family. In short, this local shrine is at some level identified with other Sengen shrines, all of which are dedicated to Princess Konohanasakuya.

13. This is *naorai,* sharing food with the deities. See Befu (1986, 160) for an analysis of how these offerings then become gifts returned by the deities to mortals, thus allowing mortals to partake of the deities' diving power.

14. Kojin is the name of a sort of demonic creature. The villagers also said that the figure was a sort of a *hotoke-sama* or bodhisattva, which comes to the same thing since in the villagers' view all ancestors become bodhisattva. To add to the confusion, the characters I was given for Koshi indicate that the figure could actually be a *konshinzuka*, or the stone image of the traveler's guardian deity. If one were to go by the pronunciation of the word *"koshi"* rather than by the characters I was given by the eager amateur village folklorists, the figure could also be that of Confucius. This sort of confusion was not unusual.

15. The bodhisattva Jizō was very popular in Kuzaki. The village had three statues devoted to him: one on Sengen; one on the spot where some old graves were moved when the village expanded, this one to protect the children from ghosts; and another near an inn. The last statue was dedicated to women who had not been

able to bear children. The grandmother of the family who owned the inn had been barren for years before she prayed to Jizō-sama. When she finally bore a son, she had the statue installed outside the household, and other women in the village who had fertility problems worshipped there. Elsewhere in Japan, Jizō is worshipped as the protector deity of aborted or miscarried fetuses or babies that die very young. As Hendry notes (1986, 43), it is only in Japan that this bodhisattva is associated with children. Originally known as Kshitigarbha (earth womb), he is the bodhisattva who in other Buddhist countries delivers souls from hell and helps people in their last moments before death (Snellgrove 1987, 340).

16. I have translated the word she used, *"shinkō,"* as "beliefs" rather than "faiths" or "creeds" because she went on to use the phrase *"shinkō shimasu,"* meaning "to believe in" or "have faith in," and it seemed best to keep the translation of her usage consistent.

17. As the word *"tendoku"* implies, the priest does not read the texts as much as he flips open an old book like a giant fan and lets it fold up again; his reading is thus a skipping through the text.

18. *Amacha* contains hydrangea, which is a diuretic, and the drink is meant to purify both one's external and internal systems. See Lebra (1986, 365) for a discussion of the tea's properties.

19. The temples at Aonomine-san were once a pilgrimage site for all the fisherfolk of Shima Peninsula. The charms from this temple were still held to be good personal protection for diving. One of the shrines was also devoted to the protection of boats. Plath notes that Fuseda *ama* and boatmen still go there regularly (personal communication).

Chapter 6. Keeping the *Ie* Afloat: Part 2

1. It is not surprising that Kuzaki men were taken as sailors. As Kalland notes (1984, 15), there was a tradition of fishing villages providing coast guard duty for the fiefs during the Edo period; this was often done in lieu of paying taxes on their fishing. The strong association in Kuzaki between fishing and the feudal tradition is examined later in this chapter in the discussion of the Hachiman-san festival.

2. See Kalland (1980, 99), Norbeck (1954, 140) and Segawa (1963, 242) for descriptions of this. Segawa (1956), however, lists several fishing villages in which entire families spent part of the year on boats; it seems clear that although menstruation was considered generally dangerous and polluting throughout Japan, maintaining the *ie* division of labor could be more important than the taboo.

3. On Japanese fishermen especially, Norbeck notes that "The god of boats, Funadama-sama, is a deity now only half believed in but who, curiously, receives offerings with unfailing regularity" (1954, 129). See also Norr (1974, 62–63) for a discussion on how south Indian fishermen's gods are linked to the larger religious tradition; Firth (1966, 49), who found that Malay fishermen denied the importance of religion and yet did enlist the aid of spirits; and Glacken (1955, 290–291) and Malinowski (1918, 92) for descriptions of fishing societies where rituals were rou-

tinely performed. Hagiwara (1973, 10–36) lists an elaborate ritual cycle for the fishermen of Kamishima, an island not far from Kuzaki, which suggests that more isolated communities rely far more on ritual than technology for luck and safety in fishing.

4. Herbert (1967, 511) describes Ebisu as "one of the most popular and one of the most controversial Kami of the whole Shintō Pantheon. . . . He is generally represented as a fat, bearded, smiling fisherman, holding a fishing-rod in one hand and a large *tai* (seabream) in the other." As with many of the *kami,* Ebisu seems to have multiple origins and identities; see Naumann (1974) for an interesting discussion of the role of Ebisu as a fishing deity.

5. According to the villagers, the three ingredients of this salad—rice, fish, and vegetables—represent the three sources of Japan's wealth: the fields, the sea, and the mountains.

6. The same sort of huge *mochi* cake is used in Kuzaki weddings, as well as on other ritual occasions. *"Sechi"* seems to be a dialect word to refer to this type of pink and white *mochi.*

7. Weber (1968 vol.2, 424) notes: "The pervasive and central theme [as religion of the gods begins to differentiate itself from simple magic or wizardry] is *do ut des.* This aspect clings to the routine and the mass religious behavior of all peoples at all times and in all religions. The normal situation is that the burden of all prayers, even in the most other-worldly religions, is the aversion of the external evils of this world and the inducement of the external advantages of this world."

8. This exhausting itinerary is typical of modern Japanese pilgrimage. Graburn gives an excellent description of this sort of tourism in his *To pray, pay and play* (1983).

9. Arne Kalland (personal communication) claims that when an attempt to introduce pearl diving in the eighteenth century was made on the mainland of Japan, male divers from Okinawa had to be imported because the local *ama* refused to engage in pearl diving.

10. As David Plath has pointed out to me, for the port and pilgrimage towns in the area, sex is not a new commodity but a traditional one.

11. Its location on a cliff overlooking the ocean was striking, and I was not able to learn why the place had been closed rather than expanded or sold to more enterprising villagers.

12. Nomura (1978, 4) refers to *tsubuki* in Kuzaki only as *kazaritsuri* (decorations or adornments). Hagiwara (1973) describes similar amulets for the New Year on Kamishima and calls them *kazari.*

13. According to the Japanese Language Dictionary (*Nihon Kokugo Daijiten* vol.12, 439), Somen Shōrai is a legendary figure. He was the poor elder brother of Kyotan Shōrai, a great lord. Somen offered hospitality to a disguised *kami* who had been turned out by his richer younger brother. As a reward, the descendants of Somen were offered protection from calamities, while Kyotan Shōrai was destroyed.

14. The Hagiwaras (1973) describe a similar event on Kamishima, but this occurs on the second day of the New Year.

15. There were some men, for example, whom the villagers regarded as alcoholics *(aruchū)*. This category was interesting, for all fishermen were heavy drinkers by 1980s U.S. standards, but only the men who drank enough to make them unreliable at their work were regarded as alcoholics.

16. In fact, according to Grapard, Hachiman was probably the very first Japanese *kami* to be assigned a Buddhist avatar based on criteria that became the model for all other *kami,* who were eventually all given Buddhist identities (1992, 80).

17. The variety of ways in which such rituals can be unraveled is shown by Ben-Ari's work (1991); his analysis of another archery ritual considers the many strategies used by the audience to record the event.

Chapter 7. Elders and Ancestors

1. To argue this, I have heard at least one scholar use Bergson and, in my understanding, incorrectly so. Bergson (1999) argues that the idea of relativity (in Einstein's sense) allows for a philosophical construction of the object as it has become, thus freeing it to be seen as relational. He also notes that a different understanding of time and memory, however, teaches us that there is a process involved in this— there is a making in the becoming: Objects and people have specific histories.

2. I would like to thank Andrew Berstein for his response to my comments on a conference paper: "I would argue that making is just as important as becoming," a remark that set me off on this train of thought.

3. For an analysis of the difference between the NHK filmed event and regular *noshi awabi*–making sessions, see Martinez 1993.

4. A bamboo or metal cylinder; the *kanji* I was given are glossed as *noshibo* in the dictionary.

5. In a paper on gift giving for funerals in urban Japan, Tsuji (forthcoming) describes how on the day after someone dies in an urban household, gift catalogs appear through the mail so that bereaved families can have a reference guide to return gifts (and, of course, they'll know where to purchase them as well). The fact is, she says, that the funeral director contacts the gift company the moment he is hired to provide his services (and what complicated financial or even kin relations might exist between these two businesses, Tsuji does not say!). Tsuji's article is about how deciding to participate or not in this gift giving defines a modern urban community and how, these days, a man's employer will also contribute toward funeral costs. Nakamaki (1995) has described how some companies go a step further and enshrine dead employees and hold yearly Obon celebrations for the company dead. I will return to these points later.

6. Note the presence of *mochi,* so often associated with Shinto rituals, in this Buddhist rite. The lived reality of offerings made it very difficult for me to place offerings into a neat little table of dichotomies.

7. The description of Obon in most works on Japan covers a page or two (cf. Beardsley 1959, 455–456; Embree 1939, 284–285; Hendry 1981, 215–216). This is not to say that the importance of Obon is ignored; rather, it is subordinated to the purely social.

8. These ghosts are ancestors whose families have died out and therefore are no longer being looked after at a *butsudan,* or they are dead who have died bad deaths and have no family to look after them. Note that all rice offerings to the *hotoke-sama* are of cooked rice, while the hungry ghosts get uncooked rice. Even *mochi,* rice cakes, are not cooked but pounded into the form they have. This would seem to place the ghosts into the category of Shinto *kami* that should always be given the freshest food and uncooked rice as offerings. Thus, properly cared for ancestors achieve enlightenment and become Buddhas, while the neglected dead also become powerful but are harmful. This seems a continuation of Shinto ideas that all dead become *kami* in one way or another.

9. Of course, Amida's paradise is in the west, and sending spirits back east is more a Shinto than a Buddhist practice. No one in Kuzaki was the least bit bothered by this.

10. Although a careful look at this list gives the idea that the past was not so deep: Some of the offerings are definitely New World crops!

11. The word *"urabon"* is often used as another term for Obon. The first part of the word, *ura,* is made up of the characters for bowl *(u)* and orchid *(ran).* However, in Kuzaki calling the time after Obon when *nembutsu* are said for the living *"urabon,"* the villagers of Kuzaki seem to be using *"ura"* in an entirely different sense—that is, as as meaning "the reverse side" or "the back, rear." While sounding the same, *"ura"* in either of these cases is represented by different characters. Whether this is a conscious differentiation made only in Kuzaki or a misunderstanding of the term by the villagers, I was unable to learn.

Chapter 8. Ritual, Gender, and Identity

1. For the two examples I discuss here, I not only use pseudonyms, but I also have combined different people into each described individual.

2. Standish (2000) has an interesting example of this from looking at Japanese postwar films. Films that made it past the U.S. military censors often had a protagonist who died. For the censors, this read as a message that "war was bad," because in just causes (or U.S. war films), the hero always survives. Of course, the hero who sacrificed all for his cause is an important theme in Japan and has nothing at all to do with the idea that war is bad.

3. This was a debate that until few years ago had occupied the Japanese medical and legal system, with organ transplants not possible since there was no admission of the concept of brain death (cf. Lock 2001).

4. Interestingly, in contrast to the standard view that Japan was and remains a highly patriarchal society, there is ample evidence that for a generation at least, women's ties with their natal families remain important. Most important in this is

the fact that all women expect to return home to their parents' for a month after giving birth. In Kuzaki, the giving of gifts to the wife's family was also important.

5. I base this part of my analysis on Jay's (1992) ideas on blood sacrifice. While Japan has long avoided spilling blood in rituals, even tantric rituals, the offering of the freshest, almost living fish and other produce allow me—I think—to follow her argument.

6. Vlastos' (1998) edited book is full of articles that appear to be describing a Japan on the verge of becoming a simulacrum.

References

Aichi Daigaku. 1965. *Ama no mura: Toba-shi, Kuzaki-chō* (An *ama* village: Toba City, Kuzaki Ward). Special Issue of the Memories [*sic*] of the Community Research Institute of Aichi University. Toyohashi City: Aichi University.

Allison, Anne. 1994. *Night work, sexuality, pleasure and corporate masculinity in a Tokyo hostess club.* Chicago: University of Chicago Press.

Anderson, Benedict. 1991. *Imagined communities.* London: Verso.

Aoki Tamotsu. 1994. Anthropology and Japan: Attempts at writing culture. *Japan Foundation Newsletter* 22(3): 1–6.

Ardener, Edwin. 1987. Remote areas: Some theoretical considerations. In *Anthropology at home,* edited by Anthony Jackson, 38–54. London: Tavistock Publications.

Ardorno, Theodor W. 1973. *The jargon of authenticity.* Translated by Kurth Tarnowski and Frederic Will. London: Routledge & Kegan Paul.

Asad, Talal. 1993. The construction of religion as an anthropological category. In *Genealogies of religion, discipline and reasons of power in Christianity and Islam,* edited by Talal Asad, 24–37. Baltimore: Johns Hopkins University Press.

Ashkenazi, Michael. 1983. Festival change and continuity in a Japanese town. Unpublished Ph.D. thesis presented to the faculty of the Graduate School of Yale University.

Asquith, Pamela J., and Arne Kalland. 1997. Japanese perceptions of nature: Ideals and illusions. In *Japanese images of nature,* edited by Pamela J. Asquith and Arne Kalland, 1–35. London: Curzon.

Augé, Marc. 1995. *Non-places: Introduction to an anthropology of supermodernity.* Translated by John Howe. London: Verso.

Bachnik, Jane. 1983. Recruitment strategies for household succesion: rethinking Japanese household organization. *Man* 18(1): 160–182.

———. 1995. Orchestrated reciprocity: Belief versus practice in Japanese funeral ritual. In *Ceremony and ritual in Japan,* edited by Jan van Bremen and D. P. Martinez, 108–145. London: Routledge.

Bachnik, Jane, and Charles Quinn, eds. 1994. *Situated meaning: Inside and outside in Japanese self, society and language.* Princeton: Princeton University Press.

Bakhtin, M. M. 1981. *The dialogic imagination: Four essays.* Edited by Michael Holquist; translated by Caryl Emerson and Michael Holquist. Austin: University of Texas Press.

Barley, Nigel. 1995. *Dancing on the grave: Encounters with death.* London: John Murray.

Beardsley, Richard K., John W. Hall, and Robert E. Ward. 1959. *Village Japan.* Chicago: University of Chicago Press.

Befu, Harumi. 1963. Patrilineal descent and personal kindred in Japan. *American Anthropologist* 65(6): 1,328–1,341.

———. 1971. *Japan: An anthropological introduction.* San Francisco: Chandler.

———. 1986. An ethnography of dinner entertainment in Japan. In *Japanese culture and behavior,* edited by Willam P. Lebra and Takie Lebra, 108–120. Honolulu: University of Hawai'i Press.

Befu, Harumi, and Josef Kreiner, eds. 1991. *Othernesses of Japan: Historical and cultural influences on Japanese studies in ten countries.* München: Iudicium.

Ben-Ari, Eyal. 1991. Posing, posturing and photographic presences: A rite of passage in a Japanese commuter village. *Man* 26(1): 87–104.

Benedict, Ruth. 1974. *The chrysanthemum and the sword: Patterns of Japanese culture.* New York: New American Library.

Bergson, Henri. 1999. *Duration and simultaneity.* Edited and with an introduction by Robin Durie. Manchester, UK: Clinamen Press.

Bernier, Bernard. 1975. *Breaking the cosmic circle: Religion in a Japanese village.* Ithaca, NY: China-Japan Program, Cornell University.

Bernstein, Gail Lee. 1983. *Haruko's world: A Japanese farm woman and her community.* Stanford: Stanford University Press.

Bestor, Theodore. 1985. Tradition and Japanese social organization: Institutional development in a Tokyo neighborhood. *Ethnology* 24(2): 121–135.

———. 1988. *Neighborhood Tokyo.* Stanford: Stanford University Press.

Bird, Isabella L. 1880. *Unbeaten tracks in Japan: An account of travels in the interior including visits to the aborigines of Yezo and the shrines of Nikko and Ise.* London: John Murray.

Birukawa, Shōhei. 1965. Geographic distribution of *ama* in Japan. In *Physiology of breath-hold diving and the ama of Japan,* edited by Herman Rahn and Yokoyama Tetsuro, 57–70. Washington, D.C.: National Academy of Sciences, National Research Council (Publication 1341).

Blacker, Carmen. 1975. *The catalpa bow: A study of shamanistic practices in Japan.* London: Allen and Unwin.

Bloch, Maurice. 1989. *Ritual, history and power: Selected papers in anthropology.* London: Athlone.

———. 1992. *Prey into hunter: The politics of religious experience.* Cambridge: Cambridge University Press.

Blood, Robert O., Jr. 1967. *Love match and arranged marriage: A Tokyo-Detroit comparison.* New York: Free Press.

Bourdieu, Pierre. 1977. *Outline of a theory of practice.* Cambridge: Cambridge University Press.

———. 1984. *Distinction.* Cambridge: Harvard University Press.

Boyer, Pascal. 1994. *The naturalness of religious ideas: A cognitive theory of religion.* Berkeley: University of California Press.

Brameld, Theodore. 1968. *Japan: Culture, education and change in two communities.* New York: Holt, Rinehart Winston.

Campbell, Alan Tormaid. 1995. *Getting to know WaiWai: An Amazonian ethnography.* London: Routledge.

Cho, Haejoang. 1979. *An ethnographic study of a female diver's village in Korea: Focused on the sexual division of labor.* Unpublished Ph.D. dissertation submitted to the University of California.

Clammer, John. 1997. *Contemporary urban Japan: A sociology of consumption.* Oxford: Blackwell.

Clifford, James, and George E. Marcus, eds. 1986. *Writing culture: The poetics and politics of ethnography.* Berkeley: University of California Press.

Cobbi, Jane. 1995. Sonaemono: Ritual gifts to the deities. In *Ceremony and ritual in Japan,* edited by Jan van Bremen and D. P. Martinez, 201–209. London: Routledge.

Cohn, B. S. 1990. *An anthropologist among historians and other essays.* New Delhi: Oxford University Press.

Csordas, Thomas J. 1994. *The sacred self: A cultural phenomenology of charismatic healing.* Berkeley: University of California Press.

Dalby, Liza Crihfield. 1983. *Geisha.* Berkeley: University of California Press.

Davis, Winston. 1977. The *miyaza* and the fisherman: Ritual status in the coastal villages of Wakayama Prefecture. *Asian Folklore Studies* 36(2): 3–29.

———. 1980. *Dojo, magic and exorcism in modern Japan.* Stanford: Stanford University Press.

Derrida, Jacques. 1976. *Of grammatology.* Translated from the French by Gayatri Chakravorty Spivak. Baltimore: Johns Hopkins University Press.

DeVos, George A., and Wagatsuna Hiroshi

———. 1961. Value attitudes toward role behavior of women in two Japanese villages. *American Anthropologist* 63(6): 1,204–1,230.

Dore, Ronald P. 1958. *City life in Japan: A study of a Tokyo ward.* London: Routledge and Kegan Paul.

———. 1978. *Shinohata: A portrait of a Japanese village.* London: Allen Lane.

DuFoureq, Elisabeth B. 1969. *Les femmes Japonaises.* Paris: Denoël/Ganthier.

Durkheim, Emile. 1915. *The elementary forms of the religious life.* Translated by Joseph Ward Swain. London: Allen and Urwin.

Ebersole, Gary. 1992. *Ritual poetry and the politics of death in early Japan.* Princeton: Princeton University Press.

Eco, Umberto. 1992. *The name of the rose.* Translated by William Weaver. London: Minerva.

Edwards, Walter. 1989. *Modern Japan through its weddings: Gender, person and society in ritual portrayal.* Stanford: Stanford University Press.

Eliade, Mircea. 1969. *Yoga, immortality and freedom.* Translated by Willard R. Trask. Princeton: Princeton University Press.

Embree, John F. 1946. *A Japanese village: Suye Mura.* London: Kegan Paul.

Evans-Pritchard, E. E. 1976. *Witchcraft oracles and magic among the Azande.* Oxford: Clarendon Press.

Fabian, Johannes. 1983. *Time and the other: How anthropology makes its object.* New York: Columbia University Press.

Firth, Raymond. 1966. *Malay fishermen: Their peasant economy.* New York: W. W. Norton.

Fleming, Ian. 1978. *You only live twice.* St. Albans, UK: Triad/Granada.

Geertz, Clifford. 1973. Religion as a cultural system. In *The interpretation of cultures,* edited by Clifford Geertz, 87–125. New York: Basic Books.

Ginzburg, Carlo. 1989. *Clues, myths and the historical method.* Translated by John and Anne C. Tedeschi. Baltimore: Johns Hopkins University Press.

Glacken, Clarence J. 1955. *The great Loocho: A study of Okinawan village life.* Berkeley: University of California Press.

Gluck, Carol. 1985. *Japan's modern myths.* Princeton: Princeton University Press.

Goffman, Erving. 1971. *The presentation of self in everyday life.* Harmondsworth, UK: Penguin.

Goldstein-Gidoni, Ofra. 1997. *Packaged Japaneseness: Weddings, business and brides.* Richmond, UK: Curzon Press.

Graburn, Nelson. 1983. *To pray, pay and play: The cultural structure of Japanese domestic tourism.* Université de Droit, d'Economie et des Sciences Centre des Hautes Etudes Touristiques, Serie B no. 26. Aix-en-Provence, France: Centre des Hautes Etudes Touristiques.

Grapard, Alan. 1992. *The protocol of the gods: A study of the Kasuga cult in Japanese history.* Berkeley: University of California Press.

Hagiwara Hidesaburo and Hagiwara Noriko. 1973. *Kamishima.* Tokyo: Ijō Shoten.

Hamabata, M. 1990. *Crested Kimono: Power and love in the Japanese business family.* Ithaca, NY: Cornell University Press.

———. 1994. The battle to belong: Self-sacrifice and self-fulfillment in the Japanese family enterprise. In *Situated meaning,* edited by Jane M. Bachnik and Charles J. Quinn, 192–208. Princeton: Princeton University Press.

Hane Mikiso. 1982. *Peasants, rebels and outcastes: The underside of modern Japan.* London: Scholar Press.

Hendry, Joy. 1981. *Marriage in changing Japan: Community and society.* London: Croom Helm.

———. 1984. Shoes: The early learning of an important distinction in Japanese society. In *Europe interprets Japan,* edited by J. Daniels, 215–222. Tenterden, UK: Paul Norbury.

————. 1986. *Becoming Japanese: The world of the pre-school child.* Manchester: Manchester University Press.

————. 1993. *Wrapping culture: Politeness, presentation, and power in Japan and other societies.* Oxford: Oxford University Press.

————. 1995. *Understanding Japanese society.* London: Routledge.

Herbert, Jean. 1967. *Shinto: The fountainhead of Japan.* London: George Allen and Unwin.

Hobsbawm, Eric, and Terence Ranger, eds. 1983. *The invention of tradition.* Cambridge, MA: Cambridge University Press.

Hori, Ichirō. 1968. *Folk religion in Japan: Continuity and change.* Edited by Joseph Kitagawa and Alan L. Miller. Chicago: University of Chicago Press.

Hunter, Janet. 1992. *Japanese women working.* London: Routledge.

Imamura, Anne E., ed. 1996. *Re-imaging Japanese women.* Berkeley: University of California Press.

Ivy, Marilyn. 1995. *Discourses of the vanishing.* Chicago: University of Chicago Press.

Iwao, Sumiko. 1993. *The Japanese woman: Traditional image and changing reality.* Cambridge, MA: Harvard University Press.

Iwata Junichi. 1931. Mie no ama sagyō no konseki (Mie diving women past and present). In *Shima: Shōwa go nen zenki* (Islands: The five years preceding Showa), edited by Yanagita Kunio, 60–122. Tokyo: Takase Sueyoshi.

————. 1961. *Shima no ama: Fu Shima no gyofu no mukashigatari* (The *ama* of Shima: With reference to the folktales of Shima fisherfolk). Toba City: Shinto Insatsu Kabushiki Kaisha.

Jay, Nancy. 1992. *Throughout your generations forever: Sacrifice, religion, and paternity.* Chicago: University of Chicago Press.

Jeremy, M., and M. E. Robinson. 1987. *Ceremony and symbolism in the Japanese home.* Manchester: Manchester University Press.

Jingū Shichō. 1986. *O-Ise mairi* (Worship at Ise). Tokyo: Otsuka Kōgeisha.

Kalland, Arne. 1980. *Shingu: A Japanese fishing community.* London: Curzon Press.

————. 1984. Sea tenure in Tokugawa Japan: The case of Fukuoka Domain. In *Maritime institutions in the western Pacific,* edited by Kenneth Ruddle and Tomoya Akimichi, 11–36. Osaka: National Museum of Ethnology (Senri Ethnological Studies 17).

————. 1988. In search of the abalone: The history of the *ama* in northern Kyūshū, Japan. Reprint from *Seinana Chi-iki no shitekig Tenkai,* 616–588.

Kamishima Jirō. 1977. Ryōsai kembo shugi (The good mother, wise wife principle). *Jidai no esupuri: Nihon no kekon* 104: 150–155.

Kato, Genchi. 1971. [1936] *A study of Shinto: The religion of the Japanese nation.* London: Curzon Press.

Kato, Shinzo. n.d. *Organ transplants and brain death: A Japanese doctor's perspec-

tive. Forthcoming in *Death in Japan,* edited by John Breen and Brian Bocking. London: Routledge.

Kawada, Minoru. 1993. *The origin of ethnography in Japan: Yanagita Kunio and his times*. London: Kegan Paul International.

Keatinge, W. R. 1969. *Survival in cold water: The physiology and treatment of immersion hypothermia and of drowning*. Oxford: Blackwell Scientific Publications.

Keene, Donald, ed. 1970. *Twenty plays of the Nō theatre*. New York: Columbia University Press.

Kelly, William W. 1992. Tractors, television and telephones: Reach out and touch someone in rural Japan. In *Re-made in Japan,* edited by J. Tobin, 77–88. New Haven: Yale University Press.

Kelsky, Karen. 2001. *Women on the verge*. Durham, NC: Duke University Press.

Kidder, J. Edward, Jr. 1956. *Ancient Japan*. London: Weidenfeld and Nicolson (Educational).

Kita, Hiromasa. 1965. Review of activities: Diving seasons and harvesting patterns. In *Physiology of breath-hold diving and the ama of Japan,* edited by Herman Rahn and Yokoyama Tetsuro, 41–55. Washington, D.C.: National Academy of Sciences, National Research Council (Publication 1341).

Kondo, D. 1990. *Crafting Selves: Power, gender, and discourses of identity in a Japanese workplace*. London: University of Chicago Press.

Koyama, Takashi. 1961. *The changing social position of women in Japan*. Geneva: UNESCO.

Kurata Masakuni. 1974. Noshi awabi no yurai (The origin of *noshi awabi*). In *Ise shima,* vol. 13 of *Nihon no minwa*. Tokyo: Rengō Insatsu Kabushiki Kaisha.

Kuwayama, Takami. 1992. The reference other orientation. In *Japanese sense of self,* edited by Nancy R. Rosenberger, 121–151. Cambridge: Cambridge University Press.

Kuzaki Kambeshi (Records of the sacred guild of Kuzaki). var. Unpublished historical records of Kuzaki ward, Toba City, Mie Prefecture, Japan. Various dates.

Lebra, Joyce, Joy Paulson, and Elizabeth Powers, eds. 1978. *Women in changing Japan*. Stanford: Stanford University Press.

Lebra, Takie. 1979. The dilemma and strategies of aging among contemporary Japanese women. *Ethnology* 18(4): 337–354.

———. 1981. Japanese women in male dominant careers: Cultural barriers and accommodations for sex-role transcendence. *Ethnology* 20(4): 291–306.

———. 1984. *Japanese women: Constraint and fulfillment*. Honolulu: University of Hawai'i Press.

———. 1986. Self-reconstruction in Japanese religion psychotherapy. In *Japanese culture and behavior: Selected readings,* edited by Takie Lebra and William Lebra, 354–368. Honolulu: University of Hawai'i Press.

Lévi-Strauss, Claude. 1976. *Tristes tropiques*. Translated from the French by John and Doreen Weightman. Harmondsworth, UK: Penguin.

Linhart, Ruth. 1988. Modern times for *ama*-divers. In *Contemporary European writings on Japan: Scholarly views from Eastern and Western Europe*, edited by Ian Nish, 114–119. Woodchurch, Ashford, UK: Paul Norbury.

Lock, M. M. 2001. *Twice dead: Organ transplants and the reinvention of death*. Berkeley: University of California Press.

Lowenthal, David. 1985. *The past is a foreign country*. Cambridge: Cambridge University Press.

Luhrmann, T. 1989. *Persuasions of the witch's craft: Ritual magic in contemporary England*. Cambridge, MA: Harvard University Press.

Lukes, Steven. 1973. *Individualism*. Oxford: Blackwells.

MacDonald, Donald. 1985. *A geography of modern Japan*. Woodchurch, Ashford, UK: Paul Norbury.

Malinowski, Bronislaw. 1918. Fishing in the Trobriand Islands. *Man* 48: 87–92.

Maraini, Fosco. 1962. *Hekura: The diving girls' island*. Translated from the Italian by Eric Mosbacher. London: Hamish Hamilton.

Martinez, D. P. 1988. The division of labour in a Japanese diving village. In *Proceedings of the British Association for Japanese Studies*, vol. 11, edited by John Chapman and David Steeds, 133–194. University of Sheffield, Centre for Japanese Studies.

———. 1989. Tourism and the *ama*: The search for a "real" Japan. In *Unwrapping Japan*, edited by Eyal Ben-Ari et al., 97–116. Manchester, UK: Manchester University Press.

———. 1993. NHK comes to Kuzaki: Ideology, mythology and documentary filmmaking. In *Ideology and Practice in Japan*, edited by Roger Goodman and Kirsten Refsing, 153–170. London: Routledge.

———. 1995. Naked divers: A case of identity and dress in Japan. In *Dress and Ethnicity*, edited by Joanne B. Eicher, 79–94. Oxford: Berg.

———. 1996. The tourist as diety: Ancient continuities in modern Japan. In *The tourist image*, edited by Tom Selwyn, 163–178. Chichester: John Wiley and Sons.

———. 1998. Redefining Kuzaki: Ritual, belief and *chō* boundaries. In *Interpreting Japanese society*, edited by Joy Hendry, 213–221. London: Routledge.

Masuda, Kōichi. 1975. Bride's progress: How a *yome* becomes a *shotome*. In *Adult episodes in Japan*, edited by David Plath, 10–19. Leiden: E. J. Brill.

Matsunaga, Kazuto. 1998. The importance of the left hand in two types of ritual activity in a Japanese village. In *Interpreting Japanese society*, edited by Joy Hendry, 147–156. London: Routledge.

Mauss, M. 1985. A category of the human mind: The notion of the person, the notion of the self. In *The category of the person*, edited by Michael Carrithers, Steven Collins, and Steven Lukes, 1–25. Cambridge: Cambridge University Press.

McCreery, Guy. 1998. Redefined selves: Individuality and community in post-bubble Japan. Unpublished Ph.D. thesis submitted to the University of London.

McVeigh, Brian. 1997. *Spirits, selves, and subjectivity in a Japanese new religion: The cultural psychology of belief in shukyo Mahikari.* Lewiston, NY: E. Mellen Press.

Mishima, Yukio. 1957. *The sound of waves.* Translated by Meredith Weatherby. London: Secker and Warbury.

Miyamoto Nobuichi. 1975. *Nihon no ama* (Japan's *ama*). Tokyo: Chunichi Shimbun.

Miyata Noboru. 1983. *Onna no reiryoku to ie no kami* (Women's spiritual powers and the household gods). Kyoto: Jinbonshoin.

Moeran, Brian. 1984. *Lost innocence: Folk craft potters of Onta Japan.* Berkeley: University of California Press.

Moon, Ok-Pyo Kim. 1986. Is the *ie* disappearing in rural Japan? The impact of tourism on a traditional Japanese village. In *Interpreting Japanese society,* edited by Joy Hendry, 185–197. Oxford: Journal of the Anthropology Society of Oxford (JASO).

———. 1989. *From paddy field to ski slope: The revitalisation of tradition in Japanese village life.* Manchester: Manchester University Press.

———. 1992. Confucianism and gender segregation in Japan and Korea. In *Ideology and practice in modern Japan,* edited by Roger Goodman and Kirsten Refsing, 196–209. London: Routledge.

Morioka Kiyomi. 1968. Religious behavior and the actor's position in his household. In *The sociology of Japanese religion,* edited by Morioka Kiyomi and William H. Newell, 25–43. Leiden: E. J. Brill.

Morris, Ivan, trans. 1971. *As I crossed a bridge of dreams: Recollections of a woman in eleventh-century Japan.* Harmondsworth, UK: Penguin Books.

Morris, Ivan, trans. and ed. 1967. *The pillow book of Sei Shōnagon.* Harmondsworth, UK: Penguin Books.

Nakamaki, Hirochika. 1995. Memorial monuments and memorial services of Japanese companies: Focusing on Mount Koya. In *Ceremony and ritual in Japan,* edited by Jan van Bremen and D. P. Martinez, 146–158. London: Routledge.

Nakane, Chie. 1967. *Kinship and economic organization in rural Japan.* London: University of London, Athlone Press.

———. 1970. *Japanese society.* Harmondsworth, UK: Penguin.

Napier, Susan. 1998. Vampires, psychic girls, flying women and sailor scouts: Four faces of the young female in Japanese popular culture. In *The worlds of Japanese popular culture,* edited by Jan van Bremen and D. P. Martinez, 91–109. Cambridge: Cambridge University Press.

Naumann, N. 1974. The whale and the fish cult in Japan: A basic feature of Ebisu worship. *Asian Folklore Studies* 33: 1–15.

Newell, William H., ed. 1976. *Ancestors.* The Hague: Mouton.

Nihon kokugo daijiten. 1976. (Japanese language dictionary). Tokyo: Nihon Daijiten Kankōkai Shōgakukan.

Nihon minzoku jiten. 1971. (Dictionary of Japanese folklore). Tokyo: Nihon Daijiten Kankōkai Shōgakukan.

Nomura C. 1978. Kuzaki no nenchū gyōji (Annual rituals in Kuzaki). *Umi to ningen* 6: 1–26.

Norbeck, Edward. 1953. Age-grading in Japan. *American Anthropologist* 55(3): 373–384.

———. 1954. *Takashima: A Japanese fishing community.* Salt Lake City: University of Utah Press.

———. 1965. *Changing Japan.* New York: Holt, Rinehart and Winston.

Norr, Kathleen Louise Fordham, and James L. Norr. 1974. Environmental and technical factors influencing power in work organizations: Ocean fishing in peasant societies. *Sociology of Work and Occupation* 1(2): 219–251.

Nukada Minoru. 1965. Historical development of the *ama*'s diving activities. In *Physiology of breath-hold diving and the ama of Japan,* edited by Herman Rahn and Yokoyama Tetsuro, 25–39. Washington, D.C.: National Academy of Sciences, National Research Council (Publication 1341).

Ohnuki-Tierney, Emiko. 1984. *Illness and culture in contemporary Japan: An anthropological view.* Cambridge: Cambridge University Press.

———. 1987. *The monkey as mirror: Symbolic transformations in Japanese history and ritual.* Princeton: Princeton University Press.

———. 1990. The historicization of anthropology. In *Culture through time,* edited by Emiko Ohnuki-Tierney, 1–25. Stanford: Stanford University Press.

Okada Teruko. 1982. Kiroku karamita kazoku kankei no hen-yō: Fusia no nenrei sa ni tsuite (A documental study of the transitive family relations: The conjugal disparity of age). *Gifu Joshi Daigako Kiyō* 10: 60–63.

Ono, Sokyo. 1962. *Shinto: The kami way.* Tokyo: Charles E. Tuttle.

Ooms, Herman. 1976. A structural analysis of Japanese ancestral rites and beliefs. In *Ancestors,* edited by William H. Newell, 62–90. The Hague: Mouton.

Paulson, Joy. 1976. Evolution of the feminine ideal. In *Women in changing Japan,* edited by Joyce Lebra and Joy Paulson, 1–24. Stanford: Stanford University Press.

Peel, J.D.Y. 1984. Making History: The past in the Ijesha present. *Man* 19: 111–132.

Pharr, Susan J. 1976. The Japanese woman: Evolving views of life and role. In *Japan: Paradox of progress,* edited by Lewis Austin, with the assistance of Adrienne Suddard and Nancy Remington, 301–328. New Haven: Yale University Press.

———. 1981. *Political woman in Japan: The search for a place in political life.* Berkeley: University of California Press.

Picone, Mary. 1984. Rites and symbols of death in Japan. Unpublished Ph.D. thesis submitted to the faculty of Social Anthropology and Geography, Oxford University.

Pierson, J. L. 1966. *Selection of Japanese poems taken from the Manyōshū*. Leiden: E. J. Brill.

———. 1969. *General index of the Manyōshū*. Leiden: E. J. Brill.

Pittau, Joseph. 1967. *Political thought in early Meiji Japan, 1868–1889*. Cambridge, MA: Harvard University Press.

Plath, David, ed. 1964. Where the family of God is the family: The role of the dead in Japanese households. *American Anthropologist* 66(2): 300–317.

———. 1975. *Adult episodes in Japan*. Leiden: E. J. Brill.

———. 1980. *Long engagements: Maturity in modern Japan*. Stanford: Stanford University Press.

Prachett, Terry. 1998. *Carpe jugulum*. London: Transworld Publishers.

Pym, Barbara. 1955. *Less than angels*. London: Pan Books.

Rappaport, Roy. 1999. *Ritual and religion in the making of humanity*. Cambridge: Cambridge University Press.

Reader, Ian. 1990. *Religion in Contemporary Japan*. Honolulu: University of Hawai'i Press.

Reader, Ian, and George Tanabe. 1998. *Practically religious: Worldly benefits and the common religion of Japan*. Honolulu: University of Hawai'i Press.

Reischauer, Edwin O. 1977. *The Japanese*. Cambridge, MA: Belknap Press of Harvard University.

Reischauer, Haru Matsukata. 1986. *Samurai and silk: A Japanese and American heritage*. Cambridge, MA: Belknap Press of Harvard University.

Ricouer, Paul. 1974. *The conflict of interpretations: Essays in hermeneutics*. Evanston, IL: Northwestern University Press.

Robertson, Jennifer. 1991. *Native and newcomer: Making and remaking a Japanese city*. Berkeley: University of California Press.

———. 1992. Doing and undoing "female" and "male" in Japan: The Takarazuka Revue. In *Japanese social organization*, edited by Takie Lebra, 165–194. Honolulu: University of Hawai'i Press.

———. 1998. *Takarazuka, sexual politics and popular culture in modern Japan*. Berkeley: University of California Press.

Rosaldo, Michelle Zimbalist, and Louis Lamphere, eds. 1975. *Woman, culture and society*. Stanford: Stanford University Press.

Rosenberger, Nancy, ed. 1992. *The Japanese sense of self*. Cambridge: Cambridge University Press.

Sahlins, M. 1985. *Islands of history*. Chicago: University of Chicago Press.

Said, Edward. 1991. *Orientalism*. London: Penguin.

Sakai Teikichirō. n.d. *Kyōdoshi, Nagaoka mura ōaza Kuzaki* (The village land records of Kuzaki, a major section of Nagaoka village). Unpublished records.

Salamon, Sonya. 1973. Stretching the limits of womanhood in contemporary Japan. *Journal of Steward Anthropological Society* 5(1): 68–82.

Sansom, G. B. 1931. *Japan: A short cultural history*. Stanford: Stanford Unversity Press.

———. 1958. *A history of Japan to 1334*. Stanford: Stanford University Press.

Segawa Kiyoko. 1956. *Ama*. Tokyo: Koken Shorin.

———. 1963. Menstrual taboos imposed upon women. In *Studies in Japanese Folklore*, edited by Richard M. Dorson, 239–250. Bloomington: Indiana University Press.

———. 1971. *Han onna, josei to shōgyō* (Female peddlers, women and trade). Tokyo: Kabushiki Kaisha Miraisha.

Simmel, Georg. 1964. The stranger. In *The sociology of Georg Simmel*, translated, edited, and with an introduction by Kurt H. Wolff, 402–408. New York: Free Press.

Smith, Robert J. 1974. *Ancestor worship in contemporary Japan*. Stanford: Stanford University Press.

———. 1978. *Kurusu: The price of progress in a Japanese village, 1951–75*. Kent, UK: Dawson.

Snellgrove, David. 1987. *Indo-Tibetan Buddhism, Indian Buddhists and their Tibetan successors*. London: Serindia Publications.

Standish, Isolde. 1998. Akira, postmodernism and resistance. In *The worlds of Japanese popular culture*, edited by Jan van Bremen and D. P. Martinez, 56–74. Cambridge: Cambridge University Press.

———. 2000. *Myth and masculinity in the Japanese cinema: Towards a political reading of the "tragic hero."* London: Curzon Press.

Stefánsson, Halldór. 1998. Media stories of bliss and mixed blessings. In *The worlds of Japanese popular culture*, edited by Jan van Bremen and D. P. Martinez, 155–166. Cambridge: Cambridge University Press.

Takeda Akira. 1995. *Sosen suhai no hikaku minzokugaku: Nikkan ryokoku ni okeru sosen saishi to shakai*. Tokyo: Yoshikawa Kobunkan.

Takeuchi, Rizō. 1982. Old and new approaches to Kamakura history. In *Court and Bakufu in Japan: Essays in Kamakura history*, edited by Jeffrey P. Mass, 268–283. New Haven: Yale University Press.

Tames, Richard. 1981. *Servant of the shogun: Being the true story of William Adams, pilot and samurai, the first Englishman in Japan*. Tenterden, UK: Paul Norbury.

Tanabe Satoru. 1990. *Nihon ama dentō no kenkyū* (Research on Japanese *ama*'s traditions). Tokyo: Hosei Daigaku Shuppankyoku.

———. 1993. *Ama*. Tokyo: Hosei Daigaku Shuppankyoku.

Tanaka Hisao. 1991. *Ujigami shinko to sosen saishi*. Tokyo: Meicho Shuppan.

Tanaka Noyo. 1983. *Amatachi no shiki* (*Ama*'s four seasons). Tokyo: Katō Masaki.

Taussig, M. 1993. *Mimesis and alterity: A particular history of the senses*. London: Routledge.

Teruoka, G. 1932. *Die ama und ihre arbeit* (The *ama* and their work). *Arbeitsphysiologie* 5: 239–251.

Thomas, N. 1989. *Out of time: History and evolution in anthropological discourse.* Cambridge: Cambridge University Press.

Tobin, J. (ed.). 1992. *Remade in Japan: Everyday life and consumer taste in a changing society.* New Haven: Yale University Press.

Tsuji, Yoko. n.d. The consuming dead: Making ritual work in a commodified world. Forthcoming in *Death in Japan,* edited by John Breen and Brian Bocking. London: Routledge.

Tsunoda, Ryūsaku, trans. 1951. *Japan in the Chinese dynastic histories: Later Han through Ming dynasties,* edited by L. Carrington Goodrich. South Pasadena, CA: P. D. and Ione Perkins.

Ueno, Chizuko. 1987. The position of Japanese women reconsidered. *Current Anthropology* (supplement) 28(4): 75–82.

Valentine, J. 1990. On the borderlines: The significance of marginality in Japanese society. In *Unwrapping Japan,* edited by Eyal Ben-Ari, Brian Moeran, and James Valentine, 36–57. Manchester, UK: Manchester University Press.

van Bremen, Jan. 1995. The myth of the secularization of industrialized societies. In *Ceremony and Ritual in Japan,* edited by Jan van Bremen and D. P. Martinez, 1–22. London: Routledge.

Vlastos, S., ed. 1998. *Mirror of modernity: Invented traditions of modern Japan.* Berkeley: University of California Press.

Vogel, Ezra. 1963. *Japan's new middle-class: The salaryman and his family in a Tokyo suburb.* Berkeley: University of California Press.

Weber, Max. 1968. *Economy and society: An outline of an interpretative sociology.* Edited by G. Roth and C. Wittich. New York: Bedminster Press.

———. 1991. Class, status and party. In *From Max Weber: Essays in sociology,* translated, edited, and with an introduction by H. H. Gerth and C. Wright Mills, 180–195. London: Routledge.

Webster, Paula. 1975. Matriarchy: A vision of power. In *Toward an anthropology of women,* edited by Rayna R. Reiter, 141–156. London: Monthly Review Press.

Wiswell, Ella, and R. J. Smith. 1978. *Women of Suye Mura.* Chicago: Chicago University Press.

Yamaguchi Masao. 1977. Kingship, theatricality and marginal reality in Japan. In *Text and context: The social anthropology of Japan,* edited by R. K. Jain, 151–179. Philadelphia: Institute for the Study of Human Issues.

———. 1990. *Kihai no jidai* (Sign of the times). Tokyo: Tsukuma Shobū.

———. 1991. The poetics of exhibition in Japanese culture. In *Exhibiting cultures,* edited by Ivan Karp and Steven D. Lavine, 57–67. Washington, D.C.: Smithsonian Institution Press.

———. 1998. Sumo in the popular culture of contemporary Japan. In *The worlds of Japanese popular culture,* edited by Jan van Bremen and D. P. Martinez, 19–29. Cambridge: Cambridge University Press.

Yanagita Kunio, ed. 1981. [1950] *Kaisan no seikatsu no kenkyū* (Research on the customs of coastal villages). Tokyo: Kokuji Kankōkai.

Yanagita Kunio and Hika H., eds. 1931. *Shima: Shōwa go nen zenki* (Islands: The five years preceding Showa). Tokyo: Takase Sueyoshi.

Yoshida, Teigo. 1983. Stranger as God. *Ethnology* 20(2): 87–99.

Yoshino, Kosaku. 1992. *Cultural nationalism in contemporary Japan: A sociological enquiry.* London: Routledge.

Zaehner, R. C. 1961. *Mysticism: Sacred and profane.* Oxford: Oxford University Press.

Index

Production Notes for
Martinez / *Identity and Ritual in a Japanese Fishing Village*

Designed by the University of Hawai'i Press Production Staff
with text in Minion and display type in Flareserif

Composition by Josie Herr in QuarkXPress

Printing and binding by The Maple-Vail Book
Manufacturing Group

Printed on 60# Text White Opaque